Annie Sullivan and the Creation of Consciousness

A Cinematic Exploration of The Archetypal Field of Transformation

Karey Pohn

Picture Credits:

Cover Collage: Annie and Helen [Cover Art from DVD] *The Miracle Worker* & Jung's Bollingen Stone, Telesphoros Face. Title of this work and collage inspired by the cover art from *The Creation of Consciousness: Jung's Myth for Modern Man*, published by Inner City Books.

Here We Go Again® is a Registered Trademark of Telesphoros Group Inc. images of the game used with permission.

Basic Perinatal Matrix Drawings courtesy of Dr. Stanislav Grof, used with permission.

Photos of Annie and Helen courtesy of American Foundation for the Blind, Helen Keller Archives.

Photos of Stanislav Grof and Richard Tarnas used with Permission.

Photo of Tewksbury State Almshouse courtesy of the Public Health Museum, Tewksbury, Massachusetts.

DEDICATION

To my mother Rhonda Pohn, who is and always will be for me The Great Mother, and to Angelique Christiansen, my inspiration — whose Annie Sullivan-like abilities have transformed me in so many ways.

To Anna Patty Duke whose iconic portrayals of Helen and later Annie immortalized the story of these amazing women. And also to the memory of Anne Bancroft for making Annie come alive and helping her to come out of the shadows. Both have continued the work of Helen and Annie, inspiring others to achieve great things against the odds.

To Dr. Stuart Brown whose dedication and vision surrounding both the importance of play and Joseph Campbell's work led to my choosing Pacifica. His mentorship and friendship over the years have been a source of much joy and happiness.

To Dr. Stanislav Grof and Dr. Richard Tarnas whose work has helped me to play more and play better and to orient myself in the stormy seas of change.

To Dr. Allen Bishop, who "Bioned" the shadow of a doubt, not only nurtured my creativity as a student, but gave me my first chance to become a t-e-a-c-h-e-r!

To Dr. Stephen Gilligan, whose sponsorship over the years has helped me to traverse the deserts of thou shalt, and begin to roar my way back to the divine child.

To Satyam Veronica Chalmers whose deep understanding of intuition has helped me to listen more deeply and learn to use intuition to help create greater consciousness in others.

And to my former colleagues at Keilty Goldsmith: Dr. Tony Smith, Dr. Marshall Goldsmith, and to the memory of Dr. Joseph Keilty, who first helped me to look for patterns and to realize the power of film and play as a teaching tools. You set the trajectory that I have followed for the past two plus decades!

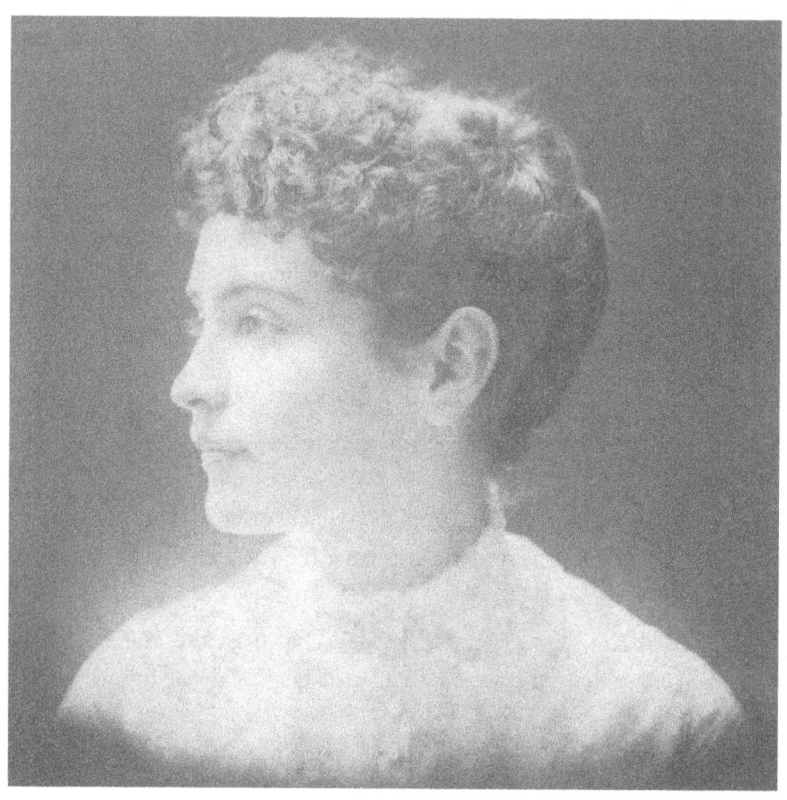

. **Figure 1: Annie Sullivan in 1886**

CONTENTS

DEDICATION i

CONTENTS iii

LIST OF FIGURES vii

ACKNOWLEDGMENTS ix

AUTHOR'S NOTE xi

PREFACE... xiii

PART I: BEHIND THE SCENES xv

Introduction and Method 1
    Purpose Statement and Research Question.................................... 2
    Rationale and Relevance: 3
    Methodology or Method to the Madness 5

Initial Conditions... 9
    Importance of Initial Conditions.. 9
    My Initial Conditions for the Project... 10
    Reiterating the Importance of Origins 12
    Initial Conditions Helen Keller.. 14
    Initial Conditions Annie Sullivan.. 18
    Initial Conditions Laura Bridgman... 29

Archetypal Beginnings... 33
    Archetypal Definitions and Understandings 33
    The Archetypal Field of the Transformation Process.................... 35

PART II: SCENE-PLAY: A CINEMATIC TOUR 45

Credits / Lost Child... 47

Nightmarish Train.. 62

Teacher Meets Student.. 67

"How Bright She Is!" 73

l-a-d-d-e-r 80

Feeling Emotions 83

"Badly Spoiled Child" 86

A Folded Napkin 96

Tolerance In 2 Weeks 100

"The Other Jimmy" 105

Reaching Out 112

"It Has a Name!" 115

"She's Not My Child!" 119

"She's Testing You!" 123

"W-a-t-e-r! " 129

"I-l-o-v-e-h-e-l-e-n! " 139

PART III: FINAL CAMPFIRE 143
   Annie and the Collective Unconscious 143
   The Miracle Worker's Enduring Legacy 144
   Dreaming My Possession Onwards. 149

APPENDICES 153

Appendix A: Learning From Legendary Lives 155
   Such Stuff As Dreams Are Made Of 155
   "More Wonderful Than Any Fiction" 157

Appendix B: The Fairytale Lives of Teacher and Student ... 159

Appendix C: Annie Sullivan Valedictory Address 163

Appendix D: Excursion Into Origins 165
   Geographic Origins 166
   Etymological Roots 168

Appendix E: Grof & Tarnas Birth Process/Planetary Archetypes . 169

Appendix F: Helene Shulman's (1997) Complex Systems model ... 170

Appendix G: Gerontomorphy/Pedamorphy Table 171

Appendix H: Extended Excursion into Initiations— Eternally
Dipping into the Chaotic Realm 173
   How Rites Of Passage Work—Relation To The Eternal Return 173
   Liminality And Thresholds Again 176
   How Chaos Theory Figures Into The Equation. 179

REFERENCE LIST 183

BIBLIOGRAPHY 195

ABOUT THE AUTHOR 199

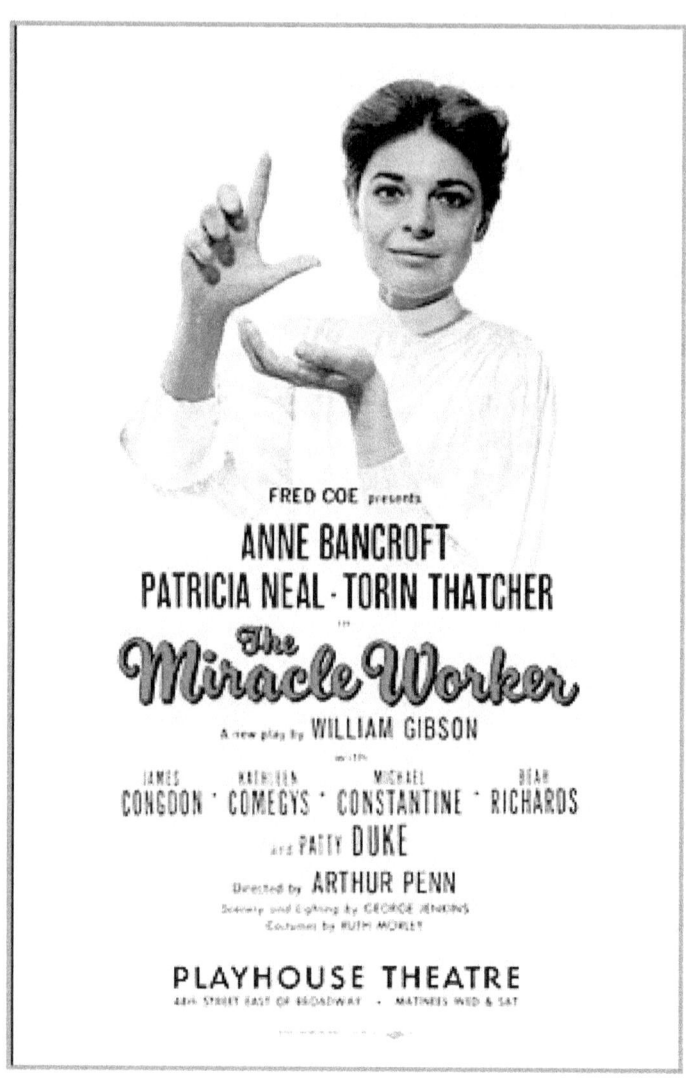

Figure 2: Miracle Worker Broadway Poster

LIST OF FIGURES

Figure 1: Annie Sullivan in 1886 ii
Figure 2: Miracle Worker Broadway Poster vi
Figure 3: Helen, Annie, and Alexander Graham Bell................................viii
Figure 4: Helen Keller and Mark Twain xvi
Figure 5: Helen Keller, age 5 14
Figure 6: Ivy Green from National Historic Landmark Application................16
Figure 7: Annie Sullivan in 1880, age 14 18
Figure 8: Laura Bridgman 29
Figure 9. Helen Keller and Annie Sullivan..31
Figure 10: Bancroft and Duke in Broadway Play version of William Gibson's
    The Miracle Worker 32
Figure 11: Grof's Perinatal Matrices..37
Figure 12: Richard Tarnas and Stanislav Grof..38
Figure 13: The Transformation Process Visually Integrated.....................40
Figure 14: Monomythopoly: Eternal Return Edition™ 41
Figure 15: Here We Go Again®..42
Figure 16: Transformation Process in Various Realms...............................43
Figure 17: Annie Sullivan, circa 1887 44
Figure 18. Wilber's Great Chain Of Being. 51
Figure 19: Mildred, Viney, and Helen...54
Figure 20: Tewksbury State Almshouse. 66
Figure 21: The Pump 130
Figure 22: Helen Keller and Patty Duke on Helen's 80th 142
Figure 23: Prelude to the Kiss 150
Figure 24: Bancroft and Duke..152
Figure 25: Anne Bancroft as Annie..154

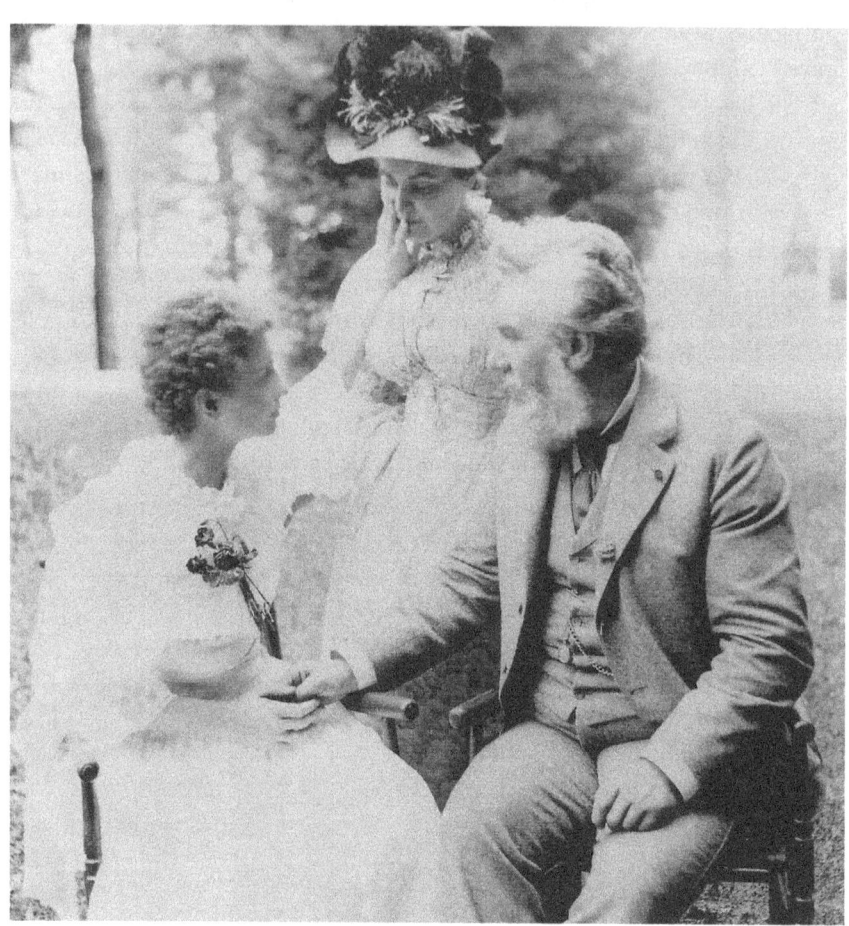

Figure 3: Helen, Annie, and Alexander Graham Bell

ACKNOWLEDGMENTS

Consciousness means "knowing with." There are many people who have helped me to become more conscious, and who I would like to acknowledge, as adding richness and joy to my journey.

First of all, I am indebted to my own lineage, Stanislav Grof and Richard Tarnas, my mentors and the Giants whose shoulders I continue to stand on. Along with Stephen Gilligan's concepts of *sponsorship* and *terrible gifts*, their work has helped me to navigate the stormy seas of change. The three of you are the Annie Sullivans of my soul and have given me language to understand this eternally returning pattern.

I would also like to acknowledge Michael Conforti and the Assisi Institute for creating the structure and container for this work. The Pattern Analyst Program provided me a wonderful playground. Thanks especially to Susan Rowland & Kevin Richards for making the material come alive, and to Robert Langs, MD, not only for his brilliance, but also for constellating this particular field so intensely in me that I had to write my way out! My "cohorts in crime": Silvia Behrend, Chris Peknic, Katrina Messenger, Letizia Amadini Lane, Katherine Best, Jonathan Keeley, Mike Tinghetelli, Kimberlyn McGreal, Bonnie Bright, Sara Wright, & Monika Reis.

For my dear family, friends, fellow playmates, and healers, thank you for your belief in me and for your help and support over the years: Diana Pohn, Ben Pohn, Jeff Pohn, Brian Levant & Alison Logan, Cheryl Creede, Lauren Rautbord, Ken Kristian, Natalia Nogales, Jonathan Sykes, Brita Martiny, David Hill, Siri Singh, Gladys Hirsch, Anna Stone, Sara Wilson, Joseph McClendon III, Greg Gibson, Ian Low, Clifton Harrison, Thomas Dann, Valeska Ramet, Agnes Regeczkey, Alenka Obal, Larry Byram, Melody Sullivan, Stacia Butterfield, Kylea Taylor, Miyera Alejo, Cary & Tav Sparks, Kris Oster, Georgena Felicia, Laurence Hillman, Perry Emge, June Katzen, Cerena Childress, Lisa Dale Miller Susan Brown, Julian Brown, Susan Reiner, Sheila Gomez Lagman, Jacqueline Valdez, Paula Tipton Healy, Greg Martin, Leigh Melander, Jake Wright, David Burston, Mike Young, Jeff, JoJo, Kendra & Rocket White, Shelly McQuerter, Michael James, Phil Cousineau, Isaac Koren & Sophie Ward, Thorald Koren, Tony & Erin Smith, Jeanne & Dan Romero, Victor & Alison Geberin, Thomas & Sasha Yakovlev-Fredricksen, Claire Zammit & Katherine Woodward Thomas. Thanks also to the writers of NCIS for their "campfire" idea.

I would also like to thank those who have gone before—my father, Maxwell Pohn for his ability to recognize patterns and trends, and to my dear friend Glenn Wilson, your senses of humor gave me great joy. Also to Dr. Walter Odajnyk, who kept me on my toes and led me to the all important question of "so what?" and "what does it matter?" Because of Walter, I am always seeking playful ways to apply what I learn.

To the memories of William Gibson for his love letter to teachers which was *The Miracle Worker*, by crafting both a script and a screenplay that stayed archetypally close to the actual events that transpired, and to Arthur Penn, the director. Also to the biographers of Helen and Annie, especially Kim Nielsen, whose scholarship in *Beyond the Miracle Worker* revealed so much and helped me to love Annie all the more.

Also, a special thanks also to Darryl Sharp, editor of Inner City Books for his advice that allowed me to feel free to play by using the word *perhaps* early on in my Pacifica Career! Inner City Books have changed my life and helped to enlighten me—especially Edinger's *The Creation of Consciousness* & John Van Eenwyk's *Archetypes and Strange Attractors*. These two books in particular led to important bifurcation points and I keep eternally returning to them. Toni D'Anca & the Pacifica Graduate Institute's Public Programs Department have provided wonderful continuing education opportunities and play space, that continues to inspire me and where I have met such wonderful new friends who I have had the opportunity to not only know with, but play with, too. I would also like to thank David Rock and his team at Neuroleadership Group, especially Robin Bowyer. Their coaching program has transformed my thinking and has helped me to more deeply understand how I might apply all of my play research.

Lastly, I must thank my beloved t-e-a-c-h-e-r-s and colleagues at Pacifica Graduate Institute, the *inspiratio conntinuo*, who continue to inspire me a decade later: to Diane Huerta who invited me in and especially Dr. Robert Romanyshyn and Dr. Veronica Goodchild, the teachers who opened my eyes to the poetic and imaginal possibilities of research; research librarians Mark Kelly & Richard Buchen; Drs. Helene Shulman & Dr. Glenn Slater, who first introduced me this eternally returning pattern—the jury is still out on this one, as I cannot seem to escape from this hermeneutic circle; & to Dr. Elizabeth Nelson, whose dissertation was my first inspiration, and whose advice, about focusing on one thing, I am never able to really follow.

AUTHOR'S NOTE

In this book, I explore the Archetype of Transformation and the role of the teacher through an archetypal analysis of *The Miracle Worker* (Penn, 1962). The film is based on the legendary lives of Helen Keller and Annie Sullivan. Playwright William Gibson wove the facts of their lives into a brilliant play (1956/2008) and later screenplay (1961), which captures the first 32 days of their relationship.

Utilizing this *healing fiction* as a cinematic canvas, I have sought to *see through* and at the same time show an example of archetypal pattern analysis at work, explicating and applying relevant concepts from the Assisi Institute Archetypal Pattern Analyst training program. This book also tells the story of a master pattern analyst and teacher—Annie Sullivan—at work, as it simultaneously brings to light, in an archetypal way, the transformation process and shows how this eternally returning archetypal pattern played out cinematically in the lives of Helen and Annie.

Utilizing Stanislav Grof's (1975, 2000) cartography of the psyche as a guide, along with Richard Tarnas's archetypal astrological insights as an additional orienting device, this study uses Yoram Kaufmann's (2009) orientational approach to hermeneutically uncover the amazing riches contained in this iconic film.

Along with the overall inspiration of Carl Jung, Joseph Campbell, and James Hillman, major concepts that helped me to navigate and make meaning of the landscape were: Stephen Gilligan's (1997) self-relations; John Van Eenwyk's (1997) and Michael Conforti's (1999, 2007) takes chaos theory and Victor Turner's (1969, 1982a, 1982b, 1988) and Arnold Van Gennep's (1909/1960) notions of liminality and rites of passage, as well as Walker Percy's (1975) triadic and tetradic notions of consciousness, and David Rock and colleagues' (2006, 2008, 2012), research and application of neuroscience principles to coaching and leadership.

Our great human adventure is the evolution of consciousness. We are in this life to enlarge the soul, liberate the spirit, and light up the brain.

— Tom Robbins
Wild Ducks Flying Backward

Real courage is risking something that might force you to rethink your thoughts and suffer change and stretch consciousness. Real courage is risking one's clichés.

— Tom Robbins
Another Roadside Attraction

In every job that must be done, there is an element of fun, you find the fun and snap, the job's a game.

— Mary Poppins
(Richard and Bob Sherman)

PREFACE

Annie Sullivan and the Creation of Consciousness is the book version of my final project for the Assisi Institute Archetypal Pattern Analyst Training Program. As such, this edition retains much of the flavor of the original, as well as its basic structure. There are two reasons for this choice.

First, it will give people unfamiliar with the process an example of how archetypal pattern analysts do what we do. Second, by having an "academic flavor," which is at the same time conversational and playful, it will hopefully inspire others to hold the tension of opposites and to blur boundaries. By showing that scholarship needn't always be so serious, it may encourage others to venture into uncharted territory and create consciousness in their own unique ways.

Tom Robbins, my favorite author, said that "life is too serious to be taken that seriously." My favorite movie is Walt Disney's masterpiece, *Mary Poppins* (Stevenson, 1964). This book seeks to add an element of fun and play into this important subject, because Annie herself employed play to teach Helen. It is my firm belief that play is vital to our survival as a species, and it is a very important ingredient in the creation of consciousness.

William Gibson wrote *The Miracle Worker* as a love letter to the teaching profession. It is my hope that this book follows on his work and enlarges our idea of teacher. I believe that teachers come in all shapes and flavors, they have the ability to help us create consciousness, to see things differently, and thus expand our own horizons.

Joseph Campbell, himself a master teacher, said that myths are collective dreams and I believe that the creations of the entertainment industry are also collective dreams. By seeing more deeply through them, we may be able to learn more about ourselves and our world. Helen Keller said of her religion that it was "the light in her darkness." For me, popular culture has that power, too. This book attempts shine a spotlight on just one piece of popular culture and the vast riches that it can provide, if we only have the archetypal eyes to see.

Karey Pohn
Encinitas, California
September 4, 2013

I have never known the deep joy of surrender to my own, I cannot say genius, since I have not that immortal gift of the gods - but to my own individual bent or powers. I have been compelled to pour myself into the spirit of another and to find satisfaction in the music of an instrument not my own and to contribute always to the mastery of that instrument by another. How often I have been asked: "If you had your life to live over, would you follow the same path?"
Would I be a teacher? If I had my life to live over I probably should have as little choice of a career as I had this time. We do not, I think, choose our destiny. It chooses us.

—Anne Sullivan Macy
(Braddy, 1933, pp. 292-293)

I need a teacher quite as much as Helen. I know that the education of this child will be the distinguishing event of my life, if I have the brains and perseverance to accomplish it.

—Annie Sullivan, in *Story of My Life*,
Letter May 22, 1887

The subject was difficult, and my knowledge inadequate; but I am glad I didn't shirk my responsibility; for, stumbling, hesitating, and incomplete as my explanation was, it touched deep responsive chords in the soul of my little pupil, and **the readiness with which she comprehended the great facts of physical life confirmed me in the opinion that the child has dormant within him, when he comes into the world, all the experiences of the race. These experiences are like photographic negatives, until language develops them and brings out the memory-images.**

—Annie Sullivan,
Letter August 28, 1887

PART I
BEHIND THE SCENES

Because I was ignorant, and felt inferior, I pretended that I was scornful and contemptuous of everybody . . . . My mind was a question mark, my heart a frustration.

– Annie Sullivan

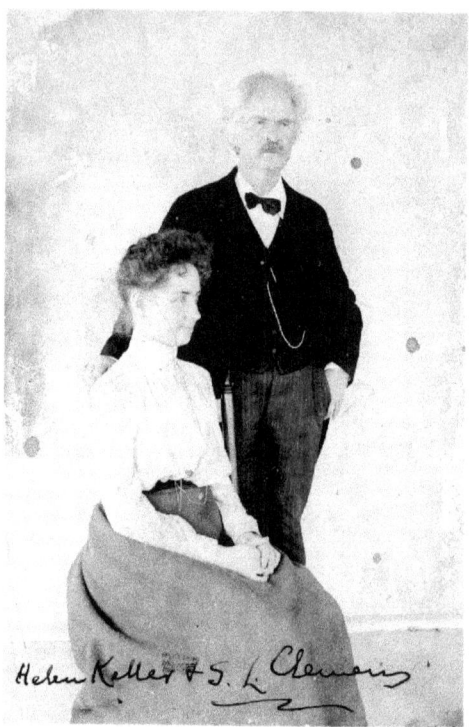

Figure 4: Helen Keller and Mark Twain

I need not go into any particulars about Helen Keller. She is fellow to Caesar, Alexander, Napoleon, Homer, Shakespeare, and the rest of the immortals. She will be as famous a thousand years from now as she is today.

– Mark Twain (Masters, 1938, p. 188)

INTRODUCTION AND METHOD

"There is a curious paradox that no one can explain who
understands the secrets of the reaping of the grain?
Who understands why spring is born out of winter's laboring pain
or why we must all die a bit before we grow again."

—El Gallo, *The Fantasticks* (Jones & Schmidt, 1990, p. 106).

Helen Keller and Annie Sullivan, the story of their relationship is the stuff of myth, fairytale, and legend. The iconic event that happened at the pump in Tuscumbia Alabama, on April 5, 1887 was a watershed moment. Although it occurred 126 years ago, the wonder of it has not faded. The "miracle moment" is etched in our collective consciousness. Helen Keller, the first deafblind woman to graduate from Radcliffe, wrote of it in her own autobiography (1903/2003) and other writings—especially in her biography *Teacher* (1955)—which have in turn inspired numerous biographies (Hermann, 1999), and hundreds of books and films (Pugh & Crow, 2000; Hamilton, 2005; Price, 2005). Helen Keller's achievements were amazing, she was a prolific and inspirational writer and speaker, a humanitarian who traveled the world helping others with her teacher Annie Sullivan Macy by her side. The recognition and honors accorded Helen are well deserved. Helen and Annie: to talk about one of them is to necessarily talk about the other, for they were inextricably entwined, as Mark Twain (Clemens, 1903), in a letter to his long time friend Helen Keller wrote:

> I am charmed with your book—enchanted. You are a wonderful creature, the most wonderful in the world—you and your other half together—Miss Sullivan, I mean, for it took the pair of you to make a complete and perfect whole. How she stands out in her letters! her brilliancy, penetration, originality, wisdom, character, and the fine literary competencies of her pen—they are all there.

Helen's brilliant light, however, overshadowed the truly remarkable efforts of her teacher Anne Sullivan Macy, although the letters that chronicle this work are contained in Helen's autobiography (1903/2003). Nella Braddy, the person Annie confided in, wrote a biography of Annie in

1933, and part of Annie's story was told by Helen herself, in 1955 her biography *Teacher*. Nielsen (2009) in her biography about Annie—*Beyond the Miracle Worker*—noted that even though biographies do exist about Annie, Helen is still the most prominent character.

It was not until 1956, when playwright William Gibson wrote *The Miracle Worker* for *Playhouse 90* (Penn, 1957), that Annie and the importance of her teaching Helen was truly presenced. William Gibson read Keller's *Story of My Life* as a child, and wrote *The Miracle Worker* as an homage to Annie, the 20-year-old teacher who freed her young student from a prison of silent darkness. Gibson called it his "love letter to the teaching profession" (Gibson, 2008).

Gibson's original teleplay went on to become a Broadway play, and a feature film in 1962. Although the original actors were different in the *Playhouse 90* television version, Anne Bancroft and Patty Duke starred in both the Broadway play and the 1962 film, winning many awards, including Tonys for Best Actress [Bancroft], and Best Newcomer [Duke], and Oscars for Best Actress [Bancroft] and Best Supporting Actress [Duke]. A Broadway revival of *The Miracle Worker* was staged in 2010, and since the original feature film (Penn, 1962), two other television versions of the film have been made in one in 1979 (Aaron, 2009), starring Patty Duke—the original Helen— as Annie; and again by Disney in 2000 (Tass, 2000). The play has never been "off the boards," a perennial favorite, it is always being performed anew somewhere (Gibson, 2008). *The Miracle Worker* is reenacted annually on summer weekends at Helen Keller's birthplace in Tuscumbia, Alabama. Another beautiful film, *Black*, by Bhansali (2005a, b) uses *The Miracle Worker* as an inspiration; set in India, it features an older man as the teacher of the young deafblind girl.

Purpose Statement and Research Question, AKA Why are We Here and What are We Going to Do?

Although several biographies have been written about Anne Sullivan Macy (Braddy, 1933, Lash, 1980, Hickok, 1961, Nielsen, 2009), none has considered the beginning of their remarkable relationship from an archetypal standpoint. Only one dissertation has been written about Annie Sullivan, and that concerned her teaching methods (Pevser, 2010). Jung (1951/1990) said, "the most we can do is to dream the myth onwards and give it a modern dress (p. 160, para 271). Similarly, this work seeks to dream

2

The Miracle Worker (Penn, 1962) in its original cinematic version onward, and give it an archetypal pattern analyst's dress.

One of the areas where Archetypal Pattern Analysts can make a contribution is in the entertainment industry. I have written elsewhere of the possibly transformative power of popular culture (Pohn, 2003, 2006). By using this film, which is based on fact, perhaps *The Miracle Worker* can continue its miraculous work, and not only shed light on the transformation process, but perhaps it can also teach us new lessons that we can apply to other areas, from our educational system to our own individual lives and relationships.

Purpose statement: The purpose of this archetypal study is to use the orientational approach (Kaufmann, 2009) to explore *The Miracle Worker* (Penn, 1962). In exploring this historically based work, this book seeks to do two things: 1) to explore the archetypal field of the transformation, its landscapes and process; and 2) to be both an example of archetypal pattern analysis at work—utilizing the film as a canvas to apply, and at the same time, to explain various important concepts in our field. Annie Sullivan, as we will see, was a consummate pattern analyst. Thus, we will not only be able to see how pattern analysis works, but also see a pattern analyst at work.

Research question: The focus of my research is: What can the film, *The Miracle Worker* (Penn, 1062) tell us about the archetypal process of transformation, with a focus on the teacher's role in the process.

Rationale and Relevance: Mythical Thinking and Archetypal Pattern Analysis

In 1962, the same year that *The Miracle Worker* came out, Levi-Strauss (1962/1966) wrote *The Savage Mind, (La Pensée Sauvage)* and coined the term *bricolage* to describe mythical thinking. Levi-Strauss saw mythical thinking as the "science of the concrete," and one of its hallmarks is that gives us objects to think with *"bonne a pensee,"*

> In its old sense the verb "bricoleur" applied to ball games and billiards, to hunting, shooting and riding. It was however always used with reference to some extraneous movement: a ball rebounding, a dog straying or a horse swerving from its direct course to avoid an obstacle. And in our own time the "bricoleur" is still someone who works with his hands and uses devious means compared to those of a craftsman.

The characteristic feature of mythical thought is that it expresses itself by means of a heterogeneous repertoire which, even if extensive, is nevertheless limited. It has to use this repertoire, however, whatever the task in hand because it has nothing else at its disposal. Mythical thought is therefore a kind of intellectual "bricolage"—which explains the relation, which can be perceived between the two. (pp. 16-17)

One of the hallmarks of depth psychology is that mythical thinking is at its heart. It is one of depth psychology's initial conditions: In Freud's self-analysis and he realized: "I am Oedipus," and Jung saw mythical themes early on in his work mentally disturbed patients at Burgholzi. Depth psychology, and in particular Archetypal Pattern Analysis, borrow concepts from many different fields in an effort to make sense of the psyche, using them as objects to think with. One of the major fields that Archetypal Pattern Analysis uses to help us understand archetypal patterns is chaos theory, the study of nonlinear dynamics, or deterministic chaos.

Michael Conforti, founder of the Assisi Institute, in *Field Form and Fate*, following on Jung's notion that "at bottom psyche is merely world" (Jung, 1951/1990, p. 173, para. 291), explicated the relationship between psyche and the new sciences, and how they can help us to see through the patterns in our lives. Conforti's (2007) book *Threshold Experiences*, showed the importance of the initial therapeutic interview, the richness of the information that is available to us, "if we only have eyes to see."

The discipline of Archetypal Pattern Analysis gives us these eyes, to understand archetypes deeply, and gives us a systematic way of entering into and exploring different realms and systems—whether occurring in the natural world, or in a personal life, from nighttime dreams to daytime dramas; in organizations and in culture. Archetypal Psychology founder, James Hillman, noted that archetypes

are cosmic perspectives in which the soul participates. They are the lords of its realm of being, the patterns for its mimesis. The soul cannot be, except in one of their patterns. All psychic reality is governed by one or another archetypal fantasy, given sanction by a God, I cannot but be in them. (Tarnas, 1995, p. 5)

Archetypal Pattern Analysis allows us know where we are, what archetypal fantasy we are participating in—allowing us to make sense of the noise, to understand what the pattern is, what is likely to happen, and to explicate those patterns. We can then either seek to live in greater accordance with them, or if called upon, to help to interrupt nongenerative patterns. The discipline can help us to ensure that there is archetypal resonance, so that we are not working at cross-purposes.

Methodology or Method to the Madness

Hermeneutics. Fittingly, I will use a hermeneutic method, as it is archetypally coherent with my topic—in that its patron god Hermes, is intimately implicated in the transformation process; he is a psychopomp traveling between realms and leads people out of the underworld. Hermes is also a bricoleur, trickster, and the god of thresholds, crossroads, and connections. He is a culture bringer, giving us the alphabet and writing. Hermes is also connected to the unconscious, a place of riches for the psyche. He is the god that brings the contents of this underworld out in the open by his synchronistic tricks (Hansen, 2001, p. 116). Hermes is the "god of significant passage, and is always present during transitions (Stein, 1983). Hermeneutics, like the eternal return, goes around in circles, iterating and feeding back what has been learned; it is also an appropriate method because I will mainly use various texts as my co-researchers, especially the biographies of Annie Sullivan and Helen Keller (Nielsen, 2009; Brady, 1933; Lash, 1980; Hickok, 1961; Waite, 1959; Hermann, 1999; Keller, 1955) the 1962 version of *The Miracle Worker* (Penn, 1962; Gibson 1961), William Gibson's (1956/2008) play by the same name, and Helen Keller's autobiography (1903/2003) which contains also contains Annie Sullivan's letters.

Transformophic episteme. Levi Strauss (1962) created a myth of mythology to describe mythical thinking, which took the form of what he was talking about—a *mythomorphic episteme*. Similarly in my dissertation (Pohn, 2006), I created a website to discuss the archetypal aspects of play using a bricolage method, which in being playful, similarly took the form of what it was talking about—a *bricoludomorphic episteme*. In the current paper I will be using an example of transformation to explore the archetypal field of transformation and in resembling what it speaks of, it will at times feel chaotic. I have coined the term *transformorphic episteme* to describe it, combining *transform*, meaning change/metamorphosis, and *morphic* meaning shape of, so *transformorphic* is the shape of transformation. *Transformorphic* also alludes to the Orphic Mysteries, as it can be rearranged into: *transform* and *orphic*. The Orphic mysteries are especially fitting here, because, as we will see later, they mirror the transformation process that Helen went through in the development of consciousness. The Orphic Mysteries were

> Rites based on the myth of Dionysus Zagreus, the son of Zeus and Persephone. When Zeus proposed to make Zagreus the ruler of the universe, the Titans were so enraged that they dismembered the boy and devoured him. Athena saved Zagreus' heart and gave it to Zeus, who thereupon swallowed the heart (from which was born the second Dionysus Zagreus) and destroyed the Titans with lightning. From the ashes of the Titans sprang the human race, who were part divine (Dionysus) and part evil (Titan). This double aspect of human nature, the Dionysian and the Titanic, is essential to the understanding of Orphism. The Orphics affirmed the divine origin of the soul, but it was through initiation into the Orphic Mysteries and through the process of transmigration that the soul could be liberated from its Titanic inheritance and could achieve eternal blessedness. (Columbia Encyclopedia, 2013)

Healing Fictions. James Hillman (1983a), in *Healing Fictions*, showed that all of our depth psychological writing is at its base poetic, and from Freud's 1905 (1905/1997) *Dora* onward, that "case histories are a way of writing fiction" (p. 5). Long before Hillman was born, both Helen Keller and Annie Sullivan realized the storied nature of life. Each eloquently expressed in similar words, that narratives of people's life are similar to dreams. Following this insight, which happened while psychoanalysis was still in its early infancy, I will examine the story that has become known to us through William Gibson's (1956/2008; Penn, 1962) play and later film *The Miracle Worker*. In separate Appendices—an excursion may be taken into "Learning from Legendary Lives" (Appendix A), where I give in detail the reason for my choice, and let both Annie and Helen express themselves on the subject, and there, too, I provide a fairytale version of their story as seen in *The Miracle Worker* (Appendix B). I highly recommend reading the first two appendices before taking the cinematic tour, as they will provide context to those who are not familiar with the story.

Nietzsche's way. Jung (1988), in expanding on the eternal return in a passage from Nietzsche's *Thus Spoke Zarathustra*, explicated: "all truth is crooked, the snake's way is the right way, every straight way lieth, time itself is a circle, the idea of the eternal return" (p. 1271). Van Eenwyk (1997) described looking at the functioning of the psyche from within the psyche "like riding a roller coaster built on a Möbius strip. It is full of paradox. It's chaotic" (p. 70). So chaos theory is a good choice! Similarly, writing about archetypes and their dynamics, especially the transformation process, is chaotic. One of the qualities of strange attractors is that they iterate or repeat, and are non linear.

Although there is an itinerary for this journey through the film, like the Latin *iter*, from which *iteration* and *itinerary* originate, journeys in Roman times were a bit more chaotic, aberrations abounded, and there was not so much certainty as to the outcome of one's journey; delays and detours were a matter of course. In describing iterative dynamics, (which this book is also an example of in its form), Van Eenwyk (1997) noted that the journeys chaotic dynamics take mirror travel in Roman times, and:

> so does life, actually. Just as life is unpredictable, so are nonlinear iterative equations. Unlike linear equations, which proceed in an orderly fashion to a predictable outcome, iterative equations determine their own destiny. Their outcome is rarely predictable" (p. 48).

The Inlaws (Hiller, 1979) provides a cinematic example, where Peter Falk (playing Vince) when trying to dodge bullets while running back to the plane advises Alan Arkin's character (Sheldon): "Serpentine, Sheldon, Serpentine." Although not dodging bullets, transformation is chaotic and nonlinear, and thus it is impossible to go in a straight line in describing various concepts and dynamics as they play out in the film.

Sometimes detours will be necessary, veering off course, and stopping to get our bearings will be necessary. Similarly, we will convene around a campfire , at the end of each film chapter, and regroup before forging ahead, although we will follow the story of the film sequentially or diachronically beginning somewhere, and ending up somewhere else, as the thru-line.

Organization of the Book

The book is divided into three parts: Behind the Scenes, The Cinematic Tour and a Final Campfire. PART I: BEHIND THE SCENES sets the stage and is comprised of three chapters: Introduction and Method, Initial Conditions and Archetypal Beginnings.

The <u>Introduction and Method</u> chapter, where we are now, gives a short backdrop explaining the book's purpose and why it is important to study *The Miracle Worker* in this way, what it hopes to achieve and the method used to achieve it.

The <u>Initial Conditions</u> chapter explains the importance of beginnings, showing how we got to where we are, while giving us the backstory of the project [aka my predisposition to the topic and autobiographical origins]. It also details the backstories of Helen, Annie, and also Laura Bridgman, the deafblind girl who was the first to be taught at Perkins by Dr. Samuel Gridley Howe. Dr. Howe's work with Laura provided the foundation of Annie's teaching (Perkins, 1843, 1845).

In the <u>Archetypal Beginnings</u> chapter, I define some key terms: *archetype*, *pattern*, *archetypal field*, and briefly sketch out and explicate the archetypal field of transformation, visual depictions of the process will be provided as well as a chart showing where this ubiquitous pattern can be seen in nature, culture, and psychology.

PART II: THE CINEMATIC TOUR, contains many smaller chapters that correspond to the movie chapters of the DVD. It is the major focus of this book, while journeying sequentially through the film, *The Miracle Worker* (Penn, 1962), a significant amount of time will be spent of focusing on and explicating the various initial conditions, thresholds, perturbations and bifurcation points, as well pointing out archetypal themes and patterns. In particular the opening scenes, the introduction of Annie and her arrival in Tuscumbia, her meeting and first interactions with Helen will be stressed. The transformation process, as it expresses itself in rites of passage provides a fractal example and explication of the process at work. This part and the cinematic canvas of the film, show us how much depth is in the details, and allows one to experience the practice of this craft, as it is an example of the archetypes and concepts it seeks to explore.

Part III: THE FINAL CAMPFIRE contains final reflections, questions, and dreams for the future. A series of appendixes follow offering excursions into Life as Legend—the choice of fiction to portray mythical lives; Annie's and Helen's mythical lives crafted as a fairytale; an excursion into origins, exploring the significance of both the etymological and geographic origins; An extended excursion into the initiation process shows the chaotic nature of liminal times. Various helpful charts and tables are included here as well.

INITIAL CONDITIONS

How should we be able to forget those ancient myths that are at the beginning of all peoples, the myths about dragons that at the last moment turn into princesses; perhaps all the dragons of our lives are princesses who are only waiting to see us once beautiful and brave. Perhaps everything terrible is in its deepest being something helpless that wants help from us.

– Rilke, *Letters to a Young Poet*, (p. 69)

This chapter discusses initial conditions: beginning with their importance; I then place myself in the research. After that, we will look at the initial conditions of Helen, Annie, and Laura Bridgman.

Importance of Initial Conditions

Michael Conforti (1999) began his book *Field Form and Fate* with a chapter, entitled "Déjà Vu All Over Again, Repetition in the Psyche and the Natural World." Conforti found a corresponding idea to the concept of the repetition compulsion in depth psychology in the natural world. Later in the book, Conforti showed that the process is akin to the notion of iteration in chaos theory. He saw repetition or iteration as having two important functions—the stabilization of form and also the evolution of form. These dynamics seem to be the universal.

When discussing Freud and the repetition compulsion, and looking at the occurrence of repetition of the natural world, Conforti (1999) noted that

> such replicative behaviors demand an expenditure of traumatizing amounts of energy and at times are carried out at the expense of individual life. These dramas are apparently subsumed in an eternal drama, which has as one of its goals, as in the case of salmon, a return to the source to accomplish renewal. (p. 8)

There is something important about coming back to the original conditions in order to effect renewal.

This eternal drama is the *eternal return*, Nietzsche's term for the endless cycle of death and rebirth (Jung, 1988). Van Eenwyk (1997) pointed out that "the eternal return is the archetype of archetypal dynamics" (p. 114). The eternal return is Nature's engine of transformation, if you will. This is the pattern [the transformation process] and the archetypal field we will be exploring and witnessing in *The Miracle Worker* (Penn, 1962).

I have written about this pattern often, eternally returning to it from various vantage points throughout my doctoral studies and beyond. This perennial pattern is ubiquitous; it shows up everywhere, expressed simply as in Goethe's "formation, transformation, eternal mind's eternal recreation" to the complex workings of chaos theory, from mythology to psychology, it eternally re-creates itself, always resembling but never the exactly the same. From rites of passage and personal development, to birth itself, the transformation process goes by many names and is found in places as different as the therapeutic container, the halls of academia, Hollywood studios, and corporate boardrooms. We can use this process in the analysis of myths, dreams, and films. As Conforti, Rubik, Abraham, Ott, and Richards have pointed out in our curriculum, the natural world abounds with examples of these nonlinear dynamics, from the caterpillar's heroic journey into a butterfly (M. Sullivan, 2011), to the carbon cycle of stars that in their spectacular supernova deaths create the building blocks of life [See Chapter 3 for a more detailed description of this archetypal pattern].

My Initial Conditions for the Project

Since 2000, I have personally been caught in the attractor site of this archetype, which is at the heart of everything, exploring it in papers ranging from the timeless TV classic *Rudolph the Red Nosed Reindeer*, to the film *Chocolat*. After a 1000+ page dissertation, where I found it in Shiva's dice game, chaos theory, and in popular culture [Disneyland, *Chicago* and *Mary Poppins*], this archetype is *not yet* done with me. It has not yet played itself out, and I believe it never will. I am currently creating a game—*Here We Go Again*® to help popularize it in a new way. And now, without intending to, I have found myself again immersed in its chaotic waters, like the tractor beam on the Death Star in *Star Wars* (Lucas, 1977), it will not loosen its grip. [By the way, Lucas credits part of *Star Wars* success to Joseph Campbell's (1968) hero's journey—yet another place this pattern shows up, and Campbell was my inspiration to go to Pacifica in the first place.]

I have chosen the cinematic presentation, the "reel lives" of two extraordinary women, in whose real lives these dynamics played out in a truly stunning way. I got there through a synchronistic event.

Suckered in by synchronicity. I have been working with an amazing teacher named Angelique Christiansen, who has been helping me with my inferior function, sensing—since late 2007 when I began studying Pilates.

Living most the time in my head, my body is like a foreign country, which I seldom visit, and I can't seem to understand how to do things— for example how to keep from moving my shoulder up when raising my arm.   After working at these kind of things for weeks and sometimes months, when I still couldn't do what Angelique was asking, I would get very frustrated, on the verge of tears and say "I can't" at which point, Angelique, would calmly and patiently say to me: "not yet." At these times, I would often say to her, "I feel like Helen Keller, or "I'm having a Helen Keller moment." By this I meant not the part where Helen Keller finally metaphorically sees the light, gets it, and understands; but the struggling, maddeningly frustrated child who is in the dark, doesn't get it, and has no clue.

When discussing my final project with Dr. Silvia Behrends, I flippantly said "maybe I should do Helen Keller." We chatted about it for a few moments and talked about iconic moment at the pump and all the rich symbolism surrounding it—the archetype of the "AHA" moment. That would be a nice contained piece of work, which could fit within the suggested 20 pages.

Tricky Hermes at work. I was excited, I had a focus, and then I rented the film, and saw that the moment at the pump was only the tip of the iceberg! The rest of the story had gone unremembered, lost in the mists of my childhood. This is the part that became the attractor site of my project. I became possessed and began to read widely about Helen and Annie Sullivan, her amazing teacher. Then I ventured again going headlong into the breach and changed my focus to The Teacher Archetype and the Field of Transformation, later this would change again, as the focus became showing the transformation process at work, using the film as a canvas and seeing an expert pattern analyst at work in Annie Sullivan.

I was also working at this time with Dr. Robert Langs, and in that work, I constantly felt like Helen Keller, as I struggled to decode the unconscious triggers in our work together. Clueless doesn't even begin to describe how I felt working with him. But that is another story. Suffice it to say that my fear was so great that I was blind and deaf to what these triggers were telling me—I couldn't make the connections. I would tearfully exclaim that I felt like Helen Keller. He was like Annie Sullivan, helping me to understand, holding the space for transformation to occur. Dr. Langs was also Michael Conforti's very influential teacher and mentor. He taught the first module I attended at the Assisi Institute on Unconscious Communication (Langs, 1983). Like Annie Sullivan, Dr. Langs is a brilliant maverick.

My work with Dr. Langs put me into this same archetypal field that I would be exploring in *The Miracle Worker*, the focus would now be on the transformation of the struggling Helen Keller. Von Franz (1977) said that when something important is trying to come into consciousness, there is often a doubling that occurs. My work with Dr. Langs provided the necessary conditions for me to birth this paper, but my psyche was not able to bear the intense heat, and went down in flames, so that perhaps this phoenix and tribute to all my teachers would rise from the ashes, as I striven to accomplish in this book.

Reiterating the Importance of Origins

Conforti (1999) explicated that repetition or iteration, has a dual nature, which Freud recognized. In the personal realm they were either (a) nongenerative, associated with the death drive, which would be expressed for example in addiction; or (b) an "adaptation towards life which is in service to maintaining and subsidizing a stable alignment with a specific face of the archetype" (p. 8). Much of Freud's work on the repetition compulsion is focused here. Conforti also pointed out that this repetition is purposeful, in that it insures the "stable and highly regulated unfolding of a preformed morphological regime." The generative form of repetition is associated with the life drive, and as Conforti (1999) noted: "Freud was forced to see the complementary nature of the repetition drive in that it also continually moves and works to renew life" (p. 8). If one asks "to what end is the repetition geared. . . we may come to learn something from this event." (p. 9). Stephen Gilligan (1997), in *The Courage to Love*, wrote:

> The problem is that an unintegrated response repeats itself until integrated. On this point, nature seems eternally patient and forever

cruel. It may take years, even generations, but a negative experience returns until human presence is brought to touch it with love and acceptance and integrate it. (p. 12)

Being a fan of popular culture, I call this the *Green Eggs and Ham* effect, where through repetition, the ability to choose something different can lead to evolution, expansion, and growth. The film *Groundhog* Day (Ramis, 1993) is a good example of this, too.

In "Déjà Vu All Over Again," Conforti (1999) described the process of iteration, which Briggs and Peat (1989) explained: "Iteration—feedback involving the continual reabsorption or enfolding of what has come before—crops up in almost everything: rolling weather systems, artificial intelligence, the cycling replacement of cells in our bodies." And it doesn't stop there, even "elementary particles generate themselves by a constant process of creation and destruction through iteration from the vacuum state" (pp. 66, 68).

Due to the vital importance of initial conditions, let us now turn to the initial conditions of Helen, Annie, and Laura Bridgman, which will set the stage for the film. They take us to the time the film begins, and provide a context.

Initial Conditions Helen Keller

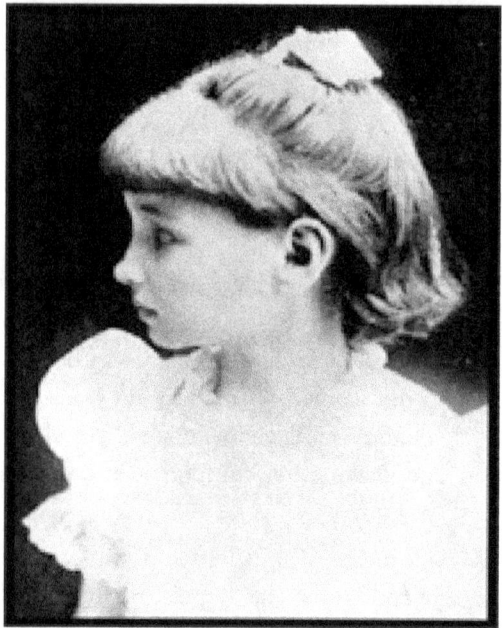

Figure 5: Helen Keller, age 5

Character cannot be developed in ease and quiet. Only through experience of trial and suffering can the soul be strengthened, vision cleared, ambition inspired, and success achieved.

– Helen Adams Keller (1938, p. 60)

Helen Keller came into the world on June 27, 1880 in Tuscumbia at 4:02 pm (Astro.com, 2013). By all accounts she was an intelligent, healthy, active child for the first 19 months of her life. Prior to February of 1882, Helen was busy assimilating the world around her; she had begun to speak and was quite precocious:

The beginning of my life was simple and much like every other little life. I came, I saw, I conquered, as the first baby in the family always does. . . . I showed many signs of an eager, self-asserting disposition. Everything that I saw other people do I insisted upon imitating. At six months I could pipe out "How d'ye," and one day I attracted every one's attention by saying "Tea, tea, tea" quite plainly. Even after my illness I remembered one of the words I had learned in these early months. It was the word "water," and I continued to make some sound for that word after all other speech was lost. I ceased making the sound "wah-wah" only when I learned to spell the word. They tell me I walked the day I was a year old. (Keller, 1903/2003, p. 15)

All this was to change, for in February 1882, a mysterious illness struck Helen leaving her blind and deaf. At the time, it was diagnosed as "an acute congestion of the stomach and brain," quite probably, it was either scarlet fever or meningitis (American Federation for the Blind, 2010).

These happy days did not last long. One brief spring, musical with the song of robin and mocking-bird, one summer rich in fruit and roses, one autumn of gold and crimson sped by and left their gifts at the feet of an eager, delighted child. Then, in the dreary month of February, came the illness which closed my eyes and ears and plunged me into the unconsciousness of a new-born baby. They called it acute congestion of the stomach and brain. The doctor thought I could not live. Early one morning, however, the fever left me as suddenly and mysteriously as it had come. There was great rejoicing in the family that morning, but no one, not even the doctor, knew that I should never see or hear again.

I fancy I still have confused recollections of that illness. I especially remember the tenderness with which my mother tried to soothe me in my waling hours of fret and pain, and the agony and bewilderment with which I awoke after a tossing half sleep, and turned my eyes, so dry and hot, to the wall away from the once-loved light, which came to me dim and yet more dim each day. But, except for these fleeting memories, if, indeed, they be memories, it all seems very unreal, like a nightmare. Gradually I got used to the silence and darkness that surrounded me and forgot that it had ever been different, until she came—my teacher—who was to set my spirit free. (Keller, 1903/2003, pp. 15-16)

Until the time of her illness, Helen and her parents lived in the "rose bower," a small cottage on the property that was a few steps from the main house of the Keller homestead, Ivy Green (See Figure 6 below) which was originally used as an office for the plantation. The cottage

was later refurnished as a bridal suite for Keller's second wife, Kate Adams Keller. Helen Keller was born here on June 27, 1880. This structure also faces south and has a large bedroom with a bay window, and a playroom on the north side of the cottage. . . . The well and pump is situated between the main house and the birthplace cottage and is covered by a four-square open structure made of cedar posts with a cedar shingle roof. (USDI, 2013)

When Helen was five years old, they moved to the main house at Ivy Green.

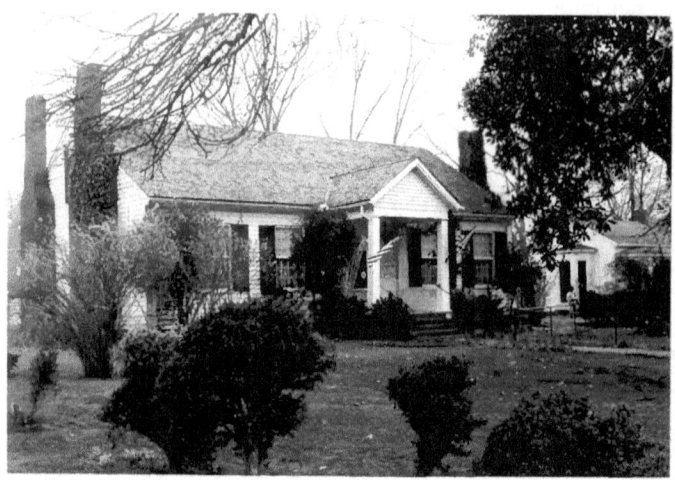

Ivy Green
Tuscumbia, AL
Main House, SW corner
Photo by: Doug Letson, 2/90

Figure 6: Ivy Green from National Historic Landmark Application

Helen (1903/3003), likened the landscape where she grew up to a paradise. The little cottage where she was born was: "completely covered with vines, climbing roses and honeysuckles. From the garden it looked like an arbour." The Keller homestead was called "Ivy Green," because

> the house and the surrounding trees and fences were covered with beautiful English ivy. Its old-fashioned garden was the paradise of my childhood. . . . .What joy it was to lose myself in that garden of flowers, to wander happily from spot to spot, until, coming suddenly upon a beautiful vine, I recognized it by its leaves and blossoms, and knew it was the vine which covered the tumble-down summer-house at the farther end of the garden! Here, also, were trailing clematis, drooping jessamine, and some rare sweet flowers called butterfly lilies, because their fragile petals resemble butterflies' wings. But the roses—they were loveliest of all. . . . . They used to hang in long festoons from our porch, filling the whole air with their fragrance, untainted by any earthy smell;

and in the early morning, washed in the dew, they felt so soft, so pure, I could not help wondering if they did not resemble the asphodels of God's garden. (pp. 14-15)

These are the initial conditions of Helen's life. [This is akin to Grof's BPM I: Intrauterine Environment, Before the Onset of Birth and the planetary archetype Neptune, see chapter 3 below].

Helen's illness was the perturbation or disturbance, which caused the system to bifurcate or diverge from its original course, and Helen was thus forced to take a dark road that was very much less travelled. In the years between her illness and Annie's arrival, Helen (1955) described herself as a *Phantom*, and then only later after the miracle at the pump did she refer to herself as *Helen*.

Helen's life will unfold as we go through the film. In 1955, Helen wrote a biography about Annie Sullivan entitled: *Teacher: Annie Sullivan Macy*. Helen always referred to Annie as *Teacher*. She does so in the book itself, and many others who knew Annie and Helen also referred to Annie as *Teacher*. It is to Annie's life, which we will now turn, and linger there a while, as it needs more illumination.

Before I begin, I wanted to mention the use of *Annie* instead of *Anne Sullivan Macy*, which has been purposefully done to presence Annie's youth. While I am aware that some could read the use of the diminutive form *Annie* as demeaning or disrespectful, this is not my intention. On the contrary, by using *Annie*, instead of *Anne* it helps the reader to remember who Annie was, and what her lived experience was as a new teacher, and in that light, not to lose sight of importance and magnitude of her accomplishments—the use of *Annie* is designed only to have us appreciate her even more.

Initial Conditions Annie Sullivan

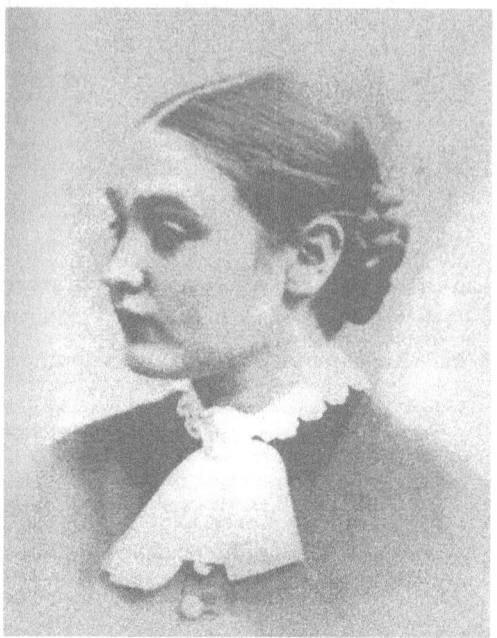

Figure 7: Annie Sullivan in 1880, age 14

I. THE BURIAL OF THE DEAD
APRIL is the cruelest month, breeding
Lilacs out of the dead land, mixing
Memory and desire, stirring
Dull roots with spring rain.

– T.S. Eliot, "The Wasteland"

Annie Sullivan's past requires more explication. Unlike Helen Keller's past, Annie comes to the tale with more age and experiences. Also unlike Keller, whose history is "an open book," part of the lexicon of history, and will unfold as we work through *The Miracle Worker* (Penn, 1962), Annie's past was shrouded in pain and anguish, shame and secrecy. It is only by showing significant events and by painting a picture of the three different fields that Annie found herself in before arriving in Tuscumbia, that we can make sense of her: Traumatic Origins in Agawam, Terrifying Tewksbury Almshouse, and Stubborn Spitfire's Education at Perkins. The above photograph of Annie was taken around 1880, the year Helen was born.

Traumatic origins at Agawam. Annie Sullivan was born in the Feeding Hills section of Agawam, Massachusetts on April 14, 1866. Her parents were poor illiterate, Irish immigrants: Thomas Sullivan and Alice Chloesy Sullivan. They emigrated from Ireland after the beginning of the Great Famine, had 5 children, and lived in poverty. Annie's life was filled with trauma and death from the beginning. Annie's mother had tuberculosis and a hip injury that occurred when Annie was very young. Tuberculosis was called consumption at the time because "the body was literally consumed by the disease" (Nielsen, 2009, p. 8). Annie's father Thomas, a hired hand, was an alcoholic.

Annie was the oldest of the 5 children. Her sister Ellen, born in 1867, died at the age of 5 from a malignant fever. Her brother Jimmie, born in 1869, died at the age of 7 from a congenitally tubercular hip. Another brother, John, born in 1872, died at the age of 2 months from "a lack of vitality." Annie's only surviving sibling, Mary, was born in 1873. Annie developed trachoma at this time, leaving her in pain with her vision significantly impaired. Trachoma is highly contagious, and resulting from exposure to bacteria, and is prevalent in impoverished communities. It causes

> inflammation and scar tissue to develop in the eye, generally on the inside of the eyelid, the blinking and rubbing of which then create additional scar tissue. Impaired eyesight and discomfort, often sever pain result. Annie's first memory of herself was hearing someone say, "she would be so pretty if it were not for her eyes. . . . Trachoma victims wore the stigma on the most prominent part of the face—the eyes. (Nielsen, 2009, p. 6)

Annie's memories of her mother Alice were intense, and in her own words they "never faded with all the years. Every detail remains distinct, and they were all vivid, and even to this day perturbing and unpleasant." Annie "remembered her mother ill and in bed, all of them desperately poor in a dark place with lots of steps" (Nielsen, 2009, p. 7). Annie's mother died of tuberculosis when Annie was 8 years old, in 1874. Annie explained:

> I do not remember what my feelings were, I know I did not cry. . . . Jimmie put his arms around me, and we both cried, I do not think from grief but because of the strangeness and stillness everywhere. (p. 9)

Annie watched her mother's body being laid out until she was discovered and jerked out of the room, and after the body was prepared, she vividly remembering the details:

> I just looked and looked at her and wondered, I saw Mary and Jimmie sobbing, and Mary was sitting on my father's knee. I didn't cry or move. Somehow they didn't seem to belong to me or I to them. They seemed more like the other people who were sitting around—strangers. I don't remember any one speaking to me or anything that happened afterwards. (Nielsen, 2009, p. 9)

Nielsen noted that "those who study bereavement characterize its initial period as one of denial, numbness, and a feeling of being on 'automatic pilot'" (p. 9).

Emily Dickenson (1830-1886) wrote a poem [#599] "There is a Pain so Utter," which describes the protective quality of the trance-like dissociation that occurs during the initial stages of grief, which may shed light on this.

> There is a pain—so utter—
> It swallows substance up—
> Then covers the Abyss with Trance—
> So Memory can step
> Around—across—upon it—
> As one within a Swoon—
> Goes safely—where an open eye—
> Would drop Him—Bone by Bone. (Wikipedia, 2013c)

Dickinson lived in Amherst, Massachusetts from 1856-1886 where the poems were found in her bedroom after she died. [Amherst is 30 miles from Agawam].

After his wife died, Annie's father Thomas fell apart. Within months, he left the children in the care of family members, abandoning them. Thomas came once to see Annie and Jimmie at Tewksbury, and after that Annie never saw him again.

Annie was illiterate and never attended school until she was 14 years old, although she was once taken to visit a local school by one of the neighbors (Nielsen, 2009). When Annie lived with her relatives the autumn after her mother died, and asked about attending school with the other children "she was told harshly, 'Don't be a fool. With your eyes, you could never learn to read or write'" (Hickok, 1961, p. 5).

Later in life, an aunt of Annie's remarked that they heard "legends of her intractability," and that Annie and Jimmie were poor and challenging children. This relative also reported that "Annie had been a "disobedient child with bad eyes" (Nielsen, 2009, p. 11). "Sometimes she was almost dangerous," biographer Nella Braddy noted (1933, p. 14).

In *The Touch of Magic*, Hickok (1961) recounted an illustrative example, which was shared in less detail by Braddy. The incident surrounded Christmas presents. For several days, packages arrived and were put into the parlor and the children were forbidden to enter. Naturally, Annie disobeying this edict, found a beautiful doll among the presents. She was convinced that the doll was for her. She would sneak in and hold the doll, and then on Christmas morning, to her shock and disbelief, the doll was given to another child.

> For an instant Annie stood frozen as the realization dawned on her that her doll had been given to someone else. Then she flew into a rage the like of which even Cousin John and Statia had never seen before. First she tried to grab the doll from her little cousin, but Cousin John seized her roughly and pushed her away. Then she stamped on her own presents and started smashing everything she could within reach—toys, Christmas-tree ornaments, a vase which Statia had received as a wedding gift. "She's just a wild animal," Statia said after they finally quieted her down and had cleaned up the debris. "I can't have her around any longer. I wont." (Hickok, 1961, pp. 6-7)

Mary, then three years old, was the only child who did not suffer from any defect, and was able to stay with Thomas Sullivan's relatives. Annie and Jimmie were abandoned and sent to Tewksbury Almshouse in February 1876. On top of all of the poverty, sickness, and death, Annie and Jimmie were now essentially orphans—Annie was not yet 10 years old, and Jimmie, having just turned 7, died within a few months of arriving at Tewksbury; Annie remained there until she was 14.

Annie's biographer, Nella Braddy, only learned of these years, almost 50 years later, in 1928. Braddy reported that Annie "talked all afternoon about the part of her life which no living being knows." Annie was 62 at the time:

> The little information Macy left behind about the first ten years of her childhood, those essential years that construct us as human beings, is anguished and disjointed. . . . To her these were shameful years for

which she had no adequate language (Nielsen, 2009, p. 12).

Crossing the threshold into Terrifying Tewksbury Almshouse.
Jimmie and Annie arrived at Tewksbury on February 22, 1876, and as was
the protocol, were to be separated and placed in the men's and women's
wards respectively. Braddy (1933) wrote: "A significant change took place in
Annie during those moments. All the dormant emotion within her woke to
life. She knew now what love was. She loved Jimmie. Loved him deeply,
passionately, tragically" (p. 18). Nielsen (2009) elaborated:

> Already, at this pivotal point, hints of Anne Sullivan Macy's tenacity and
> potential fury emerged. As an adult, Macy wrote of Johannah Dunnivan
> [her thinly disguised name for herself in an unpublished fictionalized
> memoir]: "All of the love and tenderness her nature was capable of were
> lavished upon her little brother, Jimmy." The ten-year-old had suffered
> much separation. Death had taken her mother and two siblings.
> Relatives had taken her sister but had rejected her and Jimmie. She had
> little information about her father and whether or not she would ever
> see him again. She knew virtually nothing of this loud, large, and
> frightening institution into which they had just stepped. . . . . Her
> younger brother was all she had. (p. 17)

Braddy related that Annie discussed little of what occurred during her
years there—characterizing them as "a crime against childhood," and said
"she has spent her life since the age of fourteen trying to forget what
happened up to that time" (Nielsen, 2009, p. 13).

During Annie's stay at Tewksbury, she was again surrounded by
poverty, sickness, and death. She and Jimmie spent their first night in the
death house, where the bodies were kept before they were buried, and they
would often play in there before Jimmie died.

Jimmie died on May 31, 1876, and while Annie had reacted with
dissociation and numbness to her mother's death, and death had been a
familiar to her, Jimmie's death was different. After almost fifty years,
Nielsen related that Annie wrote about her awareness that Jimmie was
going to die, and discussed his death in "greater detail than any other life
event. . . . 'An indescribable feeling of terror swept over me. It was as if
sharp, cruel fingers gripped my heart.'" A day or two later, she woke and
found a "black, empty space" where his been had been and snuck into the
death house to find him (Nielsen, 2009, p. 19). Annie explained:

It was all dark inside. I couldn't see the bed at first. I reached out my hand and touched the iron rail, and clung to it with all my strength until I could balance myself on my feet. Then I crept to the side of the bed— and touched him! Under the sheet I felt the little cold body, and something in me broke. My screams waked everyone in the hospital. Someone rushed in and tried to pull me away; but I clutched the little body and held it with all my might. [Attendants dragged her back to the ward] But I kicked and scratched and bit them until they dropped me upon the floor, and left me there, a heap of pain beyond words. After a while the first paroxysm subsided, and I lay quite still. One of the women—a poor cripple—hobbled to me, and bent down as far as she could to lift me up; but the effort hurt her so that she groaned. I got up and helped her back to bed. She made me sit beside her, and she petted me and spoke tender words of comfort to me. Then I knew the relief of passionate tears. (Nielsen, 2009, p. 20)

Nearly blind, Annie's stay at Tewksbury was interrupted only a brief six-month respite, when a benevolent priest took her to Boston to have two eye operations which were unsuccessful.

During Annie's stay at Tewksbury, some of the other inmates were kind to her and befriended Annie. She learned that there were schools that taught blind children, and her dream was to go to school. Annie learned that Mr. Sanborn, one of board members of the State Board of Charities, was to visit. Nielsen (2009), recounting Braddy's "dramatic version of the story" related that on that day, Annie followed the group of dignitaries from room to room, only being able to see vague shapes. When the visit was drawing to a close "at the last possible moment, not knowing which blurry body was his, she hurled herself forward into the group of well-dressed men and women. 'Mr. Sanborn, Mr. Sanborn, I want to go to school'" Annie pleaded (Nielsen, 2009, p. 32). Nielsen went on to comment that even if actual events were not this dramatic, "the meeting required initiative and action from Annie."

Sanborn subsequently arranged for Annie to go to the Perkins Institution, and "the final advice that Annie received from the carriage driver was: Don't ever come back to this place. Do you hear? Forget this, and you'll be all right." (p. 33). Nielsen summarized:

The difficulty of course, was that no human being could forget the Tewksbury Almshouse. The almshouse forged indelible marks on the mind, body, and future relationships of the young girl who spent the formative years between the ages of ten and fourteen there. As an adult, Macy repeatedly tried to make sense of her life at Tewksbury. She tried to draw meaning, tried to salvage a self that wasn't irreparably damaged. This past brought her much shame. (pp. 33-34)

Annie never spoke about this part of her past in public speeches, but eliminated it completely and "skipped over the almshouse going directly from her mother's death to Perkins" (Nielson, 2009, p. 34). Annie did not share these memories with anyone else before telling Braddy in 1928—not even Helen herself. Although they had lived with each other almost continually for over 40 years, in the book *Teacher*, Helen (1955) revealed that it was not until Helen herself was 50 years old and her teacher was 64, that Teacher revealed the "dark secret" of her early years (p. 53).

Years later Annie, now in her 60s, discovered that her father had committed suicide. Annie herself struggled with and suffered from depression many times during her life. Until Helen was 50, she was unable to understand her teacher's irrationality and dark moods. Knowing about Annie's past, one can understand what might have been underlying and driving Annie's depression.

Crossing the threshold—Stubborn spitfire's education at Perkins Institution. Annie arrived at the Perkins Institution on October 7, 1880. Helen Keller was three months old. Annie was an outsider and didn't fit in. Upon arriving at Perkins, Annie was asked her name and birthday; she flippantly listed her birthday as July 4. She didn't know how to spell her name, and when she was asked in front of the class, Annie was laughed at—for no one could believe that at age 14, she didn't know how to spell. The teachers and students made fun of Annie further wounding her.

Annie continued to be recalcitrant, rebellious, and difficult. Unless she wanted to learn a subject, she could not easily be compelled to do so. She disliked most of her teachers, and often found herself in trouble and at odds with either the teachers or the administration of the school. It was only because no one wanted to send her back to Tewksbury that Annie was not expelled on several occasions. Even when a conflict arose, either the teachers or the administration would take Annie's side, and thus expulsion was averted.

Tewksbury had shown Annie the seamier side of life, and thus she had nothing in common with the other pupils who were more sheltered, and largely middle class. She was older, illiterate, a liberal; she was interested in politics, was Irish and Catholic to boot. After initial skirmishes, Annie largely kept to herself, was self conscious, and socially awkward.

In spite of these initial difficulties and the lasting legacy of her traumatic origins and history, Annie quickly learned to read, and in particular had two important teachers who instilled in her a love of learning, and tamed her fury to a degree. Miss Moore understood Annie and was a caring and creative teacher; she opened up Shakespeare to Annie. Miss Moore "provided Annie with her first intellectual thrills, and with a sense of beauty of the power of words, of magic, and of the larger world as a place of potential." Annie's other favorite teacher, Cora Newton, spoke of Annie as "a wholesome, vigorously active, impulsive, self-assertive, generally happy girl, inclined to be impatient and combative towards criticisms or any opinion not in agreement with her own." Cora also remembered Annie's "executive ability and initiative" (Nielsen, 2009, pp. 43-44).

The educational philosophy at Perkins was influenced by Pestalozzian and Frobelian ideas, which were instituted the same year that Annie began at Perkins. These methods, rejected "mechanical teaching," and obligatory memorization and emphasized and sought to implement the: "many-sidedness and wisdom [of their theories] . . . physical, intellectual and moral, careful adaptation to each individual bent, capacity, and temperament; as well as to the whole idea of perfect womanhood and manhood." Nielsen (2009) explained "all available measures have been taken to increase the vital sap and suppleness of fresh life in the school, and to prevent it from running the risk of becoming petrified." Nielsen further explicated that "lyrical training mattered; play and pedagogical flexibility suited student needs" (p. 39). Michael Anagnos, the director of Perkins was strongly aligned with these principles, and during the 1880s sought to establish a permanent kindergarten at Perkins as well. This was the unconscious field in which Annie learned, although the kindergarten did not open until after Annie had graduated and left Perkins. Annie loved myth and literature, and showed an aptitude for teaching; Braddy (1933) gave an example:

> In the midst of her own difficulties she began to show her gift for teaching. She lifted a class of ten-year-olds who were struggling with ancient Greek history out of despondency by suggesting that each of

them take the name of one of the characters in the history. Thus, Eunice became Pericles, Lydia, Aristides, etc. It came to the attention of Mr. Anagnos who smiled when he heard it and said, "Not Aristides, but Aristidena." After that Mr. Anagnos, Edward Everett Hale, and a number of others dropped Lydia's name and called her Aristidena. (p. 72).

Aristidena (Miss Lydia Hayes), became head of the New Jersey Commission for the Blind, and spoke of Annie's kindness to the smaller children. Annie had shown the same kindness to her when she was "a timid little girl from the Far West, lonely and sad, at first, in her new surroundings. This was something that Annie could understand." Nielsen (2009) observed that lonely and incarcerated people everywhere tore at her heart. This was one reason why she was drawn to Laura Bridgman. Laura, when Annie entered the Institution, was a woman of fifty. (p. 72)

Annie befriended legendary Laura Bridgeman, who was living as an adult at the school. Laura was the world famous deaf-blind pupil of Dr. Samuel Gridley Howe, who at the age of 2, had been stricken deaf and blind, and who Howe discovered at age 7 in New Hampshire. Through her work with Howe, Laura had come to international attention. In 1842, Charles Dickens, when visiting the United States wanted to see two things—Niagara Falls and Laura Bridgman. Dickens visited Perkins and wrote about his visit— of meeting Laura and of her education—in *American Notes* (Dickens, 1842). Kate Keller would read Dickens' account in the mid-1880s, and thought Dr. Howe might be able to help. However, upon learning that Howe had died in 1876, she didn't pursue the matter further (Hermann, 1999).

To communicate with Laura, all of the students at the school learned the manual alphabet. Laura could not abide fools, and her language was very stilted. Annie spent hours conversing with Laura, spelling into her hand all of the gossip and goings on at the school. Howe had kept detailed records of Laura's education, and this would later serve as the primer that Annie would study in preparation for teaching Helen.

As time went on, Annie became less rebellious and was kind to others who entered estranged. Annie had two successful eye operations during her stay at Perkins, and as a result, was able to act as a guide and take some of the other students on outings. Midway through Annie's stay at Perkins, Mrs. Sophia Hopkins became a housemother for one of the cottages where

Annie lived. Hopkins was a widow whose daughter [of a similar age to Annie] had died recently. Hopkins became like a mother to Annie; Hopkins took Annie home with her in the summers and they forged a lifelong friendship. Annie's correspondence with Hopkins while Annie was in Tuscumbia is of inestimable value, and provides much of the written record that we have of Annie's teaching methods and of what transpired, as it occurred.

In 1886, Annie graduated from Perkins as valedictorian of her class. The complete text of her valedictory address is contained in Appendix C. Here are a few relevant excerpts (Sullivan, 1886):

Today we are standing face to face with the great problem of life. . . . . And now we are going out into the busy world, to take our share in life's burdens, and do our little to make that world better, wiser and happier. . . . if we obey the great law of our being.

God has placed us here to grow, to expand, to progress. To a certain extent our growth is unconscious. We receive impressions and arrive at conclusions without any effort on our part; but we also have the power of controlling the course of our lives.

We can educate ourselves; we can, by thought and perseverance, develop all the powers and capacities entrusted to us, and build for ourselves true and noble characters. Because we can, we must. It is a duty we owe to ourselves, to our country and to God. . . . Self-culture is a benefit, not only to the individual, but also to mankind. Every man who improves himself is aiding the progress of society, and every one who stands still, holds it back.

The advancement of society always has its commencement in the individual soul. It is by battling with the circumstances, temptations and failures of the world, that the individual reaches his highest possibilities.

The search for knowledge, begun in school, must be continued through life in order to give symmetrical self-culture. . . . Directors, teachers and matrons: we enter life's battle-field determined to prove our gratitude to you, by lives devoted to duty, true in thought and deed to the noble principles you have taught us. . . . Fellow-graduates: duty bids us go forth into active life.

Let us go cheerfully, hopefully, and earnestly, and set ourselves to find our especial part. When we have found it, willingly and faithfully perform it; for every obstacle we overcome, every success we achieve tends to bring man closer to God and make life more as he would have it. [emphasis added]

Annie had no idea of how she would make her way in the world, what she would do for a living, or where she would live; and she feared going back to Tewksbury. In the summer of 1886, the Kellers consulted an occulist in Baltimore, who referred them to Dr. Alexander Graham Bell. They traveled with Helen to see Dr. Bell, who recommended that Captain Keller contact Perkins. Upon returning to Tuscumbia, Keller penned the legendary letter, which is where we will leave the story for now.

Initial Conditions Laura Bridgman

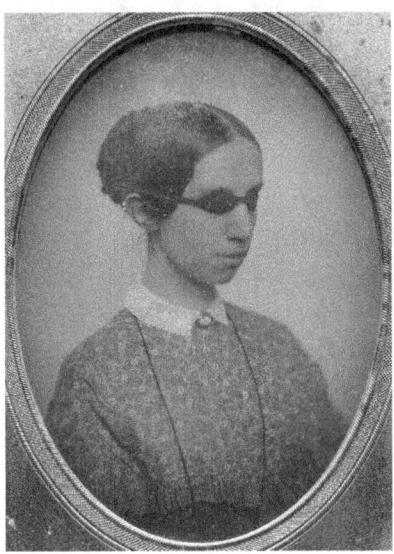

Figure 8: Laura Bridgman

I sat down . . . before a girl, blind, deaf, and dumb; destitute of smell; and nearly so of taste: before a fair young creature with every human faculty, and hope, and power of goodness and affection, enclosed within her delicate frame, and but one outward sense—the sense of touch. There she was, before me; built up, as it were, in a marble cell, impervious to any ray of light, or particle of sound; with her poor white hand peeping through a chink in the wall, beckoning to some good man for help, that an Immortal soul might be awakened. Long before I looked upon her, the help had come. Her face was radiant with intelligence and pleasure. . . . . . From the mournful ruin of such bereavement, there had slowly risen up this gentle, tender, guileless, grateful-hearted being. Like other inmates of that house, she had a green ribbon bound round her eyelids. A doll she had dressed lay near upon the ground. I took it up, and saw that she had made a green fillet such as she wore herself, and fastened it about its mimic eyes.

—Charles Dickens, *American Notes*, 1842
on his impressions of Laura Bridgman

Laura Bridgman was the third child in her family. Her mother and father had two other daughters by the time Laura was born on December 21, 1829. Although she had fragile beginnings, and was subject to seizures at first, Laura rallied at 20 months, but then got scarlet fever and was sick for many weeks. Two of her sisters also contracted the disease, but they did not survive. Laura had a long recuperation, and by age 4 she was fully recovered—her intelligence and curiosity undiminished, but the illness left her blind and deaf. Prior to being "discovered" by Dr. Howe, Laura had developed a rudimentary sign language, and this allowed only limited communication with her family. However, a hired man who lived on their farm, and was disabled seemed to understand Laura intuitively. Laura had frequent tempers, and by age 7, because of her size, this was becoming problematic. Laura loved to imitate whatever her mother did; she helped around the house and knew how to knit and crochet. Laura's father was the only one who could enforce discipline; he would indicate displeasure by stamping on the floor and thus "startle her into obedience."

In 1837, Dr. Samuel Gridley Howe met Laura and invited her to come to Perkins, which she did on October 12. Although it was difficult for Laura to be ripped away from her family and surroundings, Howe gave Laura two weeks to recuperate before he began to teach her. He began by using raised letters taped to everyday objects. He would then have Laura match the objects with the corresponding labels themselves. Initially, Laura just imitated and memorized them, so Dr. Howe changed his approach; he then cut up the letters so that Laura had to recombine them. Eventually, within three months, Laura was able to make the connection that words were the names for things; she then learned the manual alphabet.

Although Dr. Howe worked with her early on, Laura was later taught by others. Like Dr. Howe, these teachers kept very detailed notes and taught her in a structured way. Dr. Howe published reports about his work with Laura, and she was the first deaf-blind child to be taught language. In 1842, Charles Dickens visited Perkins and met Laura. He wrote about her in *American Notes*, making Laura world famous (Perkins, 1843, 1845).

Laura was a curious and demanding student, a lifelong learner and letter writer. She suffered a series of emotional and physical losses during her adolescence— being heavily impacted by the loss of teachers, and also by Howe's marriage and absence for extended periods of time. Except for a brief time back with her family, Laura was not comfortable outside of

Perkins, and so she lived there for most of her life. Although there are some similarities between the methods by which Laura and Helen were taught, Laura did not learn idiomatic English, and resulting in her speech being stilted and staccato—more peculiar and unusual, instead of the natural, flowing, and fluent way that Helen was able to express herself.

An optional excursion into origins is offered and contained in Appendix D, taking us to the beginnings of the lives of our leading ladies, Annie and Helen, and the circumstances and fields that surrounded and informed them. The excursion begins by delving into the origin of *origins* etymologically, continues looking at the places where Annie and Helen grew up, and finally goes into the origins of their very names.

We have one last stop, at archetypal beginnings, before we proceed to our Cinematic Tour. In the Archetypal Beginnings chapter that follows, we will learn more about archetypes and in particular the archetypal field of the transformation process.

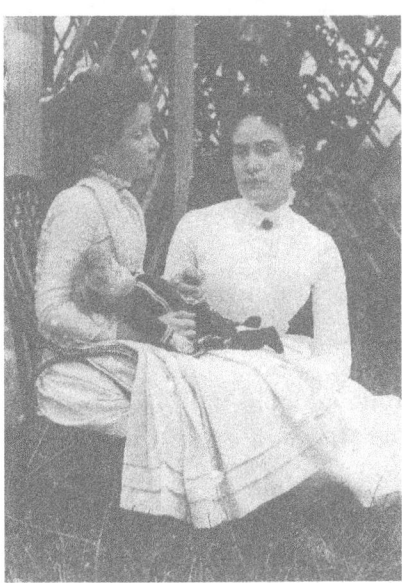

Figure 9. Helen Keller and Annie Sullivan

The readiness with which she comprehended the great facts of physical life confirmed me in the opinion that the child has dormant within him, when he comes into the world, all the experiences of the race. These experiences are like photographic negatives, until language develops them and brings out the memory-images.
—Annie Sullivan, in *Story of My Life*, Letters August 28, 1887

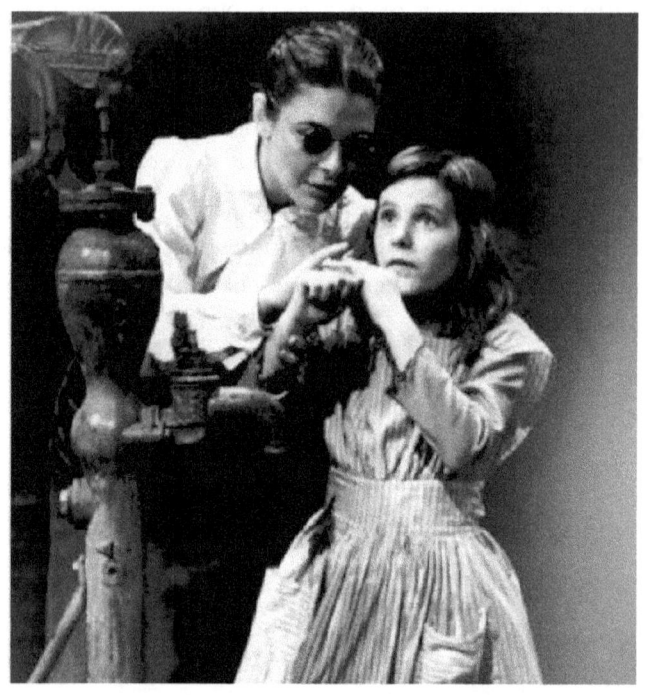

Figure 10: Bancroft and Duke in Broadway Play version of William Gibson's *The Miracle Worker* **[from cover of play, 2008]**

ARCHETYPAL BEGINNINGS

Once I knew the depth where no hope was, and darkness lay on the face of all things. Then love came and set my soul free. Once I knew only darkness and stillness. Now I know hope and joy. Once I fretted and beat myself against the wall that shut me in. Now I rejoice in the consciousness that I can think, act and attain heaven. . . . . Night fled before the day of thought, and love and joy and hope came up in a passion of obedience to knowledge. Can anyone who has escaped such captivity, who has felt the thrill and glory of freedom, be a pessimist?

—Helen Keller in *Optimism*, 1903

In this chapter, I will define some key terms: *archetype*, *pattern*, *archetypal field*, and then briefly sketch out and explicate the archetypal field of transformation. In the Cinematic Tour chapter that follows, I will hint at or allude to these archetypal roles, often implicitly. In future work, I hope to explore these archetypal roles of the teacher in education, and the metaphorical nature of the learning process, that were begun by Mayes and Ormell (Mayes 2010a, 2010b; Ormell, 1996) and show how they beautifully play out in this film, but, "not yet."

Archetypal Definitions and Understandings

As universal underlying patterns, *archetypes* are the primordial images that are common to all humanity. As organizing principles of the psyche, archetypes "are the psychic correlates of the instincts" (Odajnyk, 1976, p. 15), and allow us to perceive in patterns and categories. Jung said of them: "The primordial images are the most ancient and most universal 'thought-forms' of humanity. They are as much feelings as thoughts: indeed, they lead their own independent life" (Jung, 1943/1972, p. 66, para. 104) . . . and they are relatively autonomous. Conforti (1999) noted that an "archetype is a preexisting non-personally acquired information field in the collective unconscious" (p. 1), and that archetypes also "perhaps function to align one to some innate destiny factor" (p. 7). Jung further describes archetypes as ideas that have been stamped on the human brain for aeons. That is why it lies ready to hand in the unconscious of every man . . . . The greatest and best thoughts of man shape themselves upon these primordial images as upon a blueprint. I have often been asked where the archetypes or primordial images come from. It seems to me that their origin can only be explained by assuming them to be deposits of constantly repeated experiences of humanity . . . . The archetype is a kind of readiness to produce over and over again the same or similar mythical ideas . . . recurrent impressions made by subjective reactions." (pp. 69-70, para. 109)

Archetypes, although they are expressed in a myriad of forms, are not the forms themselves, but can be thought of as more akin to the fields out of which forms arise. Conforti has discussed extensively Ervin Laszlo's clarification that "form exists as a potential in fields even before it appears in the outer world" (1999, p. 16), and explained that Laszlo's idea better helps us comprehend

> Jung's and Hillman's notion about the primacy of the image. The image, as a representative of a specific archetypal field, carries with it its own inherent morphology and information, and when accessed works to entrain the individual or culture into that archetypal field. (p. 17)

One of the "mantras" of Archetypal Pattern Analysis is that "Patterns are a coalescing of multiple trajectories around a singularity" (Conforti, 1999, p. 21). While we cannot ever know the *archetype per se*, we can discern its presence from its footprints, in the patterns that it creates. An archetype has the power to entrain and draw individuals into its orbit (p. 23). Conforti has explained that:

> The archetype, which functions as an informational, rational and meaning carrying structure, works its influence by creating a field of influence. . . . Similar to the effect of fields in the outer world—such as gravitational or electromagnetic or in the casting of a spell—the archetype often consumes individual consciousness and works to incarnate through the types of situations, obsessions, interests, concerns, and moods we experience. The presence and existence of the archetype is felt through its effects. (p. 22)

Conforti (1999) explicated that individuals act out these archetypal influences through their complexes, which have an archetypal core, and act like an attractor site magnetically pulling things toward itself that resonate with it. This is similar to the example of a carrier shell (the symbol which adorns the first edition of *Field Form and Fate)* accreting things to it.

Luckily, there is a way to escape the gravitational hold of the complex, and that is through consciousness. Consciousness becomes, as Conforti noted "a central player when it comes to metabolizing the content and imperative of the complex. At this time one needs to step out of the spin and possessive hold of the complex and make conscious meaning of the process" (p. 25). In discussing the relatively stable forms that archetypal material takes over time, Conforti (1999) noted that they coalesce into familiar patterns, and that "pattern recognition is essential for the preservation of life" (p. 28).

Now that we have an idea about archetypes, archetypal fields, patterns, and their importance, we can now look more deeply at what I believe is the most important and ubiquitous pattern—the strange attractor that I have been orbiting around since at least the year 2000—the archetypal field of transformation, or the transformation process.

The Archetypal Field of the Transformation Process

Although the names may be changed to protect the innocent, this ubiquitous pattern is how the universe plays. One of its *nom de plume's* is the *eternal return*, which is also *"the archetype of archetypal dynamics, so to speak"* (Van Eenwyk, 1997, p. 114, emphasis added). Van Eenwyk pointed this out as when discussing the feedback dynamics generated by archetypal processes: "the eternal return is the epitome of all such aspects of archetypal processes" (p. 114). These two sentences were a huge bifurcation point for me, and reiterated to me Conforti's (1999) and colleagues' notion that "change often occurs through the presence of small rather than large perturbations" (p. 65). We will see this play out abundantly in the film, but now, back to the archetypal pattern.

Stanislav Grof's (1975) pioneering work with non-ordinary states of consciousness led him to chart a cartography of the psyche based on the experiences of his own and many co-researchers' experiences. He found that peoples' experience tended to cluster around four distinct themes.

What Grof did not realize, having grown up as an atheist in a communist country, was that this pattern was also mirrored in the *perennial philosophies* of the major religious traditions—the notions of death and rebirth. He writes about this in the book, *The Cosmic Game* (1998), and this book gave rise to my doctoral dissertation and also to my board games.

Although Otto Rank (1924/1993) had previously talked about the importance of birth in 1924, in the *Trauma of Birth*, Rank skipped over the liminal time of the actual birth process itself. For Rank, the trauma was the fall from grace, the loss of the paradisal womb, and the longing to return to it. Freud read Rank's book, and was severely shaken for several months, because Freud felt that Rank's discovery was so important that it might eventually prove more important than Freud's own work.

Freud had earlier suggested that the trauma of birth might indeed be the blueprint for all future anxiety, and Rank ran with this idea. Indeed Freud referred to Rank's book as "the most important progress since the discovery of psychoanalysis" (Grof, 1995, pp. 438-439). Grof in his charting the Rankian layer of the unconscious or the *perinatal* level [meaning around birth], gave us a wonderful way to talk about the transformation process.

In the popular PBS program and book, *The Power of Myth* Joseph Campbell, a long time friend of Grof's (1988), in speaking about Rank's initial insight said:

> everyone is a hero in birth, where he undergoes a tremendous psychological as well as physical transformation from the condition of a little water creature living in a realm of amniotic fluid into an air-breathing mammal which will ultimately be standing. That's an enormous transformation, and had it been consciously undertaken, it would have been indeed, a heroic act. (pp. 124-125)

What Grof brought to the table, metaphorically speaking, was his knowledge as a physician. Grof saw that the trauma of birth was actually the traumatic event of the physical process of birth itself, the harrowing and intense trip through the birth canal. Rank, being a layman, had not caught that the mythic pattern of the hero's journey, which Jung (1912/1976) had also written about *in Symbols of Transformation*, was precisely described in the actual process of physical birth itself. Grof was the first to make this specific connection (See Figure 11 below).

Thus Grof (1975) conceived of four different *Basic Perinatal Matrices* [BPM], or four different archetypal landscapes or subfields that make up the overarching archetypal field of transformation. I will briefly describe them here: BPM I is the intrauterine environment before the onset of birth—the amniotic universe—experienced as primal union with the mother. BPM II represents the condition once the contractions have begun and before the cervix has opened—experienced as cosmic engulfment and no exit or hell. BPM III represents the opening of the cervix and the propulsion through the birth canal—experienced as the intense death-rebirth struggle, while BPM IV represents the emergence of the child from the mother—experienced the death-rebirth experience, where the child comes into a different relationship with the mother (Grof, 2000). Since the perinatal matrices function as organizing principles for materials from other levels (Grof, 1975, p. 101), they are similar to the archetypal core, if you will, of a complex, but they may aggregate different complexes as well.

These archetypal Basic Perinatal Matrices are some of the are strange attractors of the psyche. They are also our own initial conditions, as we were all born—and while our births may have a different tone or cast depending on the experience (including caesarian)—the same archetypal field is present.

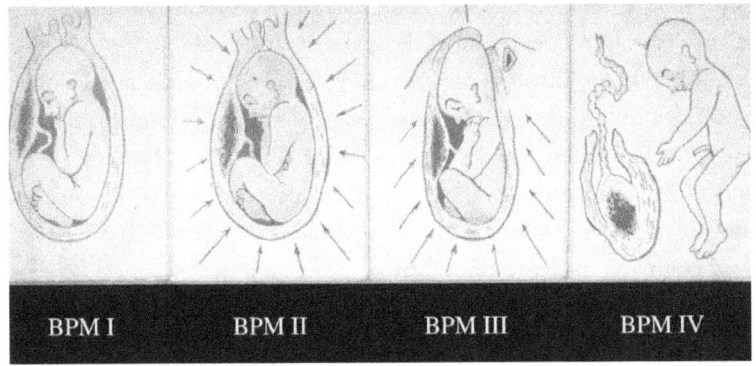

Figure 11: Grof's Perinatal Matrices

Like Nietzsche's (1892/1978) *Thus Spoke Zarathustra*, Grof's work revolves around the eternal return. Grof's (1975, 1998, 2000) work, like the eternal return, recognizes the importance of beginnings, not only our own personal beginnings with the birth process, but the ancient wisdom of primal peoples. Grof came upon the eternal return experientially, and his work allows us to go there, too. Grof's cartography is inclusive of other ideas from different depth psychology schools, and enables us to know where we are while we are on the journey of transformation and also in life itself.

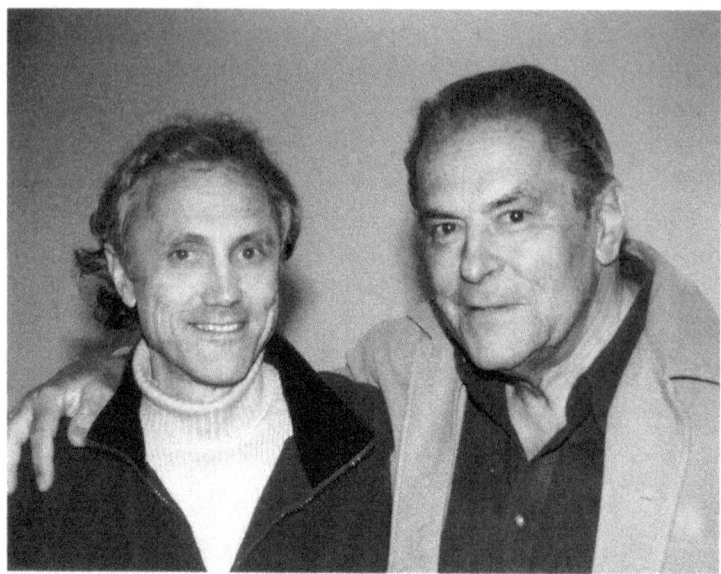

Figure 12: Richard Tarnas and Stanislav Grof

Richard Tarnas, a friend and colleague of Grof's, added another layer of understanding when, through his extensive research of archetypal astrology, Tarnas realized that the archetypal meanings of the four outer planets of the solar system correlated to the Grof's Basic Perinatal Matrices (Grof & Tarnas, 2002), and not only that, but that different configurations of the transiting planets were mirrored in the nonordinary state experiences that Grof had cognized his cartography from in the first place.

Psychology of the Future (Grof, 2000) contains a chapter on archetypal astrology, which is present in all foreign language editions of the book, but ironically not the English version. Grof noted in that chapter (2006) that "Ironically, when after years of frustrating effort I finally found a tool that made such predictions possible, it was more controversial than psychedelics themselves" (p. 1) Grof related:

> Rick is also a brilliant astrological researcher who combines impeccable scholarship and deep familiarity with holotropic states of consciousness, the subject of his doctoral dissertation. Rick also brings to his work extraordinary breadth of knowledge concerning human history and culture.
>
> We have been jointly exploring for many years the astrological correlates of mystical experiences, psychospiritual crises, psychotic episodes,

psychedelic states, and holotropic breathwork sessions. This work has shown that astrology, particularly the study of planetary transits, can predict both the archetypal content and the timing of holotropic states of consciousness. Our systematic study of the correlations between the nature and content of holotropic states and planetary transits convinced me that a combination of deep experiential therapy with archetypal psychology and transit astrology is the most promising strategy for psychiatry of the future. (pp. 1-2)

Reiterating and adding the planetary archetypes into the mix we get: the following:

BPM I is the intrauterine environment before the contractions start—the amniotic universe and primal union with the mother. Corresponding planetary archetype: Neptune.

BPM II represents the condition once the contractions have begun and before the cervix has opened—cosmic engulfment and no exit or hell. Corresponding planetary archetype: Saturn.

BPM III represents the opening of the cervix and the propulsion through the birth canal—the death-rebirth struggle Corresponding planetary archetype: Pluto.

BPM IV represents the emergence of the child from the mother—the death-rebirth experience. Corresponding planetary archetype: Uranus.

A detailed description of the interplay between the perinatal matrices and the planetary archetypal complexes can be found in the chart in Appendix E. On the following pages, are some pictorial representations: Figure 13 combines Grof's perinatal matrices, Tarnas's planetary archetypes and the process of metamorphosis. Figure 14 is my game which began everything in 2003, *Monomythopoly*™ *Eternal Return Edition*, while Figure 15 contains the latest iteration of the game. It has now fittingly been renamed as *Here We Go Again*®.

The planetary archetypes are wonderful "objects to think with," and give us useful and compelling adjectives that describe the emotional flavors of the landscape of transformation. One need not "believe in astrology," to derive benefit from them. By engaging with them from the perspective of "use value" rather than "truth value," we are able to gain insight into our lives and allow us to orient ourselves to the sometimes uncomfortable places we periodically find ourselves in.

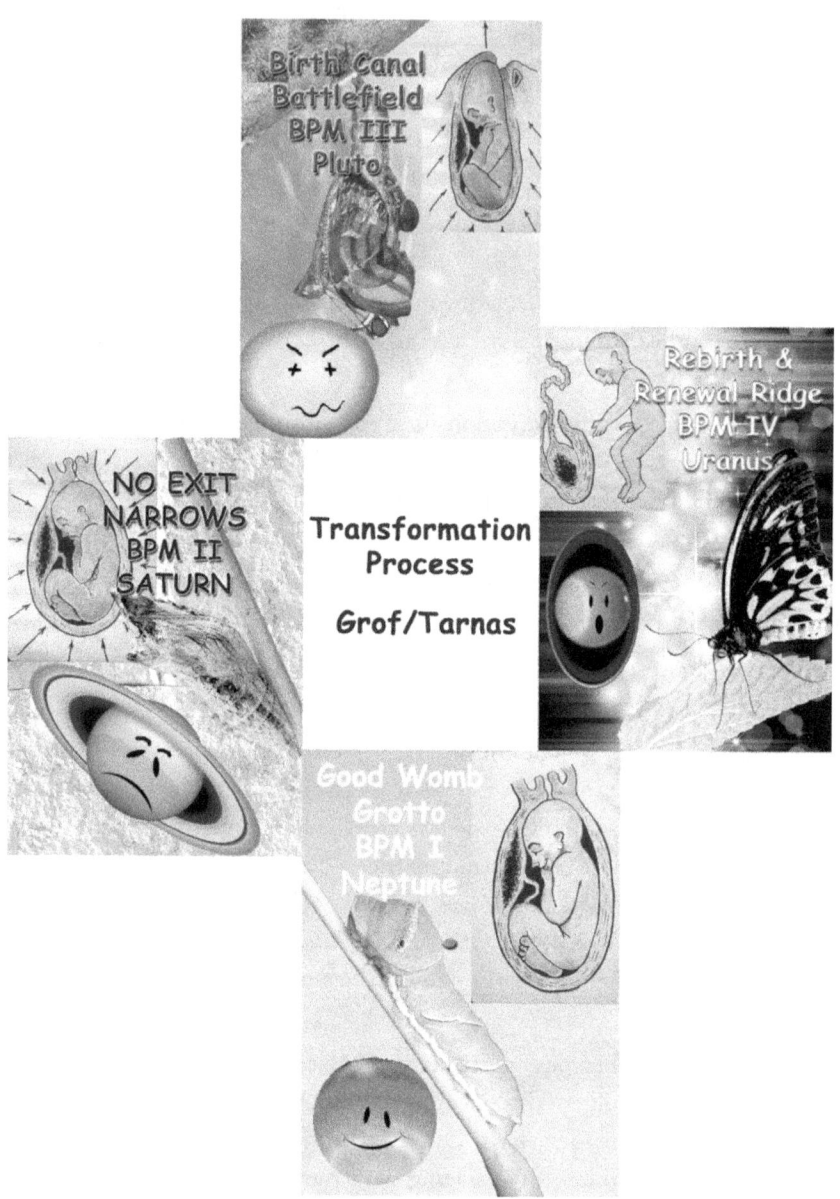

Figure 13: The Transformation Process Visually Integrated

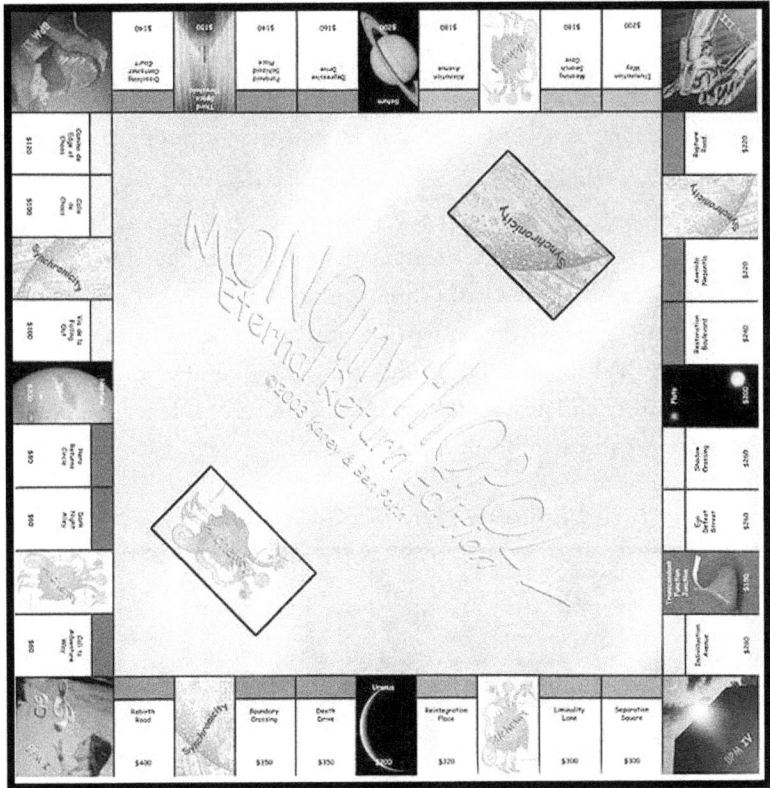

Figure 14: Monomythopoly: Eternal Return Edition™

I created the Monomythopoly™ game for my oral comprehensive exams in the Depth Psychology Department at Pacifica Graduate Institute, where we were charged with presenting on something that had deeply impacted us. I chose the work of Grof and Tarnas.

I have been caught in this pattern since my first research at Pacifica in 2000. The game showed the eternally recurring pattern of death and rebirth sequentially as it appeared in my coursework at Pacifica. This pattern has been working on me for the past 13 years, and so it is actually fitting that I would again find myself exploring it here. Fatefully, I chose the subtitle *Eternal Return Edition*, having been influenced by Van Eenwyk's (1997) book *Archetypes as Strange Attractors*, and so here "we go again," eternally returning to this same pattern!

[This version of the game, which is a part of my dissertation— a website where this cosmic play pattern plays out in many forms:

http://www.cosmicplay.net/Cosmic/Psych/psymono1.html. This link contains information on the Perinatal Matrices and the Planetary Archetypes. The following link shows the various courses, and the corresponding theorists, and their names for the different parts of the process: http://www.cosmicplay.net/Cosmic/Psych/psymono2.html]

Below, in Figure 15 is the first version of a board game *Here We Go Again*®, which I am currently creating. It synthesizes the transformation process, using the work of Grof, Tarnas, Jung, Bridges, Campbell, Vogler, and others. Fittingly, this version has recently "gone down in flames" while I have been working on this book, and is awaiting another metamorphosis into another form. The jury is still out on this one and I, too am anxious to see what phoenix will arise from these ashes.

Figure 15: Here We Go Again®

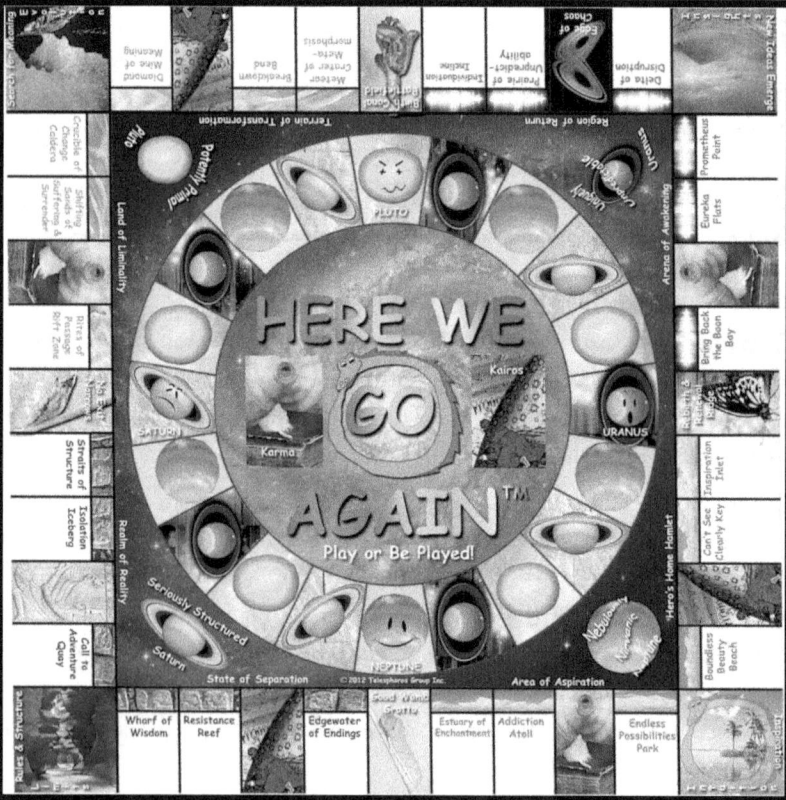

Figure 16 below shows where this pattern shows up in different realms.

Figure 16: Transformation Process in Various Realms

Nature	**Metamorphosis:** Caterpillar→Butterfly; Tadpole→Frog **Bodily Processes:** Digestion/Metabolism **Cyclical Changes:** Seasons; Day/Night; Phases of moon **Cosmic changes:** Carbon Cycle of Stars **Phase changes:** Water cycle **Cycle of Life:** Vegetation cycle; stages of life **Birth process:** mammals; birds; reptiles **Earth changes:** Volcanic activity; tectonic movements **Neurological:** Changes in neurons and neural nets **Self Organizing Systems/Chaos Theory**: see appendix F
Culture	**Rites of Passage:** [Van Gennep/Turner] traditional societies—birth/death/marriage change of status/identity **Transitions:** [Bridges]—corporate change **Coaching:** CREATE model; 4 faces of insight; [Rock] **Learning process;** belief change, 4 stages of competence- **Creative Process** **Monomyth:** Hero with 1000 Faces [Campbell] **Death/Rebirth Gods:** Demeter/Persephone; Isis/Osiris; Shiva's Dice Game; Christ **Hero's 2 Journeys:** Aristotle & Campbell [Vogler & Hauge]
Psych-ology	**Grof:** Psycho-Spiritual Death/Rebirth & Perennial Philosophy **Birth Trauma:** Rank/Freud/Grof **Jung:** Individuation, Alchemy, Creation of Consciousness **von Franz:** Dream Analysis, literature structure, fairytales **Tarnas:** Archetypal Astrology **Origin and History of Consciousness**: Neumann, Wilber **Klein:** Paranoid-Schizoid→Depressive [Object Relations] **Archetypal Dynamics:** Van Eenwyk, Conforti **Eternal Return**—Nietzsche [Chapelle: psychoanalysis], **Archetype of Renewal:** Bond

Now that we have explored the initial conditions present at the beginning of the film, have an understanding of archetypes, and a map of the archetype of transformation, we are ready to explore the film.

Figure 17: Annie Sullivan, circa 1887

[Courtesy of Perkins School for the blind]

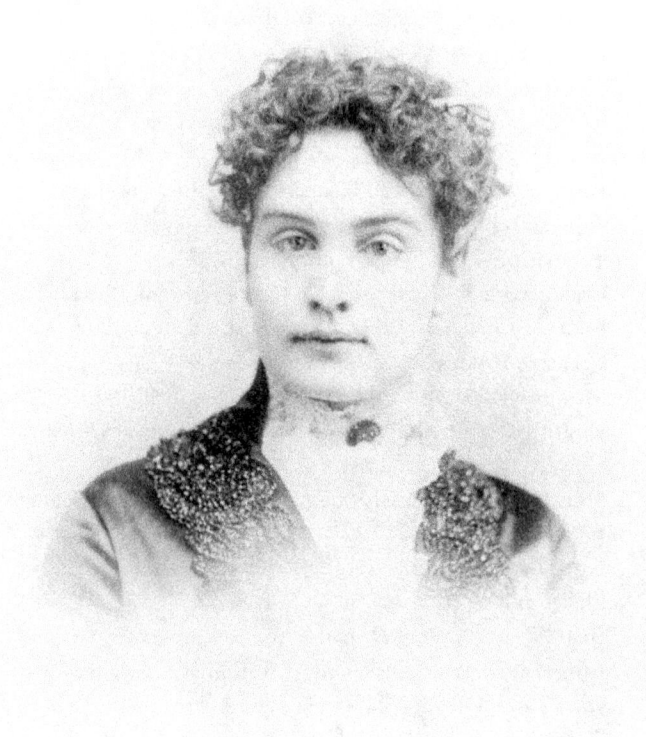

Keep on beginning and failing. Each time you fail, start all over gain, and you will grow stronger until have accomplished a purpose - not the one you began with perhaps, but one you'll be glad to remember.

– Anne Sullivan

PART II
SCENE-PLAY: A
CINEMATIC TOUR

Have you ever been at sea in a dense fog, when it seemed as if a tangible white darkness shut you in, and the great ship, tense and anxious, groped her way toward the shore with plummet and sounding-line, and you waited with beating heart for something to happen?

I was like that ship before my education began, only I was without compass or sounding-line, and had no way of knowing how near the harbour was. "Light! give me light!" was the wordless cry of my soul, and the light of love shone on me in that very hour.

– Helen Keller, *Story of My Life*, p. 25
describing the day her teacher arrived

ORIENTATION: In this part, we will proceed go through the film in a scene-play, watching the action unfold and play out; often delving deeper into different aspects of the story. To keep our bearings, I will use the chapter titles from the DVD as the major headings, with individual scenes within those chapters being discussed within them. In order not to stray too far afield, sometimes material will be placed in an appendix instead of being discussed in the main body of this chapter.

Also, as previously mentioned, along the way, we will convene around the
campfire and offer additional insights and perspectives on what has transpired.

Armed with our map for the journey of transformation—Grof's cartography of the psyche, let us boldly begin.

CREDITS / LOST CHILD

Credits Scene 1: Opening Scene-Initial Conditions—"Girl Interrupted"

The film opens with a young mother, Kate Keller, placing her daughter into a crib. Her body casts a shadow over the baby, and as she rises up and moves away, her shadow withdraws entirely from the baby, and the baby emerges into the light. Upon hearing the words, *"she'll live,"* we first see the intense emotions sweep across the mother's face: anguish, concern. She places her hand on her heart, and her much older husband Arthur comes to embrace her. The doctor who has also come into view, confesses—"I can tell you now, I thought she wouldn't." The couple is distressed to hear this. Captain Keller informs the doctor that he has been a parent before, but "this is my wife's first, she isn't battle-scarred yet." The mother inquires whether her daughter will "be alright?" The doctor reassuringly says "By morning she'll be knockin' down Captain Keller's fences again." The mother then anxiously asks: "Is there nothing we should do?" Her husband answers: "Put up stronger fencing, Hmm?" The doctor replies: "Just let her get well. She knows how better than we do." As Captain Keller escorts him out, the doctor explains, "I never saw a baby with more vitality. That's the truth."

Mother and baby are left alone. Kate tends to the nursery, walks away from the crib, and the baby begins to cry. Going to attend to her, the mother engages in a reverie with the baby, lovingly touching her and gently speaking to her, "Don't you cry now, you've been trouble enough. . ." she playfully continues talking while pulling a blanket up to cover the baby, who quiets down. Kate muses over what she has just experienced "'The wonders of modern medicine.' They don't know what they're curing even when they cure it. Men! Men and their battle scars!" We see a couple of flashes of anger when she utters: "the wonders of modern medicine" and "men and their battle scars."

Kate suddenly notices that something is not right. A bifurcation has occurred. Kate clicks her fingers and says Helen's name, but Helen is nonresponsive, through this illness something seems to have gone horribly wrong. All hell breaks loose. Kate escalates; it is horrible, she repeatedly snaps her fingers, her intensity and anxiety mounting. She speaks Helen's name again, insistently, and then Kate descends into an escalating uncontained chaos. She is totally out of control and screaming for her husband with a blood curdling scream, the agonized expression, which is a mixture of abject pain, fury, horror—indeed the screams are reminiscent of a horror film.

Captain Keller quickly comes to her and gets pulled into this chaotic whirlpool of emotion, they are cascading into chaos together; Kate is screaming about Helen's condition, and Captain Keller is furiously passing a kerosene lantern before Helen's unseeing eyes. The scene ends with Kate sinking back down into the darkness, her hands to her face, looking exactly like a black and white version of Edvard Munch's 1893, classic pastel icon, *The Scream*. In the foreground, clapping his hands furiously, then screaming at Helen, Captain Keller's face contorts in an almost murderous Molock-like wrath, all brilliantly shot through the bars of the crib. Helen, now blind and deaf, does not visibly react, unconscious of the storm of emotions that rages around her.

We are in the world of the Great Mother, the terrible mother, who possesses the masculine— "terrible male," as her aggressive and destructive aspects (Neumann, 1949/1995, p. 99). As noted, the illness has caused a bifurcation and massive chaos ensues. The illness has abducted our little Persephone into an unseeing, unhearing, unspeakable underworld, a distraught Demeter mourns and rages at the loss of her daughter, into a world of nameless dread. The good enough mother who can provide a holding environment, has vanished, and in her place is a raging gorgon. The proper container is broken and a paranoid-schizoid world is constellated. Both parents are now pulled into the underworld, with their baby, all imprisoned in this hellish dungeon of darkness. The bars of the crib, designed to keep a child safely contained, have turned into an ominous confining jail—where if their deepest fears are realized—Helen will be forced to serve a life sentence in solitary confinement.

Just as in the myth of Demeter and Persephone, the daughter has to separate from the mother in order to come into her own—although this is often a very painful process. In order for the baby to come into the light of consciousness, she will need to separate from the mother. Proper containment and distance are necessary, the ego will need to separate from the Self. We already see through the doctor's comment that Helen has a lot of vitality, and there may be issues in the future with boundaries. Captain Keller's suggestion to "put up stronger fences" will be exactly what is needed and ultimately the first step in Helen's learning—but as we will see, he will repeatedly fail to follow his own advice. Fences provide containment, protection, and security; they are used to create boundaries or reinforce them (OED, 2013, fence).

Captain Keller is pulled into the chaos by his wife, as he came to her side earlier. He is a "mere satellite" of the Great Mother:

> Thus all child-eating father figures stand for the masculine aspect of the oroboros and the masculine-negative side of the First Parents. In these figures the accent falls primarily on the devouring force i.e. the uterine cave. Even when they later appear in the patriarchate, as genuine Terrible Father figures, e.g. Cronos or Moloch, their ouroboric character is transparent so long as the symbolism of eating is in the foreground and hence their propinquity to the Great Mother. (Neumann, 1949/1995, p. 178).

There are two references in this scene to being "battle-scarred," as well as an undertone of hostility when Kate muses over Helen. In reality, Kate was regretting her marriage to Keller and "sublimated her regrets over the marriage" through avid reading and doting on Helen.

> Kate. . . . doted on her young daughter, and her intense maternal absorption was perhaps not surprising given that by the time of Helen's birth she realized that she had made a mistake. Kate was twenty years younger than her husband, Captain Arthur Keller, with whom she had little in common. (Hermann, 1999, p. 8)

Indeed, in the film, Captain Keller is not called by his first name until his sister addresses him as Arthur. Although the Civil War is long over, he still goes by *Captain*, or *Capt'n*, and even his wife calls him this.

Reading the film as a dream, this is the *exposition,* which "places us somewhere at a place and time," (Conforti, 2010): the landscape where our dream turned nightmare occurs—the family, turned from a safe haven and paradise into a paradoxical purgatory, where the child's own illness-induced sensory limitations cause a profound lack of emotional containment in which she might be lost forever. The rest of the chapter will show Helen's interaction with this field.

Arthur Lubow called Munch's *The Scream* "an icon of modern art, a Mona Lisa for our time" (Wikipedia, 2013, The Scream).

Credits Scene 2: World Of Shades

The scene changes and we see a dark bannister, looking very much like prison bars, and the shadow of a young girl, around 3 or 4 years old approaching, her arm outstretched. We next see her groping hand come into view, grasping hold of the railing. This is how she navigates her world, the only way she is able to make sense or meaning out of it is through the sense of touch. She is reaching out, something she will do through out the film. She has no vision, no hearing, no conscious, cognitive understanding.

She must literally reach out for the most part to engage with others, however this is often problematic. In this scene, we never see her actual head, it is only visible in shadow—only the hand and the body make contact with this world.

She is not whole in this world, but is paradoxically "out of touch." She is cut off from the things that the head represents:

> from the standpoint of the body image, this commanding and acting ego is a head-ego, for in man the head is in high degree the vehicle of sensory orientation in the world. The extraordinary size of the head in comparison to the rest of the body in childhood corresponds to the role of the active ego, which reaches out and later steps out into the world, and the head is experienced as the central symbol of human ego activity. . . . The ego head-pole is emancipated as center of the personality and his gives rise to a new orientation. (Neumann, 1963/1990, pp. 121-123)

In *Up from Eden*, Ken Wilber (1996, p. 12) mythically named the second stage in the great chain or nest of being, referring to it as either the "bodyego or body self or typhon." Wilber named this stage after Typhon, a titan and the youngest child of Gaea, who was half man and half snake:

> Half man, half serpent—man and animal, man and ouroboros, still intertwined. . . . There is the typhonic self, the self that has differentiated its body from the environment but not yet differentiated its own mind from its body. (p. 46)

The typhon stage is located in the subconscious (prepersonal) portion of his diagram [see Figure 18 below], prior to the mental-ego, which is located at the threshold between the preconscious and conscious portions. The bodyego stage is still magically intertwined with the environment.

Figure 18. Wilber's Great Chain Of Being.

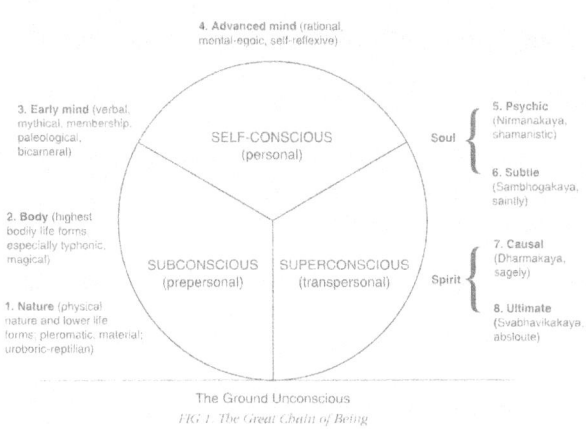

Helen's ego is at the magical-phallic stage, which covers the ages from 16 months to 4 years old. According to Neumann, at this stage the ego is still partially identified with the body-Self, and the ego is still weaker and dependent on the matriarchal world of the unconscious—"still at the mercy of the Great Mother's superiority" (1963/1990, p. 151).

The growing child is caught, imprisoned in an essentially infantile pre-linguistic state, the banister mirrors the bars of her crib, but these bars are even larger and more foreboding and cast a big shadow. This child is a like a shade—we are still in the underworld, and now the qualities are like that of a prison. She is in a kind of hell, from which there is no exit. She is in a shadow-land; reminiscent of the scene in *Lara Croft and the Cradle of Life* (de Bont, 2003): Near the cradle of life is was shadowlands, guarded by monsters and in this vicinity, there is no way to know where you are, and it is very disorienting. In describing her life, before she met Annie, Helen called herself a "phantom living in a no world" (Keller, 1955, p. 8).

Credits Scene 3: Caught In Blind Confusion

The scene shifts again, from the dark interior, mirroring the literal darkness of her world and its imprisoning quality, to the light of outside in the yard near the house. But this landscape offers no respite either. Lines of sheets hanging out to dry as they billow in the wind, become entangling obstacles, when she encounters them.

We see Helen first through the sheets, in a tactile "white shadow," her hands groping against the billowing whiteness, in blind confusion. Since the opening scene, we have not seen Helen's whole body, only in shadow or obscured. Helen is not whole. The sheets offer little resistance, she is buffeted between them and then she becomes ensnared in one of them. "Helen lashes out her face frightened, unknowing— she pulls down a sheet, becoming tangled in its folds, almost hysterical" (Gibson, 1961, p. 4). Writhing around on the ground, over and over, iterating, Helen is now entangled, like an insect in a web of meaninglessness and chaos.

These are images of the Terrible, Devouring Mother. Helen's actual mother approaches, trying to free her from the sheet's grasp, but Kate does this in an almost smothering or engulfing way; rocking her child in her arms, her own anguish is palpable—the uncontained container, too close; perhaps trying to contain herself as well in the rocking. This is the first onscreen encounter Helen has had with another person since the opening scene. The pattern is the same, groping in her darkness, oscillating between the poles of uncontained chaos of abandonment, and engulfing uncontained chaotic containing.

Stanislav Grof's BPM II—Cosmic Engulfment and No Exit or Hell—Expulsion from Paradise, the first stage of actual physical birth is the archetypal landscape that we are in at the beginning [See Appendix E]. These are the initial conditions:

WOMB AT ONSET OF LABOR BEFORE CERVIX OPENS: cosmic engulfment; immense physical and psychological suffering, helpless victim, hopelessness, agonizing guilt and inferiority; no end situation; images of hell; feeling of entrapment, devouring or entangling archetypal monsters, giant spiders or boa constrictors; apocalyptic view of world, concentration camps; meaninglessness, oppression, difficulty breathing dark night of soul begins, abysmal despair, starvation, jail, whirlpool. (Pohn, 2006).

This is only one field in the archetypal process of transformation, akin to the caterpillar building his chrysalis or cocoon, and isolating himself from the world, preparing for the intense transformation to come in the process of metamorphosis. It it the separation phase of the hero's journey and the initiation, and the beginning of the dark night of the soul.

Credits Scene 4: Reiteration—Broken Reflection

Helen is now older; we see a close-up of a Christmas tree, with an ornament hanging on a branch, a dark glass ball suspended in space. Again, we see Helen first, not directly, but as an image approaching in the reflection of the ball. At first the ball is still, but then as she approaches "with chaos in her wake" (Stevenson, 1964), the ball begins to move as she touches the branches, jerking chaotically, she grabs it with both hands, and pulls it, ripping the ornament from the tree. It shatters to the floor in a thousand pieces, reiterating the original trauma.

The Christmas tree has its origins in the "Paradise Tree" (Karas, 1991), the glass ornament representing wholeness, or her world, and the fragile state of her budding ego. The paradise of Helen's childhood was destroyed by her illness, like the unconscious hand of an unconscious god, the original paradise of the family was destroyed, torn apart, ripped off, and like the fragile globe, left in a shattered mess, a symbol of the wholeness that is now broken.

Looking closely, the inside of the ornament appears to be golden [although the film is in black and white and we can't be sure]. Stephen Gilligan (1997) in *The Courage to Love*, calls the symptoms that result from trauma a "terrible gift." Perhaps, this inner brightness is like the *prima materia* in alchemy, which through the fires of transformation, becomes the philosopher's stone. Helen is projecting her inner chaos onto the outer world.

The words "chaos in her wake" come from the film *Mary Poppins* (Stevenson, 1964). They are the lyrics in a song, "A Man Has Dreams" that George Banks sings near the end of the film. George is singing about Mary Poppins. He is about to lose his job at the bank because his children have caused a bank run. At this low-point in the film he sings: "My world was calm, well ordered, exemplary/Then came this person with chaos in her wake/And now my life's ambitions go with one fell blow/It's quite a bitter pill to take." More chaos will ensue, but then in the end a higher order will be reached. But we've gone far afield, so let's return to the story.

Credits Scene 5: Fallow Field

Helen is out in the world, walking through a field of tall light-colored grassy weeds, arms outstretched to feel what lies ahead, her mother trails behind at a distance. Helen stumbles and falls and her mother hurries toward her, but not too close; Helen rights herself and continues. The hopeful young mother is now older, careworn, aged beyond her years by the agony of her child's increasing unreachability.

Although physically proximate, they are in different worlds. The distance between them mirrors the psychic distance that lies between Helen and Kate. Although the ego must separate from the Self, and the child must separate from the mother to individuate, it is a painful process. Like Demeter, the scene ends with Kate, alone, disconsolate in the fallow field. The objective psyche is continuing the child's development, proceeding slower, and stumbling, but separation is occurring, nonetheless. The credits are finished, and the exposition is complete.

Figure 19: Mildred, Viney, and Helen

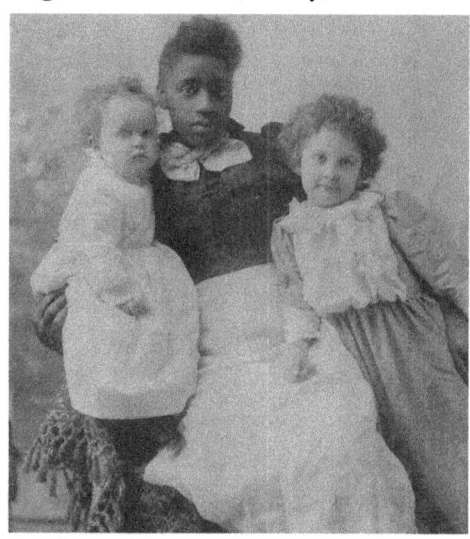

Scene 6: Cascading Chaos—Danger

We have crossed over another threshold. We have come to the current day in the story. Helen is now six years old; it is the summer of 1886. This scene and the upcoming chapters show the *development* in a dream; it is the part where the situation begins to unfold (Conforti, 2010).

Prelude to pandemonium. A young African American boy, Percy, runs up to ring a bell on the porch of the house—sounding the alarm. The four adults in Helen's family are inside the house, about to have refreshments. The ringing bell interrupts them. Aunt Ev rushes toward the door and is passed by Kate who hurries outside. As Kate comes out of the door, we see Helen on top of Percy's sister, Martha. Helen is trying to cut Martha's hair with a scissors. We see the escalation of the chaos; Kate rushes into the melee and gets between the two children, holding Helen to let Martha escape. Then Helen grabs the scissors again. Kate eventually wrestles the scissors from Helen by rocking them in her arms as if were a doll. Helen is almost a feral child; her face is strange and unnatural, her countenance like an animal; her dress and face are soiled and dirty. Finally after Helen surrenders the scissors to her mother, Kate aims her toward the house. A bench blocks Helen's way, and she unknowingly slams into it, overturning it; she howls in pain, like an animal.

Helen is growing up, she is getting stronger, and so is her frustration and rage. No longer a helpless victim, she is becoming a victimizer as well. The consequences are also more costly, it is becoming a high stakes game. Viney, Martha's mother, warns Martha off—admonishing her. This is obviously not the first time that Helen has tyrannized these children.

In this scene, we have crossed over into a different archetypal field, Grof's BPMIII—Death-Rebirth Struggle— Propulsion through the Birth Canal. This archetypal landscape is where we will be situated for most of the film.

BIRTH CANAL—DEATH-REBIRTH STRUGGLE: tremendous pressure; volcanic forces; titanic life and death struggle; aggressive and sadomasochistic aspects, scatology, pornography, especially bondage,— intense sexual orgiastic feelings: agony and ecstasy fusion; torture, war and bloody revolutions; demonic aspects, Walpurgis Night, satanic; vital threat, extreme danger; observer or identification with aggressor or victim; feelings of suffocation, anoxia, crushing and choking; Dionysian ecstasy, carnivals and harems; adrenaline rush, amusement park rides; mythological hero encounters; dying and being reborn, ego death; death-rebirth deities element of fire, phoenix rising. (Pohn, 2006)

Helen has gone from helpless victim, imprisoned and alone, to an aggressor, attacking her playmate with a scissors. Helen is perhaps on the threshold of the magical warlike stage of ego development, which occurs between approximately 7 and 14 years of age. It certainly seems to be the case, and if she hasn't yet crossed the threshold, she is very close. She is still in typhon stage of Wilber's (1996, p. 12) model (See Figure 18 above).

Failure to communicate. The family is now gathered in the living room as Helen enters, searching for her doll. Aunt Ev begins the conversation, speaking with her brother Captain Keller she begins: "Arthur, something ought to be done for that child." Aunt Ev absently hands the doll to Helen, who begins to pat the dolls blank face with her hand. Aunt Ev doesn't know what Helen is trying to communicate and so she basically ignores Helen.

As Helen gropes her way from person to person, she repeats this same gesture, imploring them. The adults in the room don't pay any attention to her. They are like the sheets; and buffet Helen around; they can't seem to understand her, so she is still essentially lost. Although Helen is actually blind and deaf, the adults are essentially blind and deaf to her as well.

From the dialog, we learn that the Kellers have been seeking help from specialists but it hasn't helped—just as Helen is seeking help now. The situation seems hopeless. Aunt Ev suggests writing to the Perkins school, and Kate is also imploring her husband, but he is resistant. A constant struggle seems to be playing out between Keller and his wife about this— Kate constantly wanting to reach out, and Keller stubbornly opposing and then reluctantly giving in. This pattern reiterates as well throughout the film—another battle of sorts. Keller seems to be "anima possessed" irrationally sticking to his guns. The women urging Keller to write a letter and Keller dismissing the idea of out of hat, declaring that they will not be able to help Helen, without any attempt to investigate the matter.

The discussion is interrupted after Helen, still groping and seeking something, succeeds in pawing all his papers from the desk onto the floor. Keller then pushes Helen toward Kate, saying "I might as well try to work in a henyard as in this house." Again, there is chaos in Helen's wake. The entire conversation becomes more charged, as James, Helen's half-brother, suggests putting Helen away somewhere. Everyone is involved and getting more emotional, the baby is now crying, too. As the chaos continues James adds:

James: Some asylum. It's the kindest thing. . . . She can't keep herself clean. It's not pleasant to see her about.

Kate: Do you dare complain of what you can see?

Keller: This discussion's at an end. The house is at sixes and sevens morning and night over this child. I want some peace here. I don't care how. But we won't have it by rushin' about the country to every new quack.

How do you solve a problem like Helen?

Keller has hit a threshold and has barked out his proclamation, lashing out verbally at others, in much the same way as Helen does physically. He acts as negative feedback on the system, trying to dampen down the chaos and keep things in place, to keep the established "order."

Keller is more *gerontomorphic* in nature—resistant to change, better adapted to the past, etc. (Montague 1983; Shulman, 1997; Pohn 2006), whereas the women are more *pedamorphic*, open to change and flexible, in their style (See Appendix G: Gerontomorphy/Pedamorphy Table). Keller has the power, but does not use it in a productive way. He is constantly seeking a *retroactive restoration of the persona*, trying to revert to an earlier state, in his case, likely to the time of the Civil War, where he felt that he was in charge. Paradoxically Keller is becoming anima possessed and out of control himself in his attempts to fight his own civil war within his family. This constant struggle is also a pattern that continues to repeat.

Meanwhile, Helen is even more insistently patting the doll's blank face. Finally Helen pulls two buttons off of her Aunt's dress and incessantly pounds them into the doll's face. Finally Kate understands, Helen wants the doll to have eyes. Kate sews them on for Helen who is overjoyed. Aunt Ev exclaims: "This child has more sense than all these men Kellers, if there's ever a way to reach that mind of hers."

This joyful calm is short-lived, as Helen proceeds to make her way to the baby's cradle and dumps her sister out, causing a new round of chaos to ensue, as tempers flare. Again, we have a lack of what small containment there is in the situation, the cradle—now upset, which mirrors the upset in both Helen and the family. Helen is perfectly unconsciously communicating, as she has no other way to express herself.

Kate shakes Helen saying: "Helen! You're not to do such things. How can I make you understand?". . . . How can I get it into your head, my darling?" They are plainly in agony, caught in a dilemma. Keller and Kate then begin arguing about disciplining Helen, and are conflicted about what to do and how to accomplish it, as their pity and love for their daughter tears at their hearts. Kate emotionally proclaims: "I don't know what to do, I don't know how to teach her."

Helen is now in the middle of it all, and as her parents are fighting; she is putting her hands now on her mother's mouth and on her own, moving her soundless mouth, then she turns to her father and does the same thing. She is increasingly frustrated, moving her mouth even more; her father restrains her, and then she ends up slapping her mother in the face. Kate understands that Helen is trying to communicate, to talk and be like other people. After this battle, which Kate finally wins, Captain Keller agrees to write the letter.

Another bifurcation point has occurred, and the bifurcations then begin bifurcating, as the system becomes chaotic. The different family members have different coping mechanisms for handling the situation.

James, disengaged, disempowered, dismissed, and devalued, wants to get rid of the problem, and dissociate from it by putting Helen in an asylum; Captain Keller oscillates between fighting and leaving the field. The dilemma they are facing is disciplining Helen, and although he talks about discipline, Keller attempts to delegate doing anything about it—constantly putting it onto Kate: "Kate, she must be taught some discipline." He disavows any responsibility, a pattern that will continue to repeat itself, just as he has just done moments before in pushing Helen towards Kate when Helen made a mess of Keller's desk.

Captain Keller either stubbornly sticks to his convictions with a focus on the past, a blustery Yahweh on high, or abdicates the role of the father completely. Jung, (1952/1976) in a discussion of the Mithras tradition, describes the archetypal role of the father:

> The father represents the world of moral commandments and prohibitions. . . . the father is the representative of the spirit, whose function it is to oppose pure instinctuality. That is his archetypal role, which falls to him regardless of his personal qualities. . . . The paradox lies in the fact that, like the mother who lives life and then takes it away again as the "terrible" or "devouring" mother, the father apparently lives

a life of unbridled instinct and yet is the living embodiment of the law that thwarts instinct. (pp. 260-262, para. 396)

Helen is reaching a point of development where the father is becoming more important, as her nascent consciousness continues to develop in the magical-phallic/magical warlike stages. Thomas Moore (1992), remarked: "Without the father there is chaos, conflict, and sadness. . . when we feel the confusion of a fatherless life and wonder where he could be, the father has been evoked. . . . He is finding his way back" (p. 34). Jung (1931/1978) discusses the importance of the father and the role he plays vis-a-vis the mother:

> The archetype of the mothers is the most immediate one for the child. But with the development of consciousness the father also enters his field of vision, and activates an archetype whose nature is in many respects opposed to that of the mother.

> Just as the mother archetype corresponds to the Chinese yin, so the father archetype corresponds to the yang. . . . It determines our relationship to man, to the law and to the state, to reason and the spirit and dynamism of nature. (p. 35, para. 65)

Jung then turns to focus on the father and goes into more detail about the father archetype, describing the nature of this powerful primordial image inside the child:

> The father is the "acutor" and represents authority, hence also law and the state. He is that which moves the world, the wind and storm, thunder and lightning, the guide and creator of invisible thought and airy images. He is the creative wind-breath—the spirit, pneuma, atman. . . .

> At first he is *the* father, an all-encompassing god image, a dynamic principle. Just as man was late in discovering nature, so he only gradually discovered law, duty, responsibility, the state the spirit. As the nascent consciousness becomes more capable of understanding, the importance of the parental personality dwindles. The place of the father is taken by the society of men and the place of the mother by the family. . . .

> The father goes about, talks with other men, hunts, travels, makes war, lets his bad moods loose like thunderstorms, and at the behest of invisible thoughts he suddenly changes the whole situation like a tempest. He is the war and the weapon, the cause of all changes; he is the bull provoked to violence or prone to apathetic laziness. He is the

image of all the helpful or harmful elemental powers. (Jung, 1931/1978, pp. 35-36, paras. 65-67)

We have another piece of the puzzle now. The dynamics have revealed that we are also dealing with the absent father, or the father as "terrible male" when he is there; the logos principle, which the father also represents can turn against him. Jung wrote: "the man becomes rigidly set in his previous attitude, while the woman remains caught in her emotional ties" (Jung, 1952/1976, p. 300, para. 458).

The women, especially Kate, are engaged, and seeking solutions. However, they are socially disempowered and cannot act on their own; as a result, they are very frustrated by their lack of knowledge and power. Helen, too, seems to be powerless; the family can't even understand what she wants. For if the women are powerless, as a disabled child Helen must be doubly so, and cannot do anything either—or can she? Although blind, deaf, and dumb, Helen takes matters into her own hands, literally and figuratively and creates chaos. Being so close to the autonomous psyche, Helen instinctually provokes the system to higher order through chaos.

Helen, as she will many times during the film, gets mad—at times she goes berserk—her anger, frustration and rage send the system into chaos. She is getting larger, harder to control. The family uses negative feedback—giving in, distracting, or even rewarding Helen for her outbursts—buying a short-term solution for a long-term heavy price.

Yet the autonomous psyche has a method to this madness. It knows that self-organizing systems, including families and individuals, very often need to be pushed far from equilibrium to change. While early in life, not so much variety is tolerated, with systems stabilizing and replicating through iteration, later on to get to greater levels of complexity, novelty is introduced through perturbations in the system—temporarily resulting in greater chaos, which ultimately results in a higher order. This is what is seeking to happen here. And in this case, Helen's tantrum and resulting family chaos have resulted in Captain Keller agreeing to write to Perkins, changing his original position and opening the door to further novelty and transformation—which will come in the person of Annie Sullivan.

At the beginning of the film the doctor said: "She knows how better than we do." He was right. Helen, in driving the system into chaos, is upsetting the established order and in this far from equilibrium state, there is a chance of moving it to a higher order. The themes of battle, chaos, searching for meaning are all present here. Gilligan (1997) sees the symptom as a solution, something is trying to awaken. If Helen did not act out in this manner, she would have ended up a passive victim, entombed in silence and darkness. Helen's rages and uncontrollable behavior are indeed the answer. What is trying to wake up in Helen is consciousness. This child who has so much vitality, is vitally doing all she can to change the course of her prior trajectory, and she is doing a really good job.

We now leave the Keller household in chaos and venture north to Boston, where Annie is beginning her journey.

NIGHTMARISH TRAIN

Scene 1: Last Minute Advice

Annie Sullivan, age 20, and Mr. Michael Anagnos, the Director of the Perkins School, arrive at the train station. Mr. Anagnos helps Annie with her luggage, giving her some advice, and a gift of a garnet ring. From the interchange between them we learn that Annie lacks all "tact, all talent to bend to others." And that she might have even been expelled from Perkins on more than one occasion except for the fact that the only option would have been sending her back to Tewksbury and that she has been deeply affected by it:

Anagnos: . . . that dreadful place where you grew up learning to be saucy! Annie, I know how unhappy it was for you there, but that battle is dead and done with. Why not let it stay buried?

Annie: I think God must owe me a resurrection.

Anagnos: What?

Annie: He keeps digging up that battle.

Anagnos: That is not a proper thing to say. Be humble. You'll need their affection working with this child.

The Tewksbury almshouse, was that "dreadful place," where Annie's "solar ego" was forged and tempered in her nearly blind condition—after the many tragedies of her initial conditions of poverty, trauma, and death. Death and trauma continued in this field as well. Annie was in her own underworld, a different region, than Helen's, but archetypally similar. Again, the battle theme persists.

The dynamics between the Keller family, which oscillate between opposites, have also been a part of Annie's past, too. On several occasions either Mr. Anagnos or the teachers would side against each other and allow Annie to stay instead of being expelled. Annie's own painful past, which is ever present with her, is presenced in this scene.

Annie's initial conditions have forged her to be headstrong, resolute, persistent, and unbending. She was alone and had suffered greatly. Again we have another allusion to battles, so Annie is in the same field as Helen—

they have both known great darkness and suffering. Conforti (1999, 2010) found that an archetypal attractor site is at the core of different dynamics, creating a preformed field, which entrains the participants to follow very specific patterns, and has an effect on the form things take. He also mentioned that there is an archetypal resonance that is created and we seem to be almost magnetically drawn to or attract dynamics that are similar to our past. In this way, we seek to recreate the initial conditions so that we might heal them. This is similar to the children's book *Green Eggs and Ham* by Dr. Seuss (Geisel, 1960). Sam I am, constantly asking the character I if he likes green eggs and ham. I keeps on saying no, and the pattern keeps on iterating, until finally it hits a chaotic breaking point, where I actually tries the green eggs and ham. I then decides that he indeed does like them and then in turn reiterates by telling all of the places he could enjoy them.

Now, let us look a bit closer at the gift that Michael Anagnos has given Annie and also at how the idea of angels fits into the picture.

The garnet ring: Fruit of the underworld. The garnet ring was an interesting choice of gift. Garnets get their name from the Latin *garanatus* meaning seedlike, referring to pomegranate seeds. One of the most popular colors of garnets is a deep purple-red like the pomegranate seed. Throughout history, they have been a popular gemstone and are hard and durable stones. Among the ancient traditions and legends surrounding garnet are:

> In medieval times, the stones were thought to cure depression, protect against bad dreams, . . . According to legend, Noah used a finely cut, glowing garnet to illuminate the ark during those dark wet days and nights. . . . Christian tradition considered the blood-red garnet as a symbol of Christ's sacrifice. The Koran holds that the garnet illuminates the Fourth Heaven of the Moslems. The Greeks said it guarded children from drowning. It was also thought to be potent against poisons. . . . In Greek mythology, a pomegranate is referenced as a gift of love and is associated with eternity. . . . . Moreover, garnet is symbolic of a quick return and separated love, since Hades had given a pomegranate to Persephone before she left him to ensure her speedy return. Therefore, garnet may be given to a beloved before embarking on a trip, as it is believed to heal the broken bonds of lovers. . . . .There may be an affinity between garnets and the warrior tradition. . . . . The history of garnet's ability to bring about transformation is found in many books. . .

They were thought to counter melancholy and act as a heart stimulant. (Jewels for me, 2013, online)

Karl Kerényi (1952/1978) in *Athene* noted that the pomegranate was sacred to Athena, that this warrior Goddess and teacher of heroes, held "a pomegranate in the right hand and a helmet in the left." The pomegranate, he explained

> with its internal richness of myriad kernels, is a miniature copy of the underworld's richness in souls, even of its fruitfulness, if it is believed that souls of the living have come here from there or have returned here from there. Internal to this symbolism is the realm of death as the realm of souls. (p. 49).

The Angel—Heralding a battle for transformation ahead. In *The Way of the Image*, Yoram Kaufmann (2009), in explicating the orientational approach to the psyche, showed how one must carefully research symbols to get to their essence. In an essay entitled "Angels," Kaufmann used angels as an example of the orientational approach. The objective dimension of a symbol Kaufmann called the *orient*, which is the sum total of all dominants (or radicals) that are inherent in it (p. 53). After taking the reader carefully through the process, Kaufmann pointed out that angels "govern and hover over a territory. They are there before we approach the territory; they precede us." When we approach anything, for example, as a person coming to live in a new country, one needs to contend with the "laws, customs, and language that is prevailing there" (p. 56). The specificity of where the angel is located is important as well.

At the beginning of Annie's train journey, Michael Anagnos gives Annie a garnet ring, symbolic of the underworld, healing, and transformation. Michael is the name of one of the archangels, the angel that governs battle (Davidson, 1971). *Michael* comes from the Hebrew *Mikha'el*

> meaning "who is like God?" This is a rhetorical question, implying no person is like God. Michael is one of the seven archangels in Hebrew tradition and the only one identified as an archangel in the Bible. In the Book of Revelation in the New Testament he is portrayed as the leader of heaven's armies, and thus is considered the patron saint of soldiers (Behind the Name, 2013, Michael)

Anagnos, this last name, is really interesting, too. It comes from the Greek *agnosia*, meaning unconsciousness, ignorance, or not knowing (von

Franz, 1994, p. 148; OED, 2013 *agnosia*). Yet, if we place the *an,* meaning without, in front of *agnosia*, it means without ignorance! Very interesting.

Translating this psychologically: the field that Annie will be entering is the transformation process, or the archetypal field of transformation. Her journey is to be one of transformation of consciousness, as she encounters the battlefield ahead. This is the strange attractor site she will encounter, and specifically the battlefield / the plutonic underworld / the liminal initiatory space. The discussion about the battle in Annie's head suggests iteration may be purposeful after all, and ultimately lead to liberation. We know the pattern, but what we don't know is the result—much as the equations that describe nonlinear dynamics are simple, but the results are unpredictable.

Scene 2: The Long Journey South

Annie then begins her journey. She travels for days, transferring trains several times. She has recently had yet another eye operation and wears dark glasses all the time, even at night. Her eyes suffer not only from the smoke and grit, but also at times the blinding light that she is painfully exposed to on the journey. Annie also has a nightmare, as she passes through a tunnel. Annie is in liminal space, having answered the call on her own hero's journey, she is on the adventure. In the nightmare, she flashes back to her childhood, the memory of entering Tewksbury and almost being separated from her brother. At the threshold of a new phase of life that she has yet to cross, Annie is reminded of another painful threshold from long ago. Annie wakes with a start as the train emerges from the tunnel into the light.

The almshouse, of which we see several glimpses during the film, is an impersonal institution, where people were essentially warehoused, reminiscent of the realm of Tartarus from Hesiod's creation myth, *Theogony*. In Greek mythology, Ouronos, seeing some of his children as hideous monsters, stuffed them back inside of Gaia and then Cronos later threw them into Tartarus, a deep abyss, a dungeon of torment and suffering. The alsmshouse can be seen as an example of this, and of Grof's BPM-II, the womb before the cervix opens, Cosmic Engulfment and No Exit-Hell.

This peek into the past, through the dream, shows us a part of Annie's initial conditions. (See Initial Conditions Chapter —Annie). However, the story doesn't stop there. Annie heroically escaped to school. Through education, she was able to transform her identity from an illiterate nearly blind inmate to valedictorian of her class, and soon to be teacher, herself. Through knowledge she gained freedom. Annie was able to break the bonds of this quintessentially terrible mother with the terrible male container by following her innate drive for meaning and knowledge. In the object relations school of psychology, Melanie Klein called this the *epistemophilic instinct* (Hinshelwood, 1991), and Bion (1962) called it the *K-link*.

This is the field that Annie brings with her. Annie was Persephone in the underworld, but through education, she was able to get out. However, Annie still has the underworld inside of her, and it haunts her throughout the film and would keep haunting her. Later in life, Annie would again visit the underworld for extended periods, in states of depression.

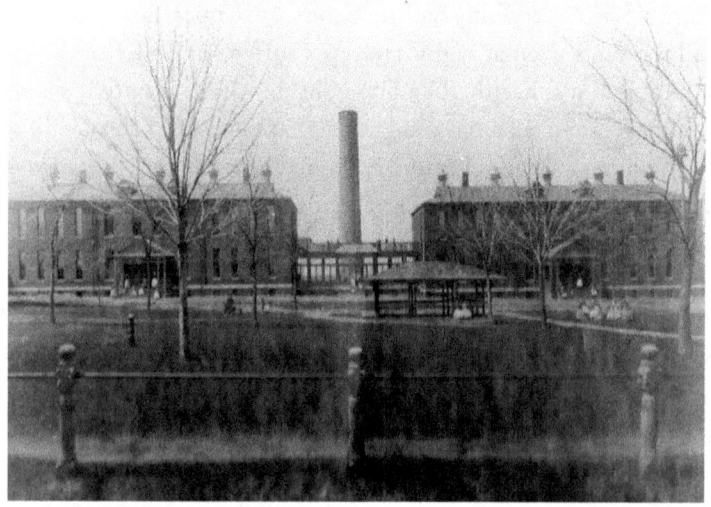

Figure 20: Tewksbury State Almshouse.

TEACHER MEETS STUDENT

Scene 1: The Threshold At Tuscumbia

As the train pulls in to the station at Tuscumbia, Alabama, Annie is standing in between the cars. She passes Kate in a horse-drawn buggy, towering above her. When Annie alights from the train, James Keller, Helen's half brother, meets her and introduces himself. She tells James that she had a brother Jimmie. He inquires, "You're to be her governess?" Annie answers, "Well, try." He replies, "You look like half a governess." Annie very independently and gingerly takes her own suitcase and leaves James to get her trunk. From this encounter, it seems to James that Annie may be inexperienced, which is indeed actually the case, as we are later informed through an exchange between Captain Keller and Kate.

Annie approaches Mrs. Keller, who is seated in a white wicker buggy pulled by a single horse. Annie is wearing black and her clothes are heavy and unsuited to the climate; perhaps alluding to the past that she cannot seem to shed. Annie does not fit in here either. Kate is wearing white and uses an umbrella to protect herself from the sun. In the scene, Kate is seated and at a higher level and looks down at Annie, who is standing below. This reflects their status and stature.

Kate is only 10 or 11 years older than Annie, and Kate's initial reaction upon seeing Annie approach is concern and a bit of irritation; we learn that Annie has been delayed and as a result, Kate and James have met every train for two days. Annie shares her disappointment that Helen is not there to meet her, and making small talk, Annie then asks Kate how far away their home is. After Kate informs her, Annie eagerly exclaims: "I suppose I could wait one more mile. But don't be surprised if I get out and push the horse." With that, Kate's mood changes and she extends a hand to Annie, who joins her in the buggy, at a more equal level, it seems.

Although we don't see it on camera, on the trip to Ivy Green, the Keller homestead, Annie has informed Kate of her background at Perkins—that she is 20 years old, and although valedictorian of her class, this is her first post as a teacher. She has also informed Kate that she was almost blind previously, and had many operations, one recently. The buggy passes by a cemetery before they arrive, too. As they arrive, in true Southern tradition, they are greeted jovially by Captain Keller. Annie eagerly inquires about

Helen, and her parents point her out: Helen, standing by herself on the porch, is unaware of Annie's arrival.

The difference in transportation and in journeys to their mutual meeting place speaks volumes. Annie has arrived alone on a large black train; it has been a long, hard journey, taking many days and requiring many changes. The journey south mirrors Annie's own life; she is an orphan and her life journey has been a long and difficult one. Kate, on the other hand, lives only a mile from the station and arrives in a small white wicker buggy with only one horse, and she has James with her for assistance. The difference in how both women arrived at the station reflects their very different upbringings and pasts. Let's delve a bit deeper into Annie's mode of transportation—the steam locomotive.

The steam engine revolutionized the world of transportation and propelled the world into a new era. Steam engines were originally used to pump water out of mines before being modified for use in locomotion. Steam locomotives run by burning combustible material. They are very powerful, take a lot of energy, and can travel much farther and faster than horses. At the time, in the late 1880s, they were a relatively new invention—being introduced in the United States only about 60 years before, in 1829. Horse-drawn transportation has been around since antiquity. Watts, who redesigned the steam engine, in the late 1700s, coined the term *horsepower* [hp] to describe a unit of measurement of power, to compare the output of steam engines with draught horses. Steam locomotives at this time averaged between 220-240 hp (Wikipedia, 2013, steam locomotive; horsepower; Yahoo, 2013; Locomotive General, 2013).

Translating psychologically, Annie's way of getting to the present moment involved a long difficult journey that took a lot of energy and also was capable of producing a lot of power. This power was produced using fire and combustion, which transforms elements from one state to another with tremendous pressure, and could bring more things from one place to another much faster than a single horse and buggy, which was what Kate had at her disposal. The revolutionary nature of this technology foreshadows the revolutionary nature of Annie's teaching, and the power that it would unleash for Helen. Annie would need this tremendous power, represented not only by the length of her journey, but also by the power by which it was accomplished in the weeks ahead. As we have only begun to see, Helen is a powerful force to be reckoned with.

Annie will need all of this plutonic power to transform Helen, and to move the system to a new order. Annie remarked to James that she "thought the trains must be backing up every time I dozed off." This presages the journey that still lies ahead, which may entail many stops along the way, and may also feel at times like it is going backwards.

The trip to Ivy Green juxtaposes youth and inexperience with a dead past. Something new is arriving, and along they way they pass by the cemetery, which contains things that are no longer alive. Something may need to die before Annie is able to reach Helen. Kate, James, and Annie are all still in their 20s, Captain Keller, is in his 40s. It seems possible that something that Keller is, or represents, or does, may need to die. This scene hints fleetingly at the old order, the old king, needing to die before we can experience renewal. This is the archetype of renewal (Bond, 2003), and the field of transformation is clearly where we are located.

Scene 2: Meeting Helen At The Threshold

Annie again gingerly takes care of her own suitcase, for she has something for Helen inside. After Annie leaves to go to Helen, Captain Keller begins to talk, and Kate stops him. We now see Annie walking towards Helen, who unaware of Annie's presence, is standing on the top step of the porch. Annie walks up, pauses for a moment and then approaches thoughtfully. She places her suitcase down heavily onto the porch with a purposeful thump, to let Helen know, through the vibration it causes, that someone is there. Annie then sits down next to the suitcase and allows Helen to come to her; Annie allows Helen to take the lead and to explore and investigate.

Helen first touches the suitcase, then Annie's hand, slowly and intently, taking it all in. Then, she sniffs Annie's hand and with her hand follows up Annie's arm to her face. Helen is not shy or reserved. She uses her hand to take in Annie's countenance similarly, and when Helen finds Annie's dark glasses, she pulls them off, and they fall away. Helen then continues to explore the rest of Annie's face and hat with both hands, at which point Annie similarly reaches her hands to Helen's face, to take it into her hands. Yet, as she does so, Helen recoils and pulls back and away.

Annie seems to be surprised by this, and studies her little pupil intensely. Helen is now holding the suitcase and begins to try to open it. Annie takes Helen's arm and motions indicating up instead. Then Helen, after a few moments, imitates the motion. Annie indicates that this is correct by taking Helen's hand and placing on her own head and nodding yes. Helen understands, and begins to take the suitcase to the door. Annie tries to take the suitcase from Helen to carry it inside, as the suitcase is quite large and difficult for Helen to manage. They struggle, Helen not allowing Annie to take the suitcase from her. Finally, half slapping, half punching Annie's hand away from the suitcase, Helen drags the suitcase upstairs. Helen has won round one.

An important moment is at hand. Kate seems to recognize this. It is the reason for her almost reverential insistence on silence; because after all, Helen cannot hear anything. Helen Keller would later say that the day she met her teacher, was "her soul's birthday" (Hermann, 1999, p. 58). In *The Story of My Life,* written in 1903, Helen wrote:

> The most important day I remember in all my life is the one on which my teacher, Anne Mansfield Sullivan, came to me. I am filled with wonder when I consider the immeasurable contrasts between the two lives which it connects. It was the third of March, 1887, three months before I was seven years old. On the afternoon of that eventful day, I stood on the porch, dumb, expectant. . . . Have you ever been at sea in a dense fog, when it seemed as if a tangible white darkness shut you in, and the great ship, tense and anxious, groped her way toward the shore with plummet and sounding-line, and you waited with beating heart for something to happen? I was like that ship before my education began, only I was without compass or sounding-line, and had no way of knowing how near the harbour was. "Light! give me light!" was the wordless cry of my soul. (Keller, 1903/2003, p. 25)

Many might assume that Helen would have picked April 5, 1887, as the most important day, the day of the "miracle" at the pump. By naming March 3rd as the most important, Helen clearly realized importance of initial conditions, too. The aforementioned description very poetically describes this bifurcation point, and the threshold was crossed at this literal threshold.

The porch is a special kind of covered and extended threshold: "an exterior structure forming a covered approach to the entrance of a building." Rather than just a doorway, where in one step you can cross it, this kind of threshold is wider and several steps will be necessary. If we translate this psychologically, it points to the fact that it will take some time to enter into Helen's psyche; it will take several steps and an additional structure will be necessary. In this case, structure itself— archetypally in the form of discipline; but we are getting ahead of ourselves.

Let us linger at this threshold, and take this time to actually explore thresholds, which signal the transition from one place or state to another. They are one of the pivotal concepts in our work as pattern analysts, and also in the transformation process [which we will discuss later].

The interactions between Annie and Helen here, as well as in their initial session together that follows, will give us a lot of information about what is likely to transpire. As Conforti (2007) in *Threshold Experiences* showed, "each of these *threshold experiences* not only introduces us to new domains, but also draws us into the realities of archetypal fields" (back cover).

Together, now Annie and Helen are entering the field of transformation. This is their threshold—the initial conditions of their relationship at this beginning—this literal place, and we have already seen from the physical structure some clues as to the nature of their relationship. Let us also consider the nature of *threshold* itself in greater depth, before proceeding to examine the nature of their actual interaction. The Oxford English Dictionary (2013) defines *threshold* as:

1. a. The piece of timber or stone which lies below the bottom of a door, and has to be crossed in entering a house; the sill of a doorway; hence, the entrance to a house or building. . . .

2. *transf.* and *fig.* a. Border, limit (of a region); the line which one crosses in entering. spec. in an airfield: the beginning of the landing area on a runway.

b. In reference to entrance, the beginning of a state or action, outset, opening.

c. In technical language, a lower limit. (a) Psychol.: esp. in phr. threshold of consciousness: In Physiol. and more widely: the limit below which a stimulus is not perceptible; the magnitude or intensity of a stimulus which has to be exceeded for it to produce a certain response.

(b) The magnitude or intensity that must be exceeded for a certain reaction or phenomenon to occur. . . .

†d. An obstacle, stumbling-block. *Obs.*

We will return to the notion of threshold later, but for now, we can learn a lot from this initial encounter between Annie and Helen, even before they begin working together. We see that Helen is able to imitate and understand certain gestures. She is intelligent and inquisitive, and Annie pays her exquisite attention. She lets Helen lead their encounter at first, as she taps into Helen's natural curiosity. What is also present is that both are strong willed, stubborn, and struggling is involved from the start.

Annie has something for Helen that will require Helen going inside and upstairs before receiving the gift Annie has brought. This metaphorically parallels the inner process that Helen will follow to receive the greater gift of consciousness that Annie will bring to Helen in their work together. Struggle will also be a part of this process of creating consciousness.

Scene 3: The Inquisition

The scene changes to a discussion between Keller and Kate, still at the buggy. Keller says that Annie is rough, yet Kate likes her—again an opposition. When asked about her age, Kate replies, "she's not in her teens, you know." Annie is 20 years old. Keller immediately begins an interrogation, wanting to know about Annie's dark glasses. We now find out from Kate that "she was blind, and had 9 operations on her eyes, one just before she left." and that although she has never taught before, Annie was the valedictorian of her class. He retorts: "A houseful of grown-ups can't cope with Helen. How can a half-blind Yankee schoolgirl manage?" James chimes in and tries to agree with Keller, but is rebuked and rebuffed, muttering: "nothing I say is right." He is on the wrong side of Kate, too. This dynamic will also continue for much of the film. Keller is dismissive to everyone, treating the other family members as underlings, as privates in his private war. The Civil War has been over for 20 years, yet he still goes by the name of Captain.

Captain Keller is questioning Annie's credentials, in his traditional paradigm, she should have qualifications, should be a teacher with a long list of accomplishments. Her lived experience, which seems to have impressed Kate, means nothing to him. Again, we see a typical patriarchal attitude. The scene changes back to Annie and Helen.

"HOW BRIGHT SHE IS!"

Helen and Annie are in Annie's room, and we see Helen now wearing Annie's hat, coat, and glasses. She picks up a hand mirror and appears to be gazing at her reflection. She is imitating what she has experienced others doing in her lifeworld. Annie watches and wryly comments "all the trouble I went to and that's how I look?"

Helen may unconsciously be identifying with and projecting onto Annie, and as Sharp (1991) noted: "Identity, denoting an unconscious conformity between subject and object, oneself and others, is the basis of identification, projection and introjection. . . . Identification facilitates early adaption to the outside world" (pp. 62-63). Quoting Jung, Sharp further explained about projection: "'so long as the libido can use these projections as agreeable and convenient bridges to the world, they will alleviate life in a positive way.' [Jung, CW8, para 507]" (p. 105).

Annie then takes the coat from Helen and interests her in the suitcase, which she opens for Helen. Helen, groping around inside, takes some clothing out and attempts to put it on her head. "Oh, no not the drawers," Annie exclaims as she tosses her undergarment out of Helen's reach. Helen is digging around again, another example of no boundaries, and she comes upon a doll.

The doll has eyes that open and close. Helen feels this and then touches her own eye and sees that they are similar and is very excited. A far cry from the blank-faced doll with the makeshift sewn on buttons that caused the commotion that got Annie here. This alludes to the fact that Annie can actually see Helen, and also that she sees Helen differently than her family has been able to.

The doll is a gift from the blind children at Perkins, and possibly represents a kind of witnessing that Annie can bring to Helen, a particular way of seeing, that Jung spoke about regarding the Telesphoros side of his Bollingen Stone. This Telesphoros figure at the center of the stone, was a tiny *homunculus*, a hooded figure that also contained the symbol for Mercury on it. Jung (1961/1989) wrote that it "corresponds to the 'little doll' (*pupilla*)—yourself—which you see in the pupil of another's eye" (p. 227). [The cover of this book has substituted out the Telesphoros with the a picture of Annie and Helen in the iconic moment where Annie identifies herself to Helen by spelling t-e-a-c-h-e-r into Helen's hand, and Helen in full understanding now, reflecting it back to her.] But we are getting way too far ahead of ourselves.

Annie has just alluded to something similar in the opening lines of this scene— Annie being able to see herself through her own new pupil! The eyes of this little doll that Annie has brought are more sophisticated and representative of real eyes than the makeshift buttons of her prior plaything.

Up to this point, Helen herself has worked out about 60 different signs to communicate with others. Helen now wants to know if the doll is for her, and so makes her gesture signifying that by, tapping the doll's face and then tapping her chest. Annie repeats the same movements with Helen's hands and then puts Helen's hand to her head and nods yes, similar to when they were on the porch. Helen is overjoyed. Annie then takes this opportunity to begin teaching Helen.

Perhaps she can also see deeper similarities between Helen and herself, as she says aloud "All right Miss O'Sullivan lets begin, with *doll*." Annie now begins to teach Helen the manual alphabet. She has met her match in Helen, as we will later see.

Annie spells out the word *doll*, with her fingers—*d-o-l-l*, and lets Helen feel each letter, very thoroughly with her left hand, and Annie puts her hand on the doll after she is finished. At this point James arrives with her trunk, momentarily interrupting her. An annoying presence that she has to deal with, Annie tersely tells James that she is showing Helen an alphabet, and turns her back on him and begins to concentrate on Helen again, spelling the letters *d-o-l-l* again into Helen's hand.

Annie begins again, going through the same sequence. Helen then imitates the letters back to Annie all together, using her right hand, touching her own right hand with her left hand to feel if she has it the same. Annie exclaims, "How bright she is!" James then shows Annie that Helen is just a good mimic, like "a monkey," and that she doesn't know what she is doing—to prove his point, he draws a cross in her left palm, which she imitates back directly into his hand.

Annie then takes the doll to begin teaching again and a tussle frantically ensues. Helen uncomprehending wants the doll back and Annie shakes her head no into Helen's hand. Helen then slaps Annie in the face as her answer. Helen continues to struggle and Annie pulls Helen up and puts her into a chair, while James is commenting on this at the door. Annie answers: "When she spells it." James then persists, pointing out that Helen doesn't realize that the thing has a name and Annie replies: "Of course not. Who expects her to now? All I want is her fingers to learn the letters." James, as he has shown by his previous demonstration with Helen, replies "Won't mean anything to her. She doesn't like that alphabet. You invent it yourself?" Annie, exasperated at having to fight this side battle, fires back: "Spanish monks under a vow of silence – which I wish you'd take."

Annie has won this skirmish, and goes to the door, shutting James out, as Helen is now frantically searching for the doll. Annie's eyesight, experience, and size allow her to keep the doll away from Helen. Annie must however re-engage Helen, and she does this by getting a piece of cake wrapped in paper, and passing it near Helen's nose, letting her smell it. Helen wants the cake and reaches out, and then Annie quickly spells the letters *c-a-k-e* into Helen's left hand. When Helen successfully spells the letters back again, this time with the left hand, Annie rewards Helen with some cake.

All Annie wants Helen to do is to imitate the letters. Helen greedily and quickly stuffs the cake into her mouth, and Annie then passes the doll under Helen's nose, and Helen quickly goes for it, but Annie will not let her have it. Annie spells *D-O-L-L* again for Helen, letting her feel the letters. Helen then spells back quickly with the left hand again, the hand that is closest to Annie. Annie places her hand on Helen's as she does this, to feel the letters. Helen, increasingly and belligerently, throws Annie's hand aside and makes the sign for the next letter in the air. Annie matches Helen's anger and intensity, and Helen throws her hand off again, and then does not finish the final *L*. Annie corrects her and emphatically makes the motion of *L* again several times, which Helen then imitates in a similar manner.

Annie knows that Helen is imitating, and not really understanding. She also knows however that this imitation is the first step to learning. Annie hands the doll back to Helen and says "imitate now, understand later. End of the first less—. . ." but Annie is unable to finish the sentence, because Helen swings a haymaker punch, which lands squarely on Annie's jaw. A *haymaker* is "a wild swing with all of a person's might to knock out the opponent" (Wikipedia, 2013, haymaker).

Helen then grabs the doll and beats a hasty retreat out of the room, locking the door behind her, and making off with the key. Annie exclaims: "Oh you little wretch, nobody's taught you any manners," as she goes to the mirror to survey the damage. Annie discovers that not only has Helen drawn blood, but she will presently find out that that the blow has knocked out Annie's tooth as well. Helen has won this battle, too: Helen 2, Annie nothing.

The struggle between Helen and Annie is escalating. Each time they engage, each time that Annie stands up to Helen, the energy increases, culminating in the injury to Annie's mouth. In the initial conditions chapter, an incident with a doll is described: Annie reacted in a similar violent way at being denied a doll. It was one of the precipitating events that landed Annie in Tewksbury. And as we have seen, Helen's doll and her desire to give it eyes and put it in the cradle were at the heart of the chaos that got Captain Keller to relent and contact Perkins. Dolls "may represent the way you relate and interact with internal and external environments," (Amar, 2007, p. 54) and are used in rituals and ceremonies as surrogates for people and deities (O'Connell & Airey, 2012 p. 220).

We have a chaotic situation here that is escalating with each iteration. There is a lot of energy in the scene, and we can anticipate other battles of wills in the future—backed up by tremendous staying power on both sides. We see how alike the two are, and this brings to mind again, the attractive nature of the archetypes and the entrainment that occurs between people that Conforti (2007) found in his doctoral work: "the existence of and dynamics of pre-formed fields (morphogenetic stabilities) which worked to entrain each member of the system into its orientation" (p. 14).

The significance of c-a-k-e and d-o-l-l. Bruno Bettelheim's (1991), book *Freud's Vienna and Other Essays*, contains an essay entitled "Master Teacher and Prodigious Pupil," written in 1980. It was based on Joseph P. Lash's (1980) book *Helen and Teacher*. The essay appeared in *The New Yorker* and was entitled "Miracles." It spoke about a treatment for severely disturbed children, which Bettelheim invented in the early 1940s and it was viewed as miraculous. Bettelheim wrote that he didn't name the method until 1948, when he as writing about it and called it *milieu therapy*.

In his essay, Bettelheim (1991) said that all of the essentials for reaching the disturbed children were used by Sullivan, although at the time he was doing his work, Bettelheim had no knowledge of Sullivan's method. Bettelheim noted the significance of the words that Annie spelled into Helen's hand on their first meeting: *doll* and *cake*. He made the astute point that

> from the very beginning of their relationship, Anne wanted Helen to have what she wanted most for herself. But Anne also knew that if we want a child to understand words, to read them, and most important, to love them, we must give the child words that signify love for him, our wish to give him what he wants most. To give the child the signifier without giving him also what it signifies is a very poor way to teach. It is, in fact, how we teach reading in our schools, with the unfavorable consequences that are well known. We still have not learned what Anne knew when she first met Helen: that food and toys symbolize love and care to the child, and that on these symbols and what they symbolize relationships can be built that truly humanize the child. (p. 161)

Bettelheim, in delving more deeply into the psychological significance of Annie's method and how it was similar to his own, gave us a sample of the still hidden riches that can help people teach and reach others in need that this book seeks to begin mining.

Locking Annie in. Keys play a major symbolic role in the film, too. They appear first in this scene, and a big fuss is made over them in the following scene, the use of keys and who possesses them tell us important things about who holds the power in various situations. *Key* comes through the Germanic from the Indo-European root *kagh*, meaning seize, hold; enclosure, (Shipley, 1984, p. 153). It is interesting that the root of this word is about holding, enclosing— focusing on the locking up aspect of keys, and not on their equally dual nature as something that opens. This is also consonant with how a key is first used here—to enclose and hold Annie inside. The first definition for *key* in the Oxford English Dictionary (2013) is: "An instrument designed to be inserted into a lock and turned." Among the figurative and allusive uses, *key* generally symbolizes "power, control, or authority, esp. over a particular place." A sample of meanings of *key* include:

- A symbol of office; a position of power or authority. . . .
- Something likened metaphorically to a key in having the power to

open or close something else; a thing which provides access or opportunity; a means to a desired objective.

• A place or position with strategic advantages which give control over or access to a territory, sea, etc.

• A means of understanding something unknown, mysterious, or obscure; a solution or explanation.

• A word or other device for encrypting or decrypting a code or cipher; something which enables the interpretation of an allegorical, cryptic, or otherwise obscure work; a means of translating a foreign text.

• A textbook or section of a textbook containing solutions to mathematical problems, translation exercises, etc.

• A list or diagram explaining the figures in a photograph or picture, the features of a map, or the symbols, abbreviations, colours, etc., used in a book, chart, or other work.

• In Bot. and Zool. A set of descriptive statements designed so that selecting those which apply to an unknown organism allows its identification or its attribution to a particular taxon.

• In Chess. The first move in the solution of a problem. (OED, 2013, *key*)

Keys thus represent power to open, contain, explain, identify, and help solve things. They give strategic advantages, and are paradoxical. Keys show us important things about learning and transformation—that in order to transform, we might first need to contain, and also that power and authority are necessary.

Helen, by locking up Annie, (and presently in the next scene throwing away the key), is trying to get rid of or resist structure—which is another pattern that will play out in the near future. One of the major problems that this film and the story itself highlights is this problematic relationship with structure. We, the audience, have already seen it play out in the lack of containment and discipline of Helen by her parents, consisting of Keller's abdication of his archetypal role in this regard, while he simultaneously remains fixed and rigid in other areas; and Kate's pity standing in the way of her ability to provide the maternal holding environment needed. Annie has not seen this yet, but she soon will.

Although Annie has only seen Helen in action for a few moments, she can tell a lot. In attempting to teach Helen and making her wait to get the doll back, Annie has found out that "nobody's taught you any manners."

From this single encounter, Annie has determined that discipline, and the structure it provides, will be the "key" to being able to teach Helen. Annie will need to put discipline and structure in place before she can do anything else. The magnitude of the problem has yet to reveal itself.

Annie has made her initial assessment, and will need to improvise. *The Perkins Report* describing how Dr. Howe taught Laura Bridgman—a more docile and willing student—is now out the window. Annie will have to find her own way. In this first teaching moment, we have another instance of the agonistic nature of their relationship, Helen is headstrong and Annie matches her intensity. The situation has escalated. When Helen does not get her way, she becomes frustrated and this quickly escalates to rage and physical struggle. Even from the beginning, however, Annie treats Helen as anything but impaired. Annie has picked a worthy opponent, often a necessary element of the Hero's Journey.

L-A-D-D-E-R

Realizing that Helen has locked her in, Annie shakes the door and calls out to Helen, and then realized the absurdity of the situation. In actuality, one of the precipitating events that convinced the Kellers to reach out to Perkins was that Helen had also locked her mother in the pantry where Kate remained trapped for more than two hours, because no one was around to hear her cries for help (Keller, 1903/2003).

Helen has essentially done to others what she feels was done to her. Helen feels locked away from their world, locked into her own world, so she locks others up and locks them in. Annie comments to herself "I'm not lost, just out of place," and knows that eventually someone will come to find her.

Meanwhile, Helen is making off with the key, and James, observing her, smiles to himself and then goes down to dinner. When Kate and Keller ask where Miss Sullivan is, James tells them matter-of-factly that "she is locked in her room and Helen has made off with the key." At this, Keller erupts and Kate also is angry. James is passive-aggressively responding to their prior chastising of him, another iteration of their pattern. Keller, Viney, and Kate scatter to try to locate Helen. Keller notifies the others, by screaming, that Helen is out by the pump. Then he goes upstairs to talk to Annie through the door, asking her if there is any key on her side. Annie tells him that "Helen took it, and that the only thing on my side is me." She later says to herself, "and even I'm not on my side," alluding to the psychological situation.

The chaos continues, everyone trying to find the key; they have searched Helen and the grounds without success. They argue about it while Helen sits on the pump rocking her doll placidly amidst the chaos—the calm at the eye of the storm she has created. James proactively goes to get a ladder, and then Keller, barking out orders irrationally sends him back to the barn with it, and then Keller decides he needs it, and commands it to be brought back. Keller's pattern is to act first, and think later.

All of his hollering has woken the baby, who is now crying. Keller next climbs up the ladder to get Annie, bellowing her name and he then tells her that he intends to carry her down. Annie protests, but then Keller commands her to follow his instructions. Keller then begins screaming at everyone down on the ground, as a large audience has gathered around to witness the commotion; he then commands them to come in to dinner.

James can't wait to get a dig in. As he enters the house, James points to the ladder and says "might as well leave the *l-a-d-d-e-r.*"

Annie has lagged behind, and stays to watch Helen, who begins to grope around the ground to find out if anyone is there. To make sure no one else is around, Helen stands up and widens her search radius. Now convinced that she is alone, Helen produces the key, which has been hidden in her mouth, and moving a stone aside, drops it into the well, smiling to herself like the cat that has just eaten the canary. Annie, with a tinge of admiration in her voice for Helen's slyness, says "you devil. . . you think I'm so easily gotten rid of, you've got a thing or two to learn first. I've got nothing else to do, and nowhere to go." Captain Keller then bellows Annie's name and she runs inside.

Helen is at the magical-warlike stage of Neumann's (1963/1990) model, [the typhon stage of Wilber's (1996) great chain of being model] and by locking Annie up and throwing away the key, she is attempting to dispose of Annie, to banish her from existence. Simultaneously, by locking Annie in, Helen is unconsciously communicating how locked in she is at present: she is locked in and cannot get out of the patterns of frustration, fighting, and uncomprehending unconsciousness. At the magical stage of ego development, the unconscious is still dominant and consciousness has not yet gained independence; "this ego is irrational and its activity in no way resembles that of the solar-rational ego. For this reason, the intentions and ritual action of the magical ego are still in part unconscious and emotion toned" (Neumann, 1963/1990, p. 149). Helen not only wishes Annie would go away, she does something about it. Neumann further explicated:

> through its activity toward the body and the unconscious, drives and emotions can be harnessed and utilized in the concentration of magical activity. . . . The magical youthful ego is productive, active, procreative and phallic. It confronts the world not with passive wishes but with active intervention. (p. 151)

James cannot win, and he is in a state of resignation—in a stagnant attractor site, in his own "damned if you do, damned if you don't" underworld.

Captain Keller, who is much better at ordering people around instead of doing anything, is the one who extricates Annie from her situation. The masculine logos is what is needed. The father is finally doing something, instead of standing in the way. By ascending the ladder, he needs to become more conscious. The masculine needs to show up to the party in order for things to move forward.

Helen, by dropping the key into the well, is unconsciously communicating that the key is in the unconscious and it is out of reach for now. She has won this battle; yet, Helen the tyrant has met her match. Yes Helen is cunning and very bright, and she does have the home court advantage; however, Annie has age, experience, size, and sight on her side. A battle of wills is brewing, and Helen's reign of terror and chaos, the "old order," is nearly over. There's a new sheriff in town, but that also means a new and probably bigger battle is in the offing.

Annie has survived much worse than this little Napoleon has to dish out. Annie has staying power, because ironically she has "nowhere else to go, and nothing else to do" but stay. She truly has no other viable choice. It is a high stakes match for Annie—because she has no way to earn a living, and returning to Tewksbury is anathema to her, and not an option. Helen is about to meet her Waterloo.

On April 10, 1903, Mark Twain said: "The two most interesting characters of the nineteenth century are; Napoleon and Helen Keller." He later continued: "Napoleon tried to conquer the world by force and failed. Helen tried to conquer the world by power of mind—and succeeded." (Keller, 2011; Clemens, 1937). Interestingly, Napoleon was actually exiled to St. Helena, an island in the mid-Atlantic. [See Appendix D: Excursion into Origins, for etymological origins of Helen's name.]

FEELING EMOTIONS

Scene 1: Trying Temperance

The scene changes, it is after dinner, an apparent truce is in place. Annie and Helen are back in Annie's room. Annie is writing a letter to her friend Sophie Hopkins about Helen, about the need to "discipline her without breaking. . . [her spirit]." Annie is interrupted by Helen's groping hand. Attempting to find out what Annie is doing, Helen heedlessly invades Annie's space. Annie pushes her away, and Helen then comes upon the inkwell and topples it, which spills ink all over the page. A little bit of liquid chaos begins, which Annie tries to initially contain and clean up. However, as Helen makes a bigger mess, Annie sees the opportunity in the chaos, and takes it as a chance to teach Helen. She firmly dabs Helen's hand further in the ink and spells *i-n-k* into Helen's other hand. Trying to indicate that this thing, this spilled liquid that is ink, has a name. Helen is of course uncomprehending, and proceeds to get the ink all over herself again, which Annie now busily wipes it off.

Annie then sits Helen down on a stool and distracts her with a sewing card, showing Helen how to work the needle, cautioning her about its sharpness. Annie goes back to cleaning up the mess from the spilled ink, and meanwhile Helen has stabbed herself with the needle and reacts violently. Helen gropes around, and finding the doll, raises it over her head, attempting to vent her rage. She is interrupted by Annie, who sits her back down, and says "Lets try temperance," to the unhearing Helen.

Taking her cue from the last encounter, Annie begins to show Helen different emotions by letting Helen feel them on her face. Annie first takes the doll and makes a violent motion with it, imitating what Helen has just done and signs *b-a-d-g-i-r-l* into Helen's uncomprehending hand, then Annie makes her face into an exaggerated mask of sadness. She lets Helen feel her face; Helen then mimics this expression with her own face, feeling to make sure she has it correct. Helen looks very unnatural and almost gruesome. Annie then has Helen kiss the doll, signs *g-o-o-d-g-i-r-l* into Helen's hand, and smiles exaggeratingly, and again Helen imitates her with her own face. Helen then goes to put her doll on the washstand near the pitcher, setting her there gently. Annie says out loud, in a surprised tone, "very good girl." In the next instant, Helen picks up the pitcher, which is next to the doll, and smashes it to the ground, with a big smile still on her face. She quickly makes her way back to Annie to read Annie's face. Annie frowns, but not as exaggeratedly and Helen copies her. Annie then nods yes, and places Helen back on the bed, engaging her with the sewing card again, spelling the word into Helen's hand as she does so.

Scene 2: Rewarding Bad Behavior

Next, Kate enters and asks Annie about what she is doing. Annie says that she is conversing with Helen. Kate asks if Helen understands the letters are a word, and Annie explains that she "won't know what spelling is until she knows what a word is," to which Kate replies that the "Capt'n says it's like spelling to a fence post. . . is it?" Annie explains to Kate drawing an analogy to how Kate talks to the baby. Neither the baby nor Helen understand what is being said, but in time, both of them will. Signing the letters to Helen, Annie is helping her to learn, the way any other child would learn, "letting Helen hear it" in the only way she can. Kate counters "other children aren't . . . impaired," and Annie tells her "Oh, there's nothing impaired in that head. It works like a mousetrap." Annie informs Kate that it might take a million words in order for Helen to make the connection between words themselves and things they signify, and she offers Kate *The Perkins Report* to read. Kate then asks to learn the letters; they seem to be forging a partnership. Kate tells Annie that it is Helen's bedtime, and Annie goes to take the card from Helen, who resists. Helen then stabs Annie with the needle, and begins throwing a violent tantrum.

Kate instinctively does what she must have done many times, she gives Helen a sweet, which acts to calm Helen down for the moment, but truly only acts to reinforce the behavior. Annie asks Kate indignantly, "Why does she get a reward, for stabbing me?" To which Kate replies: "There are so many times she simply cannot be compelled." Annie responds: "Yes, I'm the same way myself." Annie then goes over to the washstand, stepping on the remains of the broken pitcher on the way, picks up the doll and at first caresses it and then begins to throttle it, shaking it at the neck.

Again, in this chapter, we see Helen creating chaos around herself: the spilled ink and the broken pitcher, mirroring the chaos in Helen's mind, which spills out around her, as she unable to contain herself and she will not allow others to contain her either. Helen has no ability to tolerate the smallest frustration, and goes into a rage again. She is violently aggressive in her overreactions. After having stabbed herself with the needle a few minutes previously, she now viscously uses her newfound weapon against Annie, stabbing her with it.

The system has become chaotic, and instead of redirecting Helen in a positive way, Kate—attempting to dampen the chaos—continues to iterate around the same pattern, creating a negative feedback loop that actually keeps the chaotic pattern in place. Annie's intervention moments before, was to try to teach Helen about emotions, instead of actually rewarding bad behavior, as her parents have done and continue to do.

Annie reads the pattern, and has her work cut out for her. Although we, the audience, have seen this pattern of placating before, this is the first time Annie has seen Helen interact with someone in her family. Annie has seen Helen's escalation from zero to rage in an instant, but this is the first Annie has seen of Helen's parents' complicity—their part in sustaining the pattern.

This scene once again shows us the resonance between teacher and student, which Conforti spoke about in *Threshold Experiences* (2007) and their seemingly fated nature. In *Field Form and Fate*, he elaborated:

> As an archetype assumes increasing dominance over the ego, it creates situations and interactional patterns in reality which can be viewed as the physical manifestation of the archetype. . . . We are coming to the appreciation and workings of fields and their power to create entrainment patterns. (Conforti, 1999, pp. 82-84)

The dialog between Kate and Annie at the end shows us that neither Helen nor Annie can be compelled. Both Helen and Annie are headstrong and aggressive, and have the ability to use whatever is at hand to accomplish their desired objectives. They also share a similar habit of externalizing their emotions, in taking their aggression out on dolls especially—as can be seen when Helen almost smashes her doll, and later when Annie rings the doll's neck. As we have seen, dolls can be surrogates for people, and Annie is displacing her frustration toward Helen upon the doll, taking out her aggression in a safer way. Annie's unconscious communication in this instance is that she wants to wring Helen's neck, maybe not so unconscious, come to think of it!

"BADLY SPOILED CHILD"

This upcoming chapter is the turning point in the film, akin to the *crisis* in a dream: "The crisis is when something begins to happen, dramatic action. It is a call to action, a call to do something" (Conforti, 2010). This is the first time the family is all together with Annie and Helen at the same time. It can be seen as the initial conditions of their "group therapy," if you will. Annie has seen Helen in action one-on-one, but here she sees it in the context of the entire family, and assesses the situation. Annie makes important observations and takes decisive action, intervening to break up the pattern that keeps reiterating.

Scene 1: Opening Salvo

The following morning, the family is seated at breakfast, except for Helen—who is grazing, going around from plate to plate, taking whatever she wants with her bare hands. We first see Helen eating off of her father's plate. While the rest of the family are quite used to this behavior and take no notice of Helen as she does this, Annie is watching, and looks a bit shocked.

Captain Keller and James are busy debating the Civil War, and the battle of Vicksburg, which happened over 20 years before. James contends that The South was lost two years before the end of the war because Grant outthought them, and Keller contends that The South lost the war "by stupidity vergin' on treason," due to having a "half-breed Yankee traitor" in charge instead of a Southerner, like Old Stonewall (who was already deceased by that time, having died a week before the battle due to friendly fire). Once again, no one pays any attention to Helen.

James, after enduring Keller's demeaning way of conversing, gives his opinion that the reason that the Yankees won was because Grant was obstinate, and that he "wouldn't give up, he tried four ways of getting around Vicksburg."

At this point, Helen has moved all the way around the table, past her mother who is absorbed in reading *The Perkins Report*, and on towards Annie's plate. Annie has been waiting for this, and when Helen puts her hand in Annie's plate, Annie deliberately removes Helen's hand. Helen gropes again, not to be denied, and Annie again rebuffs her, this time more strongly by taking her wrists and not letting go as they struggle back and forth.

Kate interrupts and advises Annie that Helen "is accustomed to helping herself from our plates." Annie responds evenly, "Well I'm not." Keller's response is to call Viney to get Annie a new plate, while James sardonically remarks, "her table manners are the best she has." Meanwhile the struggle is mounting, because even though Kate has asked James to give Helen something to quiet her, and he tries to hand Helen a piece of bacon, Helen will have none of it and slaps the bacon away.

Keller meanwhile implores Annie "let her this time. It's the only way we get any adult conversation." He even goes so far as to try to continue to get Annie another plate, which she declines. Now Kate, too, is after Annie to give in: "What Capt'n Keller says is only too true. She'll persist in this til. . ." The following exchange ensues while Annie continues to hold Helen at bay.

Annie: I have a plate. I intend to keep it.

James: You see why they took Vicksburg?

Keller: A plate is no matter to struggle with a deprived child about.

Annie: I'd sooner have a more heroic issue.

Helen now begins to turn up the heat, and begins to kick as well. Keller insists that Annie stop, saying that Helen has hurt herself when Helen uses this as a tactic. Annie, knowing better, assures them that Helen hasn't hurt herself. Both Captain Keller and Kate both implore Annie to stop now, asking Annie to release Helen's hands—remarking that she doesn't know Helen well enough. Annie shoots back: I know a tantrum when I see one, and a badly spoiled child!" James now enters the fray on Annie's side, "Hear, hear." The verbal struggle continues as Annie continues to struggle physically with Helen. Keller is enraged and Annie rises to meet his fury, temporarily releasing Helen from her grasp. She regains her handhold and Helen continues to flail.

Keller: You'd have more understanding if you had some pity.

Annie: Pity? For this tyrant? The whole house turns on her whims. What I pity is that the sun won't rise and set for her, and you're telling her it will. What good will your pity do when you're under the strawberries Captain Keller?

Annie has now not only identified the pattern, and dared to state the likely trajectory; she asks them to consider their actions consciously. They are still very much locked into the pattern unconsciously, so they continue to be held in its sway, still trying to get Annie to cease and desist, but Annie will have none of it and continues to expose the truth. Now locking horns with Keller:

Annie: It's less trouble to feel sorry than to teach her anything. . .

Keller: You haven't taught her anything yet.

Annie: I'll begin now if you leave the room.

Keller: Leave?

Annie: Everyone, please!

Keller: You are a paid teacher, nothing more.

Annie: I can't unteach her six years of pity if you can't stand up to one tantrum. Old Stonewall indeed!

Annie beseeches Kate to hold to her promise to help. Then Annie again asks to be left alone with Helen. Keller is so upset by Annie's behavior that he storms out, ordering his wife to follow him, raging all the way. Annie has succeeded in getting the rest of the family to leave her alone with Helen. On his way out the door, James cheerfully remarks while saluting: "If it takes all summer, General!"

The entire conversation about the Civil War is an example of unconscious communication (also known as derivative or disguised communication), Robert Langs's (1983) term for

> those communicative expressions which include implicit reference to unconscious experiences. Though awareness of derivative communication was not new to psychoanalytic clinical theory, he [Langs] made listening for derivative communication a centerpiece of his theory of analytic practice. Langs differentiated "Type 1" derivatives, which refer solely to the client's internal experiences, and "Type 2" derivatives, which arise from the patient's attempts to adapt to reality, at times evoking psychic conflict. (Wikipedia, 2013, Langs).

The Battle of Vicksburg, or the Siege of Vicksburg as it was known, was the turning point of the Civil War. It lasted more than 40 days and the

South finally surrendered the city on the Fourth of July. James seems to have brought up the conversation, and he is really talking about the smaller civil war that is going on within the household. Their conversation, a mini-battle, is another battleground. Keller's blaming of Pembroke, is actually an unconscious indictment of himself and the family who have given in to Helen, surrendering their sovereignty and authority; this is indeed in Keller's own words: "stupidity vergin' on treason." He has been unable to win this civil war within his family.

The Yankee Annie has arrived and she, as we will shortly see, is just as stubborn as General Grant. She is perturbating the system, driving the situation far from equilibrium; and the others—with the exception of James— are very upset by this. Annie is coloring outside the lines, doing an unfamiliar dance, which causes the system to become unpredictable. Again, everyone except for Annie is trying to dampen down the mounting chaos, to placate Helen by giving her what she wants, or at least some reward.

James's remarks of admiration for Grant's fighting ability tell us which side James is hoping will win this battle, and ultimately put an end to the war. When James comments on Helen's table manners being the best that she has, he is reiterating the fact that she is unmannered, uncivilized.

Captain Keller, the old king stuck in the past, is pining over Old Stonewall, who was dead at the time of the battle in question, and has been gone for over 20 years. The battle ended in parole—an agreement not to take up arms for a period of time. This presages the future, when Annie, after she wins the upcoming Siege at the Breakfast Table aka "battle royale with Helen," (Keller, 1903/2003) will not have to deal with the Kellers' interference—at least for a period of time. But, once again, we are getting ahead of ourselves.

Keller's old way of being needs to die, and he is essentially "stonewalling" Annie, thwarting her attempts at disciplining Helen, although Kate, too, plays a big part in this unconscious dynamic. Due to Annie's interruption of Helen's pattern, this old pattern, unable to run its course, has sent the system cascading quickly into chaos.

This is exactly what is needed. The initial perturbation has caused a series of bifurcations, and as a result, the system moves to an entirely new place. They are now in uncharted territory. Instead of capitulating to Keller and letting Helen continue to get away with her unacceptable behavior—

the road *famila[r]*, that well-worn path—Annie takes the entire family on the *road less traveled* (Frost, 1916). And as we will see, it will make all the difference!

Scene 2: Leaving The Field Of Battle

Kate, Keller, and James now head outside; Keller, fuming about Annie, still has his napkin around his neck. He begins to dictate to Kate, telling her that she needs to deal with it, and to make it clear to Annie that her disrespectful behavior is intolerable. Kate contemptuously asks him where he will be while she is informing Annie of his orders. Keller replies "at the office," pulling off his napkin, and throwing it at James.

While trying to assert his authority by ordering his wife around and blustering on a manifest level, his unconscious communication tells a different story. He is actually surrendering. James then asks Kate if she will really follow through on Keller's orders, adding his opinion about Annie's intervention: "I thought what she said was exceptionally intelligent. I've been sayin' it for years." James absently hands Kate the napkin, without thought. Kate quips back scornfully: "to his face?" And she accepts the napkin at first and then says to him "or will you take it, Jimmie? As a flag?"

Keller is again abdicating his duty as the father and head of the household, improperly dodging his authority, essentially retreating while using a smokescreen of anger. He is taking his marbles and going somewhere else to play.

The old king, the old order needs to die, but it is not going down willingly. He is a stern Saturn, but he is not enforcing boundaries, limits, or traditions. The only tradition he is interested in is a long lost war. Once more, the absent father is absenting himself, instead of enforcing the codes of society, in the realm of logos; he once again leaves the field. The men are at odds with each other: Captain Keller is like the mythic father Cronos swallowing his children—this is indeed treacherously stupid. James, his beleaguered progeny, is caught in this no win situation. Everyone is at "sixes and sevens" with each other, and Helen isn't even in the vicinity. The pattern is holding firm.

A white flag is the symbol of surrender or truce. Keller has unconsciously communicated that he has surrendered, and he has indeed surrendered his authority to Kate, who is unwilling to assume the parental duty to discipline. Kate, as she did earlier when Annie arrived, has essentially castrated James; and through his unconscious communication, he, too, has given up and stalks away. The men have essentially surrendered their authority once again, another iteration, because of their failure to step up to the plate, the same repetitious game continues on, unchanged, or does it? Annie, the game changer, has other plans. The family and how they interact with Helen is the problem. Now that they are safely out of play, Annie can concentrate on taming this little shrew.

Scene 3: Let The "Battle Royale" Begin

Just as Vicksburg was the turning point of the Civil War, the upcoming scene will be the turning point of Helen's war—although she doesn't know it yet. This scene lasts for over 8 minutes, with not a word being uttered, although there is plenty of noise and action. The physicality demanded of the actors was astounding. But back to the story.

Meanwhile, in the dining room, Annie is readying the field for battle. She has had to rethink her original plan; she needs to teach Helen to be civilized, to be a human instead of an animal, before she can teach her what language is. The breakfast table will be a perfect classroom.

Taking all the chairs away from the table except hers and Helen's, Annie also locks the doors and put the keys where Helen cannot get to them. While she is doing this, Helen is busy having a full-blown temper tantrum laying on the floor, kicking her legs wildly like a baby. Annie waits Helen out, knowing that she can't keep this up forever; she lets Helen blow off steam, exhausting herself and essentially fighting against herself, for Helen is in inner turmoil.

Annie readies a plate for herself and sits down to eat. Helen finally gets sick of the tantrum and decides to investigate. Upon finding Annie sitting in her chair, Helen tries to pull it out from under Annie, nearly succeeding. Annie reestablishes her position and continues to eat, and Helen then pinches Annie on the thigh, and getting up off the floor, stands up. Annie quickly shows Helen that she is eating another bite with her spoon and Helen reaches at Annie's plate.

Annie stops Helen, placing Helen firmly into Helen's own rarely used chair—putting Helen literally and figuratively in her place. Helen again comes over to Annie and now pinches Annie on the arm; this happens again, with Annie again putting Helen in her chair.

The next time Helen tries it, Annie slaps her hand. Helen escalates, slapping Annie's face, and Annie slaps her back; this happens a couple more times, each time the slapping getting stronger. Then Helen, suddenly, about to come at Annie swinging both arms, stops in mid-air and swings her arms around the air—choosing this time, to take the road less traveled. Instead of striking Annie, Helen wraps her arms around herself, trying to contain or soothe herself. Helen is now learning and has changed her behavior, for the moment.

Then Helen goes around the table to where her mother would be and finds that her mother is gone. Indeed everyone is gone, and Helen no longer has the home court advantage. It's a whole new ballgame. As Helen is gesturing wildly and frantically for her mother, Annie goes to engage Helen. Helen rebukes her, and tries to leave the room, but then discovers that she is locked in, further amping up the frenetic energy.

Next Annie grabs Helen, returning Helen to her seat, and Helen pops up and runs away, with Annie bringing her back again. This pattern iterates several times, at first Helen is able to get away, and then Annie grabs her and pull her back by her pinafore. Helen is on a shorter and shorter leash. Occasionally Helen breaks free, and Annie carries her back to the chair. Now Helen begins to mix it up, going over and under the table to try to get away. Not to be deterred, Annie then gets out in front of Helen, blocking her path like NBA basketball's future legendary defensive players Bill Russell, Hakeem Olajuwon, or Dennis Rodman (Mihajlovski, 2010).

After a while, Helen, realizing she can't win, stops. Annie again eats another bite of food, and Helen again tries to eat the food with her hands. Annie succeeds in putting Helen back in the chair and Helen remains there. Helen then starts banging her hands on the table and her feet on the floor, now in a seated tantrum. Annie scrapes some scrambled eggs off the floor and onto a plate and shoves them under Helen's nose, which breaks Helen's tantrum mid stomp. Helen, still seated, then is able to eat some eggs off the plate with her hand. Helen insistently bangs on the plate with her hand for more. Then Helen bangs on the table while Annie refills the plate, coming back with a full plate and a spoon.

Annie now places the spoon in Helen's hand with some eggs in it, and puts the spoon to Helen's mouth and Helen takes the eggs off the spoon with her hand, and puts them into her mouth. Annie forces Helen to disgorge the eggs and repeats filling the spoon a couple of times, unsuccessfully trying to get Helen to use it. Helen finally throws the spoon away. Jerking Helen out of the chair, Annie carries Helen to retrieve the spoon. Annie will not be deterred; Helen has picked the wrong person to do battle with. Annie succeeds in wrestling Helen back to her chair, spoon in hand, and again the pattern iterates, and Helen gets away, and then ends up back in the chair, this time, fastening herself onto it.

Now the pattern is beginning to change once again. Although still iterating around the chair, the Annie vs. Helen battle is beginning to show some more novelty. Now Annie cannot get Helen out of the chair—an *enantiodromia* something turning into its opposite. Annie finally succeeds in breaking Helen out of the chair by picking up the chair, with Helen firmly attached, and crashing it into the wall. Annie is trying to break this pattern of chaotic acting out, which is proving very intractable. However, Annie has more behavioral flexibility than Helen, and even has to somersault out of the way once! Annie's difficult past and her own intractable behavior as a child now hold her in good stead. This tortured tango plays on for a while, Helen baring her teeth, and flinging the spoon away again in a fury. However, when Annie has finally succeeded in reseating her, Helen stays seated.

Now, Annie goes to get more provisions from the service board, and comes back with all of the spoons and some food. Helen flings them away, one by one, eight times. Annie finally loads a spoon and forces it into Helen's mouth, by holding her by the head. When Helen suddenly opens her mouth, Annie shoves the food in, at which point Helen then turns around and spits it into Annie's face. Helen then sits in the chair, her arms crossed over her chest, savoring her victory, but it is short lived.

Annie then takes the water pitcher and throws its contents on Helen. Before she has a chance to recover from the shock, Annie forces a spoonful of eggs into Helen's mouth, and spells *g-o-o-d g-i-r-l* into Helen's hand. Then Annie makes the mistake of putting Helen's hand to her head and nodding. Helen seizes the moment to retaliate, and grabs Annie's hair and pulls it. The clock begins to strike as Annie regroups.

The scene then switches to outside, we hear the clock beginning to strike again, as we see Kate and the Baby, Aunt Ev, Viney, and her children outside. Before we follow them outside, let's pause and look more closely at what has happened, and also look at two symbols—chair and spoon.

Where previously there was no container, Helen is contained now, and she doesn't like it. She is enraged. Helen's behavior is a huge *creode* in this liminal landscape, a stubborn, long standing persistent pattern that has become a deep channel that keeps behavior or development regulated within certain limits (Wikipedia, 2013, creode). Many perturbations occurred in this scene, with bifurcations wildly bifurcating, creating novelty and creativity, in this far from equilibrium place. Annie has created chaos in Helen, paradoxically by bringing order. Annie also matches Helen's energetic intensity, and constantly destabilizes Helen's increasingly intensifying chaotic behavior—Helen is in unfamilia[r] territory as well, and is totally disoriented. Her family has never acted this way with her.

According to recent research in neuroscience research (Rock, 2006) old patterns are not easily extinguished; instead it is necessary to create new ones, and then strengthen them over time so that they can become dominant. In this way, the new pattern can serve as a new attractor site. This battle scene is a magnificent example of the power, pervasiveness, and persistency of patterns. It shows a simple bifurcation point and how the system careens quickly toward chaos and the creativity, commitment, and tenacity that are needed to change.

Chair symbolically. Chairs have been around since ancient times. As far back as the old Kingdom of Ancient Egypt. "In addition, apart from simply elevating humans, humans of elevated status, in particular, have long been associated with the early history of chairs" (Randomhistory.com, 2013). Thus, chairs "are universally regarded as a symbol of authority" (Chevalier & Gilbrant, 1996, p. 177). Chairs were mainly used in the ancient world by the higher strata of society and the gods, especially as thrones, with stools being used by the more common people. Even in the Middle Ages, chairs were mostly used by the masters of the household and beyond, they were often reserved for the upper classes. Etymologically speaking:

> The Greek language lends to the Romantic languages a contraction of *kathedra* (also into Latin, *cathedra*), which is derived from *kata*, for "down," and *hedra*, for "to sit." The word passed into Middle English from the Old French *chaiere* and the variant *chaise*, which is variously in use in English for styles of chairs today (OED, 2001, *chair*).

By remaining seated and letting Helen come to her as she continues to eat, Annie begins to unconsciously communicate her authority. Annie subsequently "puts Helen in her place, literally and figuratively, and tries to keep Helen there, in an attempt unconsciously communicate the desire to raise to raise Helen's status from that of an instinctual animal to a person of culture. Annie, through her authority, is attempting to not only to bring discipline to Helen, she is also trying to raise Helen's stature.

Helen, on the other hand, when she latches onto the chair, is attempting to assert her authority as the chaos queen. Annie's response to Helen's latest ploy, when she breaks Helen out of the chair, is essentially to dethrone this not so diminutive dictator.

Spoon symbolically. A spoon is a piece of cutlery used to contain foods that are not formed enough to be eaten with a fork because of their more fluid nature, such as soups. "Spoons are used to sip, stir, and sup," an online etiquette site remarked. They are the most prolific cutlery, with 14 different kinds for various uses being identified (Lininger, 2013). An online dream dictionary shared that psychologically, *spoons* are:

> tools of the absorption of nutrients. The soul is hungry and would like to take up new impressions. Spoon often points out to the fact that one must carry the consequences for his behaviour. If one eats with it, this can also announce that the worries and problems soon decrease. (dreamtation.com, 2013)

By insisting that Helen use a spoon instead of her hands, Annie is again trying to get Helen to move into a more civilized situation, to enforce discipline and impose structure. Helen is vehement in her disobedience, but luckily Annie, like General Grant, is obstinate and will not be defeated.

Having come to a new fork in the road, metaphorically speaking—a bifurcation point that has never before been traveled—we now join the rest of the family outside, where previously napkins were flying.

A FOLDED NAPKIN

Scene 1: The Moment Of Triumph

Aunt Ev begins to complain about the long, seemingly interminable wait; it is nearly lunchtime. Aunt Ev goes off and Viney, also about to leave, takes the baby and goes back inside. Kate is left alone momentarily, when Helen and Annie come barging out of the door. Helen immediately goes for her mother, clinging intensely to her and Kate gutterally demands, "What happened?" Annie reports: "She ate from her own plate. She ate with a spoon. . . herself. And she folded her napkin." Kate is stunned, and disbelievingly asks, "Folded her napkin?" Annie then says "the room's a wreck but her napkin is folded." And then Annie goes inside. As she leaves, Annie hears Viney tell her that lunch is almost ready, so don't be long. Almost three hours have passed. Kate is now alone holding Helen, and she marvels softly and whispers to herself, "folded her napkin. My Helen folded her napkin?" She then begins to cry, and Helen noticing, puts her hand to her mother's face. Kate bends down to further embrace Helen.

Napkins are intimately connected with the hand and the mouth, used in connection with eating, the first step in the assimilation process. Napkins can thus be seen as a symbol of order, culture, and civility— protecting and containing messes— keeping them from spreading (Von Drachenfels, 2013; OED, 2013, *napkin*). In Helen's case, this was the beginning of the beginning, the initial conditions for the first step of her learning. In her correspondence with Mrs. Hopkins, Annie wrote that she had to first discipline Helen before she could really teach Helen anything. The breakfast battle, and folding her napkin in particular, was the first step in this process.

Learning has been compared to the digestive process. Christopher Ormell (1996) developed eight metaphors "to represent the invariant features of education. Four liken it to the planning, preparation, consumption, and digestion of mental meals; the other four relate to the improved vision gained by the learner" (p. 67).

Before one can begin to digest food, one needs to eat it, and digestion goes better if done mindfully, in a calm, stress-free atmosphere, instead of just stuffing one's face. The napkin symbolizes this order. The digestive process is alchemical—done in a specific place in a specific way. This leads eventually to food being transformed, so that it can be used by the body, which combines and recombines elements, creating, destroying, eliminating, and growing—renewing itself. The food is the *prima materia* from which this process begins.

"Stress can affect every part of the digestive system," says Kenneth Koch, MD, ... "Johann Wolfgang von Goethe, the great German writer and philosopher, believed that the gut was the seat of all human emotions."

Digestion is controlled by the enteric nervous system, a system composed of hundreds of millions of nerves that communicate with the central nervous system. When stress activates the "flight or fight" response in your central nervous system, digestion can shut down because your central nervous system shuts down blood flow, affects the contractions of your digestive muscles, and decreases secretions needed for digestion. (Iliades, 2013, online)

If we take the education as digestion metaphor to heart, it stands to reason that Helen will need to be in an approach or *toward* state for learning to occur, not in an *away* or threat state (Rock, 2008). Because she cannot see or hear, Helen goes into an escalated threat response very quickly and easily, as there is a lot of uncertainty in her world. Helen's ability to think and learn will be impaired if she is not able to lower the threat level. The brain, being very social, has certain needs, which Rock has given the acronym SCARF. It stands for: status, certainty, autonomy, relatedness and fairness. (Rock, 2008; Davachi, Kiefer, Rock, & Rock, 2011; Rock & Cox, 2012). Due to Helen's lack of the very important senses of seeing and hearing, her levels of status, certainty, autonomy, and relatedness are heavily impacted. As previously mentioned, without this sensory input, she doesn't know where she fits in, and has little certainty about her environment, this affects her autonomy or ability to choose and to be able to do things independently. Helen's ability to relate to others is also severely impacted—thus her survival is threatened due to her brain's inability to make sense of the world and her place in it.

Scene 2: Ghosts Of The Past

Annie goes back inside the house and we see the chaotic state of the room—chairs are askew, the tablecloth is all bunched up, but the napkin is folded amidst the upheaval. Annie now goes inside her own consciousness and flashes back to another meal that cascaded into chaos at Tewksbury. A bunch of old crones are talking and arguing about whether or not there is a school where they teach blind children. As the argument escalates, people begin throwing food at each other and we hear screaming. Then we hear Jimmie's voice from an earlier time pleading with Annie not to leave him. Annie's brother Jimmie died within months of their arrival at Tewksbury, and he still haunts Annie, more than a decade later.

Jimmie: You ain't going to school, Annie?

Annie: When I grow up.

Jimmie: You ain't either, Annie. You're going to stay here, take care of me.

Annie: I'm going to school when I grow up.

Jimmie: You said we'd be together for ever and ever and ever.

Annie: I'm going to school when I grow up! Now leave me be.

The flashback visions fade and now Annie goes and picks up *The Perkins Report* and begins reading. This is the same report that contains the story of Laura Bridgman, and her work with Dr. Howe. Annie reads:

Can nothing be done to disinter this human soul? The whole neighbourhood would rush to save this woman if she were buried alive by the caving in of a pit, and labour with zeal until she were dug out. Now, if there were one who had as much patience as zeal. . .

While she is reading, the scene switches again to the crones, someone alerting Annie to the presence of Mr. Sanborn, saying if she talks to him, she might get out. Sanborn is the man who will be her ticket out of Tewksbury. In her mind's eye, Annie goes blindly groping toward him, pleading "Mr. Sanborn, Mr. Sanborn, I want to go to school." Then suddenly, Annie is back in the present day and she continues reading where she left off:

might awaken her to a consciousness of her immortal nature. The chance is small indeed, but with a smaller chance they would have dug desperately for her in the pit. And is the life of the soul of less import than that of the body?

Clutching the report, Annie then puts it down on the table, her determination is renewed. She is resolute, after winning this decisive battle; Annie gets an idea and quickly proceeds to execute it. Through a montage sequence, we see Annie searching for a place where she can teach Helen. She finds several buildings, all unsuitable—too dark, too dirty. She must find the proper environment, one where she won't be interfered with. Then, taking a rest against a tree, Annie spies a small house. She finds that it is mostly empty, except for random items from around the homestead, and although full of cobwebs, it is perfect.

The flashback has reminded Annie of her embattled past, where she lost the person she most loved—her brother Jimmie. Annie needs to find a proper ritual space to initiate this young being, Helen, into another identity, another field. Like the grieving Demeter, Annie has a found something to engage her, to take her mind off of her own painful grief; she has found her own Demaphoon, she will now go about the process of being the nursemaid to another child. And unlike Demaphoon, although no one knows it yet, in years to come, this child will actually become immortal.

Coming back down to earth from the rarified air of the archetypal realm, we return to the Keller homestead. Annie must now get the Kellers to agree to her plan.

Karey Pohn

TOLERANCE IN 2 WEEKS

Scene 1: A Hopeless Situation

Captain Keller is seen lighting a lamp in the study, and complaining about Annie, who is in his eyes a troublesome burden: "incompetent, impertinent, ineffectual, and immodest. Kate presences the fact that Annie is not ineffectual, because Helen did fold her napkin, which Kate points out, "is more than you did, Capt'n." Concerned that Annie has "scuttled any chance she has of getting along with the child," Keller again abdicates responsibility to his wife to give Annie notice. Kate firmly declines, and he says, "then if you won't, I must."

Annie knocks on the study door, interrupting their conversation, which she could hear from upstairs through the shut door. When Keller opens the door, Annie announces that she wants to have a talk. Keller begins to talk of his dissatisfaction in a blustery tone, and Annie interrupts him, asking about the small house she has found. Keller is not to be deterred and interrupts Annie. He begins to attempt to give her a "dressing down." He is stopped and troubled by her dark glasses; she obligingly taking them off. When he asks why she is wearing them at night, Annie replies "any kind of light hurts my eyes." This causes Keller to reconsider and he momentarily softens, deciding to give Annie another chance to remain in their employ.

Then Keller changes back to his quarrelsome persona. He demands that Annie change her rude attitude and that she persuade him that there is "a hope of your teaching a child who flees from you like the plague to anyone in this house." Annie agrees with Keller that it "is hopeless here."

This statement shocks Kate, who very intensely and forcefully—like a mother lion protecting her cub—pleads her case. Kate tries to persuade Annie that it is not hopeless, that Helen was a bright outgoing child who learns. Kate tells Annie that Helen even began talking at six months old and was even able to say "wah wah." She begs Annie to reconsider to "put up with her and with us" and says "Like the lost lamb in the parable, I love her all the more." While there are glimpses of the ferocity of Kate's love, her pain and pity cause her to collapse into a more helpless place.

This gives Annie the opening she needs. Annie names the pattern, getting them to see the current reality, the graveness of the situation. Their way of relatedness is the problem, their sympathy with Helen does not

100

allow them to give her what she needs most—structure and containment. Annie tells them that their love and pity is Helen's worst handicap, not her deafness or blindness: "All of you are so sorry for her, you've kept her like a pet. Why, even a dog you housebreak. It's useless for me to try to teach her language or anything else *here*."

Kate and Keller then share that before Annie came, they talked about putting Helen in an asylum for mental defectives, but that Kate visited there once. Kate relates "I can't tell you what I saw, people like animals with rats in the halls." Kate seems resigned to this if Annie were to give up.

Annie however has no intention of giving up, she has only said that it is "hopeless *here*." This time she places more emphasis on the word *here*. Annie, a consummate pattern analyst, says: "Give up, I've only now just seen what needs to be done." Annie then begins to explicate what she believes is necessary—her proposed intervention, and her reasoning:

I want complete charge of her . . . . day and night. She has to be dependent on me [for] everything. The food she eats, the clothes she wears, fresh. . . air. Yes, the air she breathes. Whatever her body needs is a primer to teach her out of. The one who lets her have it should be her teacher, not anyone who loves her.

Kate points out that Helen runs from Annie to them, but Annie has already considered this and factored it into her solution.

Annie is half-packed and ready to execute her intervention, which she informs Keller meets both of his conditions: (1) her attitude and (2) of getting "back in touch with Helen." As for her rude attitude Annie declares forcefully "I don't see how I can be rude to you if you're not there to interfere with me." Keller then returns her salvo with his own, asking Annie if she will abandon Helen if he doesn't capitulate to her terms?

The scene begins with the now familiar struggle between Keller and Kate. These skirmishes between the Kellers are priming the pump of transformation.

In choosing to begin the discussion with who is going to pay for the broken dishware, Keller's unconscious communication tells us that he is concerned that Annie has broken up the old order, and he, as the Old King, is threatened by her. Annie's very presence perturbs Keller. When she complies with his wishes without arguing, Annie is like an aikido master, she doesn't engage his pattern, but lets it slip past her; and in not engaging and pushing back, Keller is temporarily off balance and his humanity breaks through.

Annie turns the tables on Keller, reminiscent of a scene in *Mary Poppins* (Stevenson, 1964) where George Banks, who is similarly unconscious and inattentive to the family situation, attempts the same thing with Mary. Both Annie and Mary artfully redirect the pattern to a road less traveled by unexpectedly agreeing with their adversary. This has the effect of evoking different behavior from Kate. Kate's questioning of Annie gets her associated to the need to change. Kate in this interaction is beginning to change, tapping into the fire of her inner passion, which has been put out previously by the waters of grief.

Annie knows that the way that the family has had of relating with Helen is the problem. She cannot stay at the level of the problem and solve it, to paraphrase the future Einstein. The gravitational pull of the family pattern, of pity and pandemonium, is too strong and too well established. It is like the Grand Canyon, a deep creode (or pattern of possibility), which is etched into the landscape, the course of which will not be changed easily. Annie's solution is to exit that playing field, and go to a new neutral place, where she can create a new pattern. She needs to take Helen away to live with her somewhere else, and Annie will need to do this until Helen "learns to listen to and depend on" her.

Scene 2: Weapon Of Mass Disruption

To accomplish her goal of extricating Helen from the *pattern familia[r]*, Annie uses her secret weapon—her past. In describing the horrors of her past in graphic detail, delivered in a staccato gunfire-like pace, Annie is pulling no punches, and going for the knockout:

> The asylum, I grew up in such an asylum. The state almshouse. Rats? My brother Jimmie and I used to play with the rats because we didn't have toys. Maybe you'd like to know what Helen will find not on visiting days.

> One ward was full of the old women–crippled, blind, most of them dying, but there was nowhere to move them. That's where they put us. There were younger ones–prostitutes mostly, with TB and epileptic fits, and a couple of the kind who keep after other girls, especially young

ones. And some insane. Some just had the DT's.

The youngest were in another ward to have babies. They started at thirteen, fourteen. They'd leave, but we played with the babies, though a lot had sores from diseases you're not supposed to talk about. But not many of them lived. The first year we had eighty, seventy died. Jimmie and I played in the dead-house where they kept the bodies until they could dig the graves . . . . No. It made me strong. But I don't think you need send Helen there. She's strong enough.

Annie's presencing of her disturbing past has had the desired effect, like the water she splashed into Helen's face during the breakfast battle, this cruel reality check has snapped the Kellers out of their dreamland of denial. They agree to let Annie implement her plan, which she then further explicates. As she begins to explain, the typical dynamics accompany even this decision. Kate is hopeful and characteristically looks for solutions, while Keller stereotypically and stubbornly stands in the way of progress — the irascible old King irrationally resisting the new order, and then petulantly giving in. In the end, Keller grudgingly gives Annie two weeks, saying "it will be a miracle if you can get that child to tolerate you."

Kate asks Annie if she can accomplish anything in two weeks. Keller throws down the gauntlet, and reiterates his demands, which were arrived at by him alone, imperiously in his usual anima possessed state of arbitrary emotionality. Annie picks up the gauntlet and agrees to the Captain's irrational terms. She will get Helen to tolerate her in two weeks. The pressure is on. As the scene ends, after Keller walks out, Kate extends her hand in partnership, or friendship. Annie puts her closed fist into it, which puzzles Kate, then Annie says "A, it's the first of many, twenty-six," showing her the sign for the first letter in the alphabet.

Annie has no choice, but to graphically describe the consequences of the current trajectory by telling about her own past. For Annie to do this is huge. She has tried valiantly to put the past behind her. Although it plainly still haunts her, Annie would not talk about her time at Tewksbury with anyone else publically or privately until she was in her 60s—40 years hence.

This is the magnitude of change that is necessary to move this pattern. Annie has begun to teach Kate as well. The power has now shifted to Annie; the ball is now in her court, well played!

By interrupting the previous pattern and going somewhere new, the system is destabilized. Similar to and following on her intervention with Helen at the breakfast table, Annie is taking the system to a place it has never been before. An actual physical place to do the work is thus necessary. Annie needs to move the system to a new attractor site—in which she can tend the far from equilibrium state of the pattern: A place that is free from the intense gravitational pull of the old family order. In interrupting the familiar family unity, and isolating Helen, Annie hopes to be able to help Helen change. The system is too one-sided, and so Annie needs to put a bit of play back into it. Not our familiar notion of play as fun, but play as in leeway, *spielraum*—room to play, as in the play of a wheel.

"THE OTHER JIMMY"

Scene 1: The Initiation Begins

After preparing the small house, Annie meets Helen and the Kellers there. As per Annie's instructions, Helen's parents have taken Helen on a long carriage ride in the country for several hours so that she will not know where she is.

Her parents have a hard time leaving, as Helen is disoriented and making the sign for her mother. As they leave, Kate implores Annie, "be very good to her." After they are gone, the bedlam begins, slowly at first, then building.

Helen goes berserk, she is thrashing around like a cornered animal, her inner turmoil mirrored in the increasingly chaotic surroundings, as she destroys or throws around everything she comes into contact with. Annie has no choice but to let Helen's tornadic torment run its course. Helen, finding her doll, finally collapses in tears, and inconsolably sobs herself to sleep.

Annie is intuitively setting the stage for a *rite of passage*. [With only 6 years at most of schooling in her life, very poor vision, and no internet connection, she most likely was unconscious of it, since Arnold van Gennep didn't even coin this term until 1908]. Since rites of passage are one guise of the transformation process, we will linger a while at this campfire and talk about rites of passage—their origins, etymology, and stages; then briefly mention how they work and allude to their relation to chaos theory. As we do, we will apply these insights to our story.

An extended excursion, well worth the trip, is available in Appendix H: Extended Excursion into Initiations—Eternally Dipping into the Chaotic Realm. [*This excursion, should you choose to take it later, will reiterate and deepen understanding. First, by going into much greater detail, we will learn how rites of passage work their magic and their fascinating relation to the eternal return. Then we will revisit the notion of thresholds and learn about liminality; and how this all relates more deeply to chaos theory.*] However now, we must get back to the campfire at hand.

Rites of passage. *Rites of passage* have existed from time immemorial and virtually all societies and cultures have them in some form. In my dissertation (Pohn, 2006), I explored liminality and rites of passage in relation to the transformative power and possibilities of play. The following discussion is a follow-on from that work.

Origins. Van Gennep coined the term (1908/1960) *rites de passage* or *rites of passage*, which applied to all rituals of transition: from calendrical and cyclical rites involving entire societies, to life transitions involving the change in status of individuals or groups; initiation rites such as puberty, marriage, and death, but also including pilgrimages, and visionquests. van Gennep saw that these rites had in common three different phases, which he labeled: *separation, transition,* and *incorporation.* [Victor Turner called these stages *separation, liminality,* and *return* (1969, 1982), and we will use Turner's terminology going forward].

Etymology. Etymologically speaking, *rite* or *ritual* may come from the Indo-European root, **rtá,* from *ar,* which means to fit together, from which we get different categories of words **ar I:** *army, harmony, artisan, art*; **ar II:** *order, ordo*—as a row of threads in a loom, *primordial, ordiri,* —as in begin to weave. The fourth form, **ar IV** dropped the *a* and from it we get *rite* and *ritus,* meaning custom or usage (AHD, 2000, p. 2021), Wikipedia's widely referenced article stated:

> The original concept of *ritus* may be related to the Sanskrit ऋतá ("visible order)" in Vedic religion, "the lawful and regular order of the normal, and therefore proper, natural and true structure of cosmic, worldly, human and ritual events." (2013, *ritual*)

Rites of passage mark times of change, especially times in life when a person's identity is changing. Van Gennep (1908/1960) noted that different rites would focus on different phases of the process. Marriage rites, for example, would typically focus on the incorporation phase, while funeral rites would typically focus on the separation phase.

Phases. In the separation phase, the focus is on clearly demarcating a space and time from the profane, or the construction of a cultural realm that was defined as out of time (van Gennep, 1908/1960, p. 24). In the separation phase, the old order is symbolically ended in some way. It represents the death of old identity, the old way of being, the old status. The separation phase of Helen's rite of passage occurred in taking Helen away from the house on a long ride, and leaving her in a new place with Annie.

The transition phase, also referred to as margin or *limen* is a period or area of ambiguity, or in-betweenness, which Victor Turner (1969) later characterized as *antistructure,* where symbolic behavior continued to involve inversion and reversal. During the liminal phase, old statuses are no more, and new statuses are yet to be.

Helen will be in this phase the entire time in the garden house. Initially Helen is in complete chaos when she arrives, however, this does not last very long. Over time, Annie will introduce Helen to order and discipline. Because Helen's old way of being, or the "old order" is essentially chaotic—paradoxically, order for her will the new chaos, thus *antistructure* in this case will actually ironically be structure—Helen's liminal state will have a much more ordered flavor—this will be the inversion and reversal. In other words because the liminal state is a reversal of the previous state, and Helen's previous state was chaos, it stands to reason that her liminal state would be order: For Helen, order is the new chaos!!!

Hanson (2001) pointed out the dangers inherent in liminal periods, and quoting anthropologist Mary Douglas noted:

"Ritual recognizes the potency of disorder. In the disorder of the mind, in dreams, faints and frenzies, ritual expects to find powers and truths which cannot be reached by conscious effort. Energy to command and special powers of healing come to those who can abandon rational control for a time." In disorder, comes power, too, in disorder there is danger. . . . All this is directly applicable to the trickster because he is a denizen of the interstitial realm. (pp. 66-67)

Annie will have to think outside of the box, and find some different ways to reach Helen than the ones that Dr. Howe used with Laura Bridgman. Time is of the essence, and she has things to do.

Lastly, the incorporation phase concerns a return to a new status and relatively well-defined positions. Hansen (2001) explained that rituals serve to assist individuals with psychological changes that occur as a result of these changes in status and that they also help to solidify the new structure. Helen will not get to this phase while she is in the garden house, because her initiation will be incomplete when she has to return to her parents.

How rites of passage work, in brief. Rites of passage are essentially engines of the transformation process. Through ritual they bring us back to a chaotic place, so that we can shed the old outworn order, renew ourselves and come to a new place—a new order, a new identity. Rites of passage are a ritualized form of the transformation process and bring us back to origins, and hence partake in the eternal return. The *eternal return* is "a cyclical recurrence of what has been before, the periodic reversion to a timeless beginning. . . . It is repetition, and *anakuklosis*, eternal return" (Eliade, 1954/1991, p. 89).

Helen, too, has reverted to her own beginnings, although she does not realize that she is returning to the scene of the crime as it were. The garden house is actually the same house where Helen was born and that she lived in as a baby and young child, both before and after her illness. Indeed, William Gibson author of the play and screenplay did not realize that this was the same house either, until he visited Tuscumbia in 2008! It is not known whether Annie knew this or not. In Helen's biography (1903/2003), she never identifies the garden house as such, and other biographers did not either. Now, on to the next phase, liminality.

Crossing the threshold into liminality. Liminality, the transition phase of rites of passage come from the Latin *limen*, meaning in between, which van Gennep (1908/1960) noted means threshold, a doorway, or entranceway. The word *threshold* has ancient roots. The first part of the word, *thresh*, is "the earlier and etymological form of *thrash*; still frequent in the sense of beating out corn" (OED, 2013, *thresh*).

Helen's old way of being, the old order [which is anything but orderly], needs to die, but it is not going down without a fight. Helen's thrashing around like a typhonic tornado clearly shows the chaotic nature of this stage. During the time that she in in the garden house with Annie, Helen will be learning a secret language, and nonverbal symbolic gestures, as well as learning through playful events. But that will not happen until after Annie reestablishes contact with Helen in the upcoming chapter.

Being trapped alone with Annie, in an unfamiliar place with no way out, has pushed Helen far from equilibrium. This perturbation is the attempt to introduce the beginnings of order. Paradoxically, it initially leads the system— Helen— into more chaos, deterministic chaos, which sends her far from equilibrium. In the end, a transformation will occur, bringing the system to a new order. But, in the immortal words of my Pilates teacher, Angelique—"not yet."

Although Helen is currently at odds with her, Annie will be Helen's guide, like Hermes the psychopomp, as Helen traverses this chaotic space. Annie, as we have seen, is very familiar with this territory, having essentially grown up here. Annie spent the majority of her formative years until she was fourteen years old in the liminal landscape of illness, death, more death, and abandonment, then more death, topped off by the unmentioned other the traumas of Tewksbury, and to add insult to injury, she was almost literally blind most of the time, with a very painful eye condition.

van Gennep (1908/1960) found that the idea of a renewal, a periodic death and rebirth, is present in these different rituals and ceremonies. He noted that almost all cultures have realized that in biological and social activities "energies become exhausted, and they have to be regenerated at more or less close intervals. The rites of passage ultimately correspond to this fundamental necessity, sometimes so closely, that they take the form of death and rebirth" (p. 182). Giving up an old life and "turning over a new leaf is also an example of this same dynamic" (p. 183). "Death gives way to a new order. Configurations and patterns that replace—and sometimes improve upon the old ones" (p. 159). Bond (2003), although not using van Gennep's work directly, calls this pattern the "archetype of renewal," and shows in detail how understanding these old rites of the aging, death, and rebirth of the king can assist one in better navigating everyday life.

Annie's own initial conditions keep returning to her as well, and now that our brief initial initiation into initiations and the eternal return is finally finished, we will now turn to see what transpires next. Remember, the Extended Excursion, in to Initiations in Appendix H beckons, don't forget to visit there at some point. However, we will now move on to find out how our two heroines are doing in their underworld adventure.

Scene 2: Annie's Anguish

Annie, viewing all of Helen's traumatic thrashing and tearful heartwrenching and sorrowful sobs, wonders what has she gotten herself into. The scene changes, yet we still hear sobbing. However, we see that Helen is fast asleep, and seems to be peaceful for the moment, at least. Helen's terror and turmoil have dredged up deep, dark memories of Annie's own underworld anguish, and it becomes apparent that it is Annie's sobs that we hear.

In a dream, Annie is haunted by the tortured reminiscences of her brother Jimmie's death. The empty bed and crutch, her blindly running and groping into the death house to find and then touch his lifeless body. She is so deep into her nightmare it that she calls out his name in her sleep, waking herself in the process.

James is passing close by, close enough that he can hear Annie call, and thus comes to the window, asking if she has called him. Then he realizes, without her saying anything about it, that Annie has been dreaming about her brother, who had died more than a decade before. James then asks Annie "how old was he, the other Jimmie?" Annie tells him "about Helen's age," and she goes on to tell him a bit about her brother Jimmie, and how long ago he died. James remarks "you don't let go of things easily, do you?"

The conversation then turns to the task of teaching Helen. James asks Annie how she plans on winning Helen's affection, and Annie confesses that doesn't really know: "I lost my temper and here we are." Annie continues:

Annie: I'm counting on her. That little head is dying to know.
James: Know what?
Annie: Anything. Any and every crumb in God's creation. I've got to use that appetite too.
James: Maybe she'll teach you.
Annie: Of course.

James then goes on to intimate that Helen is beyond help, and that Annie really needs to learn to give up on Helen and accept that she is unreachable, and that Annie ought to let Helen be, and pity her as he does. Annie is incensed by this. For Annie, giving up is her idea of the original sin, because if she ever thought like that she would be dead. Annie refuses to throw in the towel; surrender is not in her vocabulary. Once again, James seems to momentarily show care and concern, but quickly turns pessimistic and combative. Annie shuts the window on him. She can ill afford his unwanted thoughts and unhelpful attitude.

When Annie speaks of using everything to teach Helen, and in this scene talks about using "every crumb in god's creation," she is instinctively onto something. As previously mentioned, one of the metaphors for education is digestion (Ormell, 1996). In object relations, Bion (Ogden, 2004) described the mother/baby interaction in these terms as well. The mother serves as the *alpha function*—which takes the baby's undigested experiences and digests them and then feeds them back to the baby so that they can be assimilated. This is similar to a pelican putting food into its pouch and then regurgitating it, half digested for the hatchlings.

Teachers do this archetypally, as well. They take things that are overwhelming and complex and make them more manageable by breaking them down into sensible portions, so that the student will be able to learn the material. Using their experience, they are able to help orient their students and provide strategies that will allow the students to find their way through the material without having to reinvent the wheel or to randomly try to see the forest for the trees (Julian Brown, personal communication, July 3, 2013).

Although beyond the present scope of this paper, the work of object relations theorists Klein (Hinshelwood, 1991) and Bion (1962) on the *epistemophillic* instinct and the *K-link* or knowledge instinct, might shed light on Annie's work in teaching Helen, too. Both Annie, Helen, and Laura Bridgman were all "voracious" readers. Their sensory limitations possibly increased the intensity of this instinct in them. The epistemophillic instinct is linked with aggression, and perhaps their intense frustration of being without language so long, helped to fuel their later love of learning.

Annie's intensity comes from the trauma of her childhood. It drives her; she has survived many traumas and cannot give up. She knows from lived experience the value of what she has to offer Helen. The Self, or as Annie would say God, has brought up the battle in her head again here—through this nightmare. As Annie alluded, when we first saw her saying goodbye to Michael Anagnos, God does owe her a resurrection—and Annie will fight for it.

James is stuck in the same cynical pattern, and their interaction return to their same oppositional dynamic. Annie can't afford to fight with James; she needs all of her energy to focus on reaching Helen.

REACHING OUT

Scene 1: Playing With Percy

Annie now approaches Helen, who is still sleeping. Annie vows that she will have no pity on either one of them. Annie touches Helen lightly, and Helen suddenly awakens, and recoils in horror at Annie's touch. Annie passionately proclaims aloud to the unhearing Helen, "I will touch you," and her voice trails off, "but how" and then a new fervent energy grabs her as she says, "do I?"

Annie has an idea; a plan of attack has formed in her mind, and she goes to fetch Percy, who is asleep in the next room. Rousing him insistently out of sleep, Annie will get Percy to be a rather unwilling playmate, and get to Helen through him! Annie lights the lamp as Percy sleepily enters the room. Annie gets him to touch Helen, who initially recoils, and then when Annie approaches with Percy again, Helen realizes who he is, and treats Percy like a big doll. She hugs him and then begins to put her hands on his lips, while moving her lips simultaneously.

It appears that Percy has played this game before, and he doesn't like the likely outcome. "She try and talk. She gonna hit me," Percy exclaims fearfully. Annie cheerfully tells him that Helen can talk, but doesn't know how yet, and Annie shows Percy how Helen makes letters. Annie explains: "She's mad at me. She won't play. But she knows lots of letters." Annie then proceeds to begin to show Percy how to spell *cake*, but during the process, Helen approaches burning with curiosity to find out what is happening. Helen find's Annie's hand, and again, she recoils. Annie once again begins to spell *cake*, and Helen approaches once more; she realizes what Annie is doing, and grabs Percy away, quickly spelling *c-a-k-e* into his hand. Annie then goes and gets a piece of cake for both of the children.

Annie informs Percy " She doesn't know it means this. Isn't that funny? She knows how to spell it, but doesn't know she knows." Helen declines the cake, and Annie continues to play with Percy, now she begins to teach him a new word that Helen doesn't know, *milk*, and begins spelling it into Percy's hand: *m-i*— Helen interrupts them. Now, Annie brushes Helen's hand away. This happens a couple of times, with Helen more insistently trying to engage each time. Annie talking aloud says: "Oh, why should I talk to you? I'm teaching a new word to Percy."

Helen has had enough, she now gets between Annie and Percy, shooing Percy away. Helen's curiosity is too strong, it has gotten the best of her, luckily. Annie has been counting on this and although struggling with herself, Helen extends her hand to Annie, who says softly: "So you're jealous, are you?" Helen's hand hangs in the air, waiting, and finally, she allows Annie to touch her. Annie spells *m-i-l-k* into Helen's hand and then gently taps Helen's hand and Helen spells it back to Annie, who then gives Helen a glass of milk. Annie now thanks Percy and sends him back to sleep. The first step has been taken. Annie has been able to reestablish contact.

Annie has seen how bright Helen is and how fast she learns and how wily she can be. Annie is now the trickster. Like Hermes, Annie is also a bricoleur, using whatever means necessary and whatever is at hand to get through to Helen. She is the psychopomp accompanying Helen on her journey. The lighting of the lamp symbolizes what language will do for Helen, bringing light to the darkness of her mind. In this case, Annie fittingly uses play as the gamechanger. Victor Turner, whose work on ritual we have referenced previously, also talks about the power of play:

> In a nutshell, Turner (1987) says that play is dangerous. It may subvert left/right hemispheric switching. Like a trickster it breaks taboos and it is liminal, existing betwixt and between. It mimics, mocks, and teases. It is a meta-language and a form of meta-communication. It is a transcendent potpourri of incongruous elements where both hemispheres intermingle. Play is educative, and speaks to us "as-if," in the subjunctive mood. It is an example of the transcendent function, the union of opposites; it can change our perceptions and perhaps even the world. It's a paradox. (Pohn 2002, p. 7)

Percy is a transitional object for Helen, like a security blanket. Transitional objects take the place of the mother when she is gone, helping the child to tolerate the fear evoked by her absence (Ogden, 2004). Donald Winnicott (1999) in *Playing and Reality* goes into depth about this, and said that transitional objects and transitional space—the space between the mother and the infant—are the root of symbolism, and also that art and culture stem from and are based on this in-between space.

When Annie tells Percy that Helen "knows but doesn't know she knows" this is known as *tacit knowing* (Moustakas, 1990; Polanyi, 1966), and it is one of the main elements of heuristic research. By *tacit knowing*, Polanyi (1966) means "we know more than we can tell" (p. 4). The neural networks are still fragile, and the connections not yet strong enough to surface into consciousness (Rock, 2006). Annie's work with Helen will be to make and strengthen these connections, so that they can lead to the aha moment of insight.

Scene 2: Long Journey Ahead

Now that the bridge of communication has been reformed between Annie and Helen, Annie gives the doll to Helen and puts her to bed. As she tucks Helen in, Annie says to herself "now I have to teach you one word, everything."

As Annie douses the light, she takes the doll and goes to sit in the rocking chair and sings a lullaby "Hush little baby," holding the doll in her arms. We then see the Kellers' the main house, Kate is sitting on the porch holding her arms around herself thinking about her separation, and Captain Keller is in the nursery, alone in the dark, holding the featureless cloth doll.

This poignant moment, where we fleetingly see the pain of Helen's parents in the darkness, which is their own inner darkness— is easily missed. It goes by in a flash, hardly noticeable, showing the nature of their situation through unconscious communication. It gives us a look at what is driving these two people, alone and in their own dark underworlds. We see the isolation and desperation for relatedness, no matter the cost, that fuel Kate's behavior, and we also see behind the curtain of bluster and bravado and find the suffering and helpless father who cannot help his family.

The terrible mother and the terrible male from the opening scene are seen in a new light. Rilke's poetic words come to mind: "perhaps all the dragons of our lives are princesses who are only waiting to see us once beautiful and brave. Perhaps everything terrible in its deepest being is something helpless that wants help from us" (Rilke, 1934/1993, p. 69). Helen's own typhonic struggling can also be seen in this way. This scene is a potent reminder to ourselves as well.

"IT HAS A NAME!"

Scene 1: The Siege Lifts

A new day brings new struggles. Annie is determined and has staying power, but Helen is supremely stubborn. The lyrics of a song come to mind: "When an irresistible force such as you / Meets and old immovable object like me / You can bet as sure as you live / Something's gotta give, something's gotta give, / Something's gotta give" (Mercer, 1954). Helen at first refuses to dress herself, misses her mother, and is forlorn. Time passes, in montage, with Helen tolerating Annie as Annie combs Helen's hair; Helen is slowly bending, "the windmills are weakening." Captain Keller, on his way to work, stops by to check Helen's progress and finds her breakfast uneaten; it is already 10am. He is characteristically churlish.

Keller: Why haven't you given it to her?
Annie: I will, when she dresses herself. She's thinking it over.
Keller: You intend to starve her into obeyin'?
Annie: She won't starve, she'll learn. You never cut supplies? All's fair in love and war, Captain Keller.
Keller This is hardly a war.
Annie: Well, it's not love. A siege is a siege.
Keller: Miss Sullivan, do you like the child?
Keller: Do you?

As Helen finally puts on her sock, Annie says: "I'm beginning to." Annie, too, is bending.

Transformation doesn't occur in a vacuum. We have a bifurcation here with Annie herself in this scene. Her defenses have begun to soften a bit. As will be described in more detail later, in the scene at the pump, *consciousness* means "knowing with" (Edinger, 1984). *Eros*, the principle of relatedness is a major player in this drama. It is the connecting principle. Eros is not only about human love, but corresponds to the larger archetype of relatedness. Logos is that which separates from and gives us distance, while eros creates connection with and between. Both of these principles are necessary for consciousness. These opposites are what fuel the transcendent function. The ancients were well aware of the power of relatedness. In Hesiod's *Theogony*, Eros was the

> Protogenos (primordial deity) of procreation who emerged self-formed at the beginning of time. He was the driving force behind the generation of new life in the early cosmos. The Orphics knew him as Phanes, a primal being hatched from the world egg at creation. He was also equivalent to Thesis, "Creation," and Physis "Nature." (Theoi, 2013, *eros*)

Eros is necessary before we can have logos; the relatedness of the ouroboric phase is all about eros. In the above-mentioned quote, another name for this cosmic principle is Thesis. A *thesis* is a statement, which serves as a premise to an argument, which then needs an *antithesis*, the opposite of the thesis, before a *synthesis* is created. Here again we see the oppositional dynamics of the principles of eros and logos, which are necessary to create something new—a synthesis. But we are getting ahead of ourselves. We need to create more eros. More connections and oppositions are also intrinsic to the process.

Scene 2: Montage—The World As Classroom

Annie then proceeds to teach Helen many words, following the same procedure. Following Helen's curiosity, Annie patiently names the things in the world that Helen encounters and is interested in. Annie constantly presents new experiences through play. As they play with beads, Annie spells *b-e-a-d-s*, climbing a tree, Helen is able to feel its many aspects and Annie spells *t-r-e-e*. Everything that Helen touches, Annie names: *bird*, *water*—all are experiences. Helen and Annie interact with the world around them, Helen, still imitating, and not knowing what the words mean.

On one occasion, Helen and Annie are wading in a stream and Annie slips and falls into the water; when Helen happens upon Annie and finds her seated in the water, Helen follows suit and sits down in the water, too. Annie patiently spells *w-a-t-e-r* into her hand. Physical exercises, walks around the property are included and provide the important physical component that was stressed at Perkins, and that Kate innately provided for Helen as a younger child.

Kate stops by with Helen's plate and sees the transformation. Helen is now well-behaved. She uses her napkin properly and eats with utensils. Her mother is very happy with all that has been accomplished. Annie is not satisfied, "obedience is not enough." Although Helen has learned the words *key* and *water* today, Annie informs Kate that Helen does not yet know what they mean. Kate asks to take Helen for a walk, and Annie deflects, by asking Kate to play their "finger game." Kate is almost beside herself, "next week seems so far off," she laments. Annie holds firm.

In the next sequence, Annie gives Helen a chick to hold, so she can experience it hatching out of its egg. Annie says aloud: "Egg. It has a name. The name stands for the thing. Oh, it's so simple. Simple as birth to explain. Helen, the chick has to come out of its shell sometime." As the chick breaks free of the egg, Annie gasps. Helen smiles genuinely, Annie beseeches her unhearing pupil, "you come out, too." Touched by the moment, Annie tries to tenderly kiss Helen's cheek, but Helen pulls back and shies away from affection.

The learning continues through play and exploration, Annie reinforcing the words Helen already knows, priming the pump, so to speak. Annie knows from reading about Dr. Howe's work with Laura Bridgman in *The Perkins Report*, that it may take a long time to break through, and she persistently keeps on. Helen is even spelling in her sleep. Annie becomes worried that she will not have enough time to get Helen to understand before her parents take Helen back.

The scene changes and Helen sits in the foreground, her face covered by a sheer dark scarf. Annie is reading a letter she is writing to her friend, Sophia Hopkins: "I feel every day more and more inadequate. My letters must show that I need a teacher as much as Helen. I need help too." Annie now paces angrily and goes to Helen, asking herself aloud, "Who? In all the world there isn't a soul who can tell me how to reach you." She angrily yanks a dark scarf that is covering Helen's face. "How do I reach you?" she beseeches.

Annie's unconscious communication is that she wants to lift this veil off of Helen, and through the vehemence with which she does this, it seems that this passionate intensity might be the way. Passionate intensity, the fire that fuels transformation, is a necessary ingredient in many processes of transformation.

The chick coming out of the egg is classical rebirth symbolism. It is like the butterfly emerging from the darkness and confinement of its self-created alchemical container—the chrysalis, The *prima materia* that has undergone many processes to become the philosopher's stone, and the rising sun that has going through the night sea journey, are also symbols of rebirth.

The land of liminality is a place of transformation. In the darkness, all are transformed—in the case of the chick and the butterfly, they undergo physical transformation of their form, moving from one state to another. Intensity is needed. The caterpillar dissolves itself into a soup of imaginal cells before its body is reformed as a butterfly. The chick begins as a single cell that must first multiply and replicate itself, and then differentiate into different organs, limbs, etcetera.

The *prima materia* and the sun undergo both physical and metaphorical deaths; both of them involve chemical reactions that involve heat. The light that we see is literally the light of transformation, as the sun chemically changes, dying and being reborn in each moment, bit by bit. At some point, billions of years in the future, this process will end in the physical death of the entire sun, but "not yet." So we see that life itself is not possible without transformation.

"SHE'S NOT MY CHILD!"

Scene 1: Last Ditch Effort

As the two weeks draw to a close, the Kellers come back to get Helen. Annie asks for more time, but the Kellers are more than satisfied with Helen's progress, because she behaves, and is cleaner and more manageable. Annie, however, is not satisfied.

Keller notices that Helen is playing with the dog's paw, spelling into it. Kate translates uncertainly, "water," for she has learned the manual alphabet from Annie. Keller remarks that the dog, Belle, "doesn't know what she [Helen] means anymore than she knows what you mean. I think you ask too much of her, and yourself. God may not have meant Helen to have the . . . eyes you speak of." Annie wants it for Helen, with all of her heart and soul. "I mean her to," Annie says fervently.

Unwilling to go concede, Annie presses for more time, but Keller holds firm. Kate, craving Helen back, will not agree either. Annie holds the line and demands that she have the rest of the day, until 6 o'clock, and the Kellers leave, only to return a few hours later.

Annie is furious that all the Kellers seem to want is to have their child housebroken; she laments: "Everyone's satisfied but me. And you. Feel it. Reach," Annie implores Helen. Helen cannot hear and still does not understand, although the light comes in through the window, bathing Helen's face in luminosity. Annie continues—the passion, pressure, and intensity palpable in her voice—explaining the world that she wants to open up for Helen, the strange attractor she is seeking to shift Helen into. The world of meaning and understanding, that means the world to Annie. Helen is on the verge of consciousness, but she has not yet achieved escape velocity. Annie explains aloud:

> I wanted to teach you. Oh. . . Everything the earth is full of, Helen. Everything on it that's ours for a wink. And what we are on it. The light we bring to it and leave behind in words. You can see five thousand years back in the light of words. Everything we feel, think, know, and share in words. So not a soul is in darkness, or done with even in the grave. But I know. I know one word and I can put the world in your hand. And whatever it is to me, I won't take less.

Now, almost frantic, with passion, fury, and frustration, Annie goes around the room trying to make Helen understand that the things around her, which she places in Helen's hands and then spells the letters, "mean a word. And the word means this thing." By now, Annie is forcing things into Helen's hands. The clock chimes in the distance, signaling that Annie's time is running out, there are only a couple of hours to go. Annie continues to hurriedly spell words into Helen's hand, iterating and reiterating, over and over, she spells many words, linking them, albeit unconsciously to various objects, until finally Annie's time alone with Helen is up. Annie even makes Helen's sign for mother, touching Helen's cheek and then spelling out *m-o-t-h-e-r*, but to no avail.

Kate comes to the door. Her voice is low and harsh, volcanic emotions seething just below the surface. Trembling, Kate is possessed, and in a fury demands of Annie "Let her come!" Annie reluctantly lets Helen go. Helen then reunites with her mother, jumping into Kate's arms; Kate carries Helen away, as if she were a toddler.

The room is now stripped bare—all of the toys, clothing, and belongings, have been taken to the house. "Annie is alone in it, and she is bidding it farewell, gazing around, impassively, a defeated general on the deserted battlefield" (Gibson, 1961, p. 102).

Annie then takes her eyecup and dejectedly bathes her eyes as the scene draws to a close.

Up until the last possible moment, Annie is strengthening the neural networks, embedding the learning, albeit unconsciously, as she repeatedly and insistently spells into Helen's hand and as yet ungrasping mind. Annie is trying to get Helen to experience an insight.

Helen's parents will not allow this new pattern to fully emerge. Kate has transformed back into the devouring terrible mother, keeping her child from consciousness. The ouroboric pull of total eros needs to be counterbalanced by logos—which is missing. Annie has been providing the logos, but the Kellers are only concerned with obedience, which is merely the first step on the journey. Annie wants the destination of consciousness for Helen, and they are only partway there. Obedience will keep Helen frozen in the animal state that she currently inhabits. Helen is now a tamed animal, but an animal nonetheless.

The initiation process has been cut short; Helen has not yet achieved the transformation of this rite of passage into the realm of the consciousness of language. She remains frozen in a pre-linguistic wasteland; it is April, indeed the cruelest month. Just as Demeter was interrupted by Demaphoon's mother, as she was trying to make the child immortal, Helen's transformation is incomplete, the immortality of language has been aborted, denied "for now." However, Annie is "not yet" finished, and she will not give up the fight. Annie has only lost this battle, not the war.

Scene 2: The Calm Before The Storm

Helen is being feted on the porch; the family showers her with gifts and attention. Annie hears it from her room while she is unpacking her clothes. Captain Keller comes to give Annie her first month's check, and expresses his hope for her continued presence. As he expresses his thanks and gratitude, we see that Captain Keller has changed, softened, if only a bit. He has a new respect for Annie. His daughter has changed; the miracle, in his eyes, has been achieved. Keller's long years of frustration and fear for his child, which walled him off and hardened his persona, have relaxed and softened a bit.

Annie explains that all she did was to teach Helen "no." Keller tells Annie that it was more than anyone else could do, but Annie will not let go, she is not satisfied. Annie wanted to teach Helen what language is, because without language, "obedience without understanding is a blindness." Annie hopes that Helen has not merely traded one form of blindness for another and all that Annie can do is "simply go on and keep doing what I've done and have faith that inside she's. . . that inside it's waiting, like water underground."

Annie then asks Captain Keller to help his daughter, explaining that "the world is not an easy place for anyone. . . . But to let her have her way in everything is a lie. To her. And I don't even love her. She's not my child." Annie beseeches Keller "to stand between that lie and her," and he solemnly agrees and escorts Annie down to dinner, jovially joking with her along the way.

Again, Annie is aware of and states the trajectory that the system will likely take, now that this interruption has occurred. If the Kellers do not realign around the new attractor, Helen will be nothing more than an obedient animal. Annie has taught her discipline, given Helen boundaries, the spirit of logos, but not yet the word. Annie has given Helen many words, but she doesn't understand them to be this. To Helen, they are a finger game she plays. Helen has "not yet" grasped the concept of language.

The reference to water waiting underground is an allusion to the unconscious, and the tacit knowing that is accumulating there (Polanyi, 1966). If only Annie can find a way to bring these connections up to consciousness! Annie intuitively senses that there are unconscious process occurring that will enable Helen to make the leap. However, she also correctly senses that certain conditions need to be provided for the insights to manifest, for consciousness to be created, and these are the conditions that she had created in the garden house.

"SHE'S TESTING YOU!"

In this chapter, instead of having a campfire, in this scene, all the relevant observations will occur in line, in a **different font** as they unfold in the story.

Scene 1: Old Patterns Die Hard

Dinner preparations are underway. Helen is in the dining room checking that the doors aren't locked, as this was the location of the "Battle Royale" at breakfast a few weeks previously. Helen gives the keys to her mother, who puts them in her pocket motioning to Helen that they are safe with her. Kate says aloud, "I think we've had enough of locked doors too." **Helen is unconsciously communicating that she wants things back the way they were, uncontained; she essentially has tried to unsecure the frame.**

As they sit down for the meal, Captain Keller holds Annie's chair for her and Kate brightly asks James: "Will you say the grace, Jimmy?" He obliges with a very interesting choice:

And Jacob was left alone and wrestled with an angel till the breaking of the day. And the hollow of Jacob's thigh was out of joint as he wrestled with him. And the angel said "Let me go, for the day breaketh." And Jacob said "I will not let thee go, except thou bless me." Amen.

James winks approvingly at Annie after he is done, and tilts his head at Helen, saying "oh you angel." Aunt Ev, who has joined the meal, remarks how strange the grace seems. **In the Bible, after the encounter with the angel, Jacob then became Israel, meaning, "one who struggles with god"—his identity changed. James' choice of this passage for the grace tells us a lot. He, too, is hoping that a transformation has occurred from this struggle. However, as we will see, the transformation is not yet complete, because the initiation was interrupted.**

As the adults make small talk, and Annie fills Helen's glass, Helen drops her napkin. Annie retrieves it and puts it around Helen's neck. The talk continues, uninterrupted and Helen does it again, and Kate notices this time as well, and Annie motions to Kate that she will take care of it. Annie then picks the napkin up and refastens it around Helen's neck. When it happens a third time, the conversation grinds to a halt.

Now the whole family is silent, the air is filled with suspense. A battle is brewing. Helen has created a perturbation, hoping to reestablish the previous "order," where she is the queen who rules supreme in chaotic darkness. Her unconscious communication signals that the truce is now over. Let the battle begin.

Annie will not brook this defiance, she draws the line and removes Helen's plate from the table. Helen begins to bang on the table, and things seem to have reverted back to where they were previously. *La plus ça change, plus la meme chose*—the more things change, the more they remain the same. We seem to be back in the old pattern again, Hurricane Helen is about to make landfall. The butterfly effect is about to take effect, and the small dropping of a napkin is about to fling things into chaos again rather quickly.

True to the old pattern's form, Annie's worst fears for Helen are materializing before her eyes. The fragile foothold that Annie has been patiently carving out, from which she had hoped to build a foundation for Helen's ascent into language, appears to be eroding and we are on very shaky ground. The family begins to re-enact the same periodic pattern of placating Helen to quell her chaos. The family is sucked into the Charybdis of the Terrible Mother once again. It is like the tractor beam on the Death Star (Lucas, 1977). James, however, is approaching escape velocity.

Kate begs Annie, holding Helen to her breast, "it's a very special day." To which Annie firmly counters, "It will be, when I give in to that." Kate again follows the prior pattern of giving in to Helen's tantrums, and Keller explains to Kate that Annie feels that indulging Helen will be detrimental. Aunt Ev then chimes in putting her weight behind the old pattern, the Terrible Mother is rearing its ugly head and enlisting allies, Aunt Ev, in the grip of this archetype will continue to egg Keller on, adding fuel to the fire. The old pattern is reasserting itself through Ev, as she incites her brother, fanning the flames, which leads the system into a more intense state; we are on the way to far from equilibrium. The tension of opposites is mounting. Annie acknowledges this by saying she doesn't want to play tug of war with Helen, and Kate refuses to let go of Helen.

A bifurcation point is at hand. Annie requests that Kate discipline Helen herself or allow Annie to do it, by taking Helen from the table, and not allowing anyone to interfere. Kate, again slides back into being the overly permissive mother aka Terrible Mother-lite, asking, "Will this once hurt so much, Miss Annie? I've made all of Helen's favorite foods." Annie unfortunately knows that it will. **Captain Keller has now joined Camp Terrible Mother, he could hold out only so long.** "It's her homecomin' party, Miss Annie." Akin to an alcoholic having just one drink that sets off a bender, **Annie knows where this will end up**, and tells Kate "she's testing you, you realize." **Annie again explicates what is occurring.** James now chimes in and tells Annie—"She's testing you."

Captain Keller reverts backwards to his old pattern and dismisses James, albeit the delivery is a little nicer, and Keller tries to dampen down the chaos, and mediate the situation. Keller is not strong enough however to begin a new behavior in the face of the massive staying power of this prior pattern, this dead Stonewall pattern is too entrenched.

Cascading into chaos/far from equilibrium, bifurcating bifurcation points take us again to places we've never been before.

Before proceeding on, it is important to get an idea of what is driving Annie. In his book, Gilligan (1997) used Annie Sullivan as an example of sponsorship. In Gilligan's Self-Relations psychotherapy, *sponsorship* is how one forges a relationship between the cognitive self and the somatic self, and this gives rise to the relational self—this is similar to the idea of the transcendent function being constellated out of holding the tension of opposites between consciousness and the unconscious—or in our case Annie and Helen.

Gilligan gives a wonderful metaphor regarding eating to describe these energies that represent the two selves. He tells us that by understanding the difference between two German words for eating, *essen* and *fressen*, we can understand

> how the connection between the somatic self and the cognitive self awakens the relational self . . . . *Fressen* is "to pig out," to eat like an animal; *essen* is to eat like a person. Using this distinction in a more general way we might say that we begin with "fressen" energy or "nature" and then bring human presence or "mind" to transform it into "essen" or human expressions. The nature of fressen energy may be seen in a child's spontaneous joy, temper tantrums, expressive art, whining, innocent kindness, and innocent cruelty. It is apparent in the challenging psychological experiences of intense anger, irrational fear,

inappropriate but compulsive behaviors, and psychological symptoms. It is also in the nature of storms, sunny days, animals, and flowers, and in wild celebrations, intense sexuality, and political rallies. Fressen energy is sometimes beautiful, sometimes horrible, sometimes both. Fressen energies carry the rhythms of time and change, as well as the archetypal forms of generational learnings. (p. 16)

Having this understanding of sponsorship in mind, let us now see how it plays out as we continue into the chaos.

Scene 2: Helen's Last Stand: AKA "Not On My Watch!"

Annie holds firm with Keller, telling him that Helen "wants to see what will happen at your hands, I told you it was my main worry." Again, Annie has read the field and knows what the trajectory is. A free-fall back into the prior state looms large. Keller tries to calm the waters, pointing out that Helen is not kicking now. Yet Annie will not give in.

> Annie: And not learning not to. She'll live up to what you demand and no more.
> James: [to Annie again] She's testing you.
> Keller: Jimmy. [testily]
> James: I have an opinion.
> Keller: No one's interested in it.
> Annie: I'm interested. Of course she's testing me. Let me keep her to what she's learned and she'll go on learning. Take her out of my hands and it all comes apart.

Annie, now goes to support this change in James. He is attempting to break free from this pattern of being dismissed. He has redoubled his effort and now Annie shows him respect, listening to him, enlisting his aid and energy. This positive feedback creates a positive feedback loop increasing the energy, enabling James to finally fully break free from the old relationship dynamics that have held him powerless.

Kate is also taking in what Annie said, reconsidering. Annie continues unrelentingly: "Be bountiful. It's at her expense. Please pass me more of her favorite food." Kate now surrenders Helen to Annie, and this causes Helen to go into another rage. Keller, again trying to buy peace at any cost (a strategy that never works out well) comes to the fore, and tells Annie that *she* seems to be the difficulty. Keller says that he will hold Helen to what she's learned, and he attempts to put things back in order, asking for

Helen's plate to be brought back.

Annie attempts to interrupt the pattern, although at least Keller seems to have made some changes, and is temporarily more tempered in his approach. Yet Annie knows that Helen's chaos is no match for Keller's cosmos [order]. She presences the invisible double standard, the elephant in the room: "If she were a seeing child, none of you would tolerate any of this. " Keller expresses that some compromise is called for, because Helen is not a seeing child. This is a case of too little, too late. He then reverts back to barking an order at Annie to bring back Helen's plate. Then Keller places the plate in front of Helen and fastens the napkin, attempting to hit the reset button, saying "There. Now, shall we start all over?" His attempt at discipline lasts only for a moment. He is no match for Helen's typhonic tyranny, and his budding disciplinary skills are not strong enough to keep Helen in check. As Keller utters this sentence and then goes back to his chair, Helen is up and Annie restrains her, Helen then bites Annie's hand, and groping for some more ammunition, finds the water pitcher and throws it in Annie's face.

This is the last straw, the war is on, the battle of Waterloo part deux has begun. As this is occurring, James cannot pass up commenting: "I think we've started all over—I think we've started all over." Keller glares at James. James is now boldly stating the pattern, twice, for emphasis, as he did when he made his "she's testing you" comments. According to von Franz (1977), when something important is about to come into consciousness, it will appear in consciousness as a double:

> In general, if a symbol appears in a double form it means that what it symbolizes is approaching the threshold of consciousness. . . . So doubleness means touching the threshold of consciousness, being still a little ambiguous, consciousness not yet knowing how to say what is what, partly still mixed up with the continuum of other unconscious contents. (pp. 26-27).

Annie has had it. She is leaving the field, with Helen in tow. Annie has a steely savage fierceness in her voice that has been forged and tempered in the furnaces of trauma. Annie warns the others not to interfere, she explains that she treats Helen "like a seeing child because I ask her to see. I expect her to see! Don't undo what I do!" And with that, she drags Helen off to fill the pitcher.

Aunt Ev, mouthpiece of the terrible mother, incites Keller by shaming him about letting "the help" talk to him like that. This old queen/aunt needs to die, too. James now springs into action. He shuts the door and bars the way, interrupting the old pattern once and for all. He is making his stand. He has transformed. This is James' *lysis*: the solution of the dream. Conforti (2010) explained that there are two aspects to the lysis, the first being to return to the habitual patterns. "The second aspect," he explicated:

> on a more profound level, offers the dreamer an approach towards life which expands the conscious attitude of the dream. It is very, very different from our habitual patterns, and is a solution offered by the Self. The dream is alerting you to think about responding in a different, more generative way.

James forcefully stands up to Keller: "Let her go," he says shocking everyone, probably including himself. Keller is taken aback. With an intensity we have never seen before, James stands firm, against the door and against Keller: "I said let her go! She's right. She's right. Kate's right, I'm right, and you're wrong. Has it never occurred to you that on one occasion you might be consummately wrong?" Keller stares unbelievingly.

A coup has occurred, and the new king has been crowned; a *coniunctio* has occurred. Annie and James have joined forces in interrupting this pattern, finally putting an end to the rule of the old king. Helen's rule as the dark queen of chaos is almost finished as well. The divine child is about to be born/reborn. Jung (1951/1990) said the divine child or child archetype:

> represents the preconscious, childhood aspect of the collective psyche. . . . it is not just a vestige. But a system functioning in the present whose purpose is to compensate or correct, in a meaningful manner, the inevitable one-sidedness and extravagances of the conscious mind. . . . our differentiated consciousness is in continual danger of being uprooted; hence it needs compensation through the still existing state of childhood. (pp. 161-162)

Now, let us follow Annie and Helen out to the pump, for the miracle moment is at hand.

"W-A-T-E-R!"

Scene 1: Meanwhile Back At The Pump

Annie is on the warpath now, and has dragged Helen out to the pump and is making her literally prime the pump. Helen does this with her right hand, and gestures for her mother with her left. Annie says aloud, "no she's not here." When the water begins to flow, Annie repositions Helen with her left hand holding the pitcher and her right hand in Annie's. Helen is no longer fighting. Helen is now outside, and also outside of the field of the Devouring Mother, and back in this strange new field that Annie is fighting to reconstitute. Annie furiously spells *w-a-t-e-r* into Helen's right hand a few times, as the cold water comes up from under the ground, splashing into Helen's left hand.

All of a sudden something is happening, Annie pauses, midword: "*w-a-t . . . ;*" Helen throws the pitcher aside, but not in anger, a new emotion flashes on her face; she is transfixed, and she struggles to bring out the words, "*wah wah.*" They gush to the surface haltingly and laboriously, being brought up from the depths of Helen's unconscious. Helen has made the connection, the iconic miracle moment has occurred. Helen understands.

Now Helen hits the pump, repeatedly and insistently signaling Annie to keep pumping. Annie obliges. Helen feels the water with both hands and then signs to Annie with her right hand, *w-a-t-e-r.* Annie nods yes, almost transfixed. Helen now begins to pump the water herself, and after it begins to flow again, she places her hands under the flow and spells *w-a-t-e-r* into her own hand. Annie nods yes vigorously, placing both of Helen's hands on her face, exclaiming "Yes, Oh my dear." Helen, then in a frenzy, wants to know the names of all the things around her. She first drops to the ground, Annie spells *g-r-o-u-n-d*, and Helen repeats it back to her—now knowing that the word means ground.

This is Helen's lysis; Annie's lysis will come at the end. This is the iconic moment everyone remembers, we are 1 hour and 39 minutes into the film, with only 7 ½ minutes to go. This perhaps points to how much effort and energy it has taken to get to this point. When Annie dragged Helen out to the pump; they were both angry and frustrated.

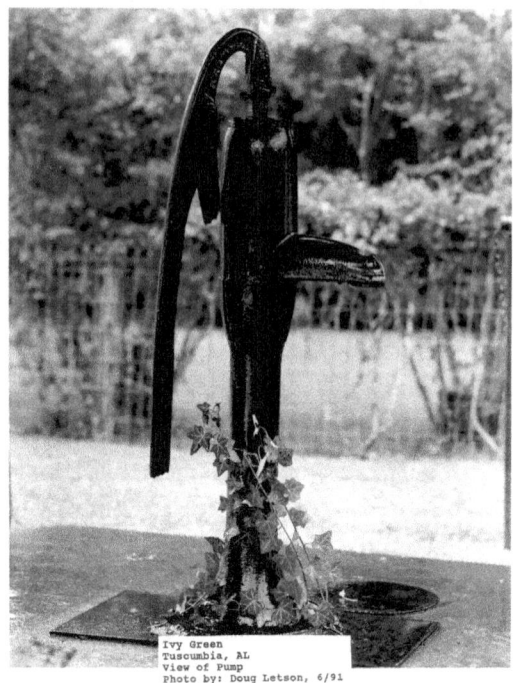

Ivy Green
Tuscumbia, AL
View of Pump
Photo by: Doug Letson, 6/91

Figure 21: The Pump

[Note: The events as portrayed in the film are archetypally correct, as to the archetypal tone but not exactly factually correct. Remember we are dealing with archetypes and healing fictions, and so some latitude is allowed.]

They differ, in that first of all, Helen did not actually utter the words *wah wah*, but instead, she spelled it. Like the silver slippers in *The Wizard of Oz* (Fleming, 1939) being switched to ruby slippers for cinematic effect; the filmmakers, following on the Broadway play, chose to underscore the transformation by adding sound.

The pump scene also differs from the actual facts that occurred in that: (1) the scene did not occur after a battle as portrayed nor (2) did it occur on the evening of Helen's homecoming; rather than being ignited by a momentary flash of anger and frustration, it was more like a long slow burn—the frustration had been mounting, for a couple of weeks, and both Helen and Annie were frustrated over the fact that Helen could not tell the difference between the container/mug and the contained/water, and kept mixing up the two.

This "aha moment," is the creation of consciousness, the creation of meaning. This is why it is the immortal moment everyone remembers. Helen has finally crossed over into a new landscape, reached the light of consciousness at the end of the tunnel. She has entered a new state of being, the landscape in Grof's (1975) cartography

BPM IV—DEATH-REBIRTH EXPERIENCE—TERMINATION OF THE BIRTH PROCESS: Crowning, final expulsion from birth canal; death-rebirth experience; ego death, total annihilation; union with the goddess—identification or encounter with Christ, Shiva, other deities; epiphanic ecstasy, expansion of space, visions of gigantic halls, sensory enhancement; illuminative ecstasy—radiant light, beautiful colors, peacock feathers, or white and golden light; feelings of rebirth and redemption—escape from dangerous circumstance; divine epiphany; enormous decompression;—appreciation of simple way of life—humanitarian tendencies, brotherly feelings—manic activity, grandiose feelings, transition to elements of BPM I. (Pohn, 2006) [See Appendix E]

It is the moment of rebirth after the intense struggle of transformation. It is the moment of the transcendent function. After holding the tension of the oscillating opposites, Helen, with Annie's help, has finally reached escape velocity and Helen is at last able to, as lyrically expressed by The Doors (1967), "break on through to the other side," together with Annie. The old king/order has died and after the night sea journey, and the dark night of the soul, the dawn has come, renewal has occurred, and consciousness has arisen from the unconscious. Hermes has brought Persephone back from the underworld, no longer the Kore, but the Queen of the Underworld. Helen's life is forever inalterably changed. Her initiation is complete, and she will also achieve immortality.

Helen now knows the meaning of words, and Annie truly has given her the world. How Annie did this, how she facilitated the creation of consciousness in Helen was the subject of fascination for Walker Percy, as it is for me. In 1954, Percy, formulated a theory about language and consciousness that he called the *Delta Factor*, after the Greek letter Δ, because of the triadic nature of language. [The Greek Δ is also shorthand in mathematics for change, and is the fourth letter in the Greek alphabet, and four is the Jungian number for completion].

Percy's essay is subtitled: "How I Discovered the Delta Factor Sitting at my Desk One Summer Day in Louisiana in the 1950s Thinking About an Event in the Life of Helen Keller on Another Summer Day in Alabama in 1887." Percy saw a link between man's dissatisfaction and his uniquely human activity of being a "symbol-monger trafficking in symbols," and Percy's desire to understand the "Helen Keller phenomenon," led to a 25-year study. When Percy wrote that essay, *The Miracle Worker* (Gibson, 1956/2008) had yet to be written.

The Message in the Bottle (Percy, 1975) contains various essays on the subject sparked by the miracle moment, but, the bottom line is: "the word *names* something. The symbol symbolizes something." Percy felt that "naming is unique in natural history," and that, agreeing with Suzanne Langer, "symbols are the vehicles of meaning" (Percy, pp. 153, 155, 156). Percy asserted "*I think* is only made possible by a prior mutuality, *we know!*" (p. 275). He also thought that consciousness is relational, and symbols and naming are what create consciousness.

> Awareness is thus not only intentional in character, it is also symbolic. . . I am not only conscious of something; I am conscious of it being what it is for you and me. If there is a wisdom in etymologies, the word *consciousness* is surely a case in point; for consciousness, one suddenly realizes, means a knowing with! In truth it could not be otherwise. The act of consciousness is the intending of the object as being what it is for both of us under the auspices of the symbol. (p. 274)

> The extraordinary characteristic of symbolization is that the symbol denotes something it is the name of something. It is the vehicle by which we are able to speak and perhaps think about something. The relationship between symbol and conception is generically and irreducibly different from the purely causal order of signal-significatum. (p. 280).

> Consciousness is of its nature intersubjective. The originary act of consciousness is the joint affirmation that the object is there of you and me. (p. 282).

Interestingly, in my dissertation, I used this symbol Δ, to mark out behind the scenes running conversations, a forerunner of the campfire; to engage the reader along the way in applying various ideas and concepts to their lives. This same iconic scene, which captured Walker Percy's imagination, has fascinated me and has led me on my own odyssey, which is quite probably only beginning. But let us get back to the portrayal of miracle moment.

Something however was clearly in the air, in the 1950s, because this is the same time that Jung (1957/1981) revised and republished "The Transcendent Function." The 1950s was archetypally similar to the time of the iconic moment at the pump. Richard Tarnas, in his masterwork, *Cosmos and Psyche* (2006) traced the movement and cycles of the outer planets, and my doctoral work relied heavily on his work to show the synchronistic events happening at the times both portrayed by cultural pieces and the time in which they were created.

Here, the same pattern of coincidence of cultural portrayal and appearance in culture hold true as well. Very briefly, the planetary archetye Uranus—the planet of sudden breakthrough, illumination, revolution, technology, awakenings, synchronicity, and rebirth—and the planetary archetype Neptune—the planet of the unconscious and watery things were in hard alignment in the sky during these two times—in 1887, they were in opposition (180 degrees apart), and in the 1950s they were in a square (90 degrees apart). In the future, I will do an extensive archetypal astrological reading of the film. Reading this combination psychologically, we can see that a sudden breakthrough (Uranus) of consciousness from the unconscious (Neptune) having to do with water (Neptune) and technology [the pump] (Uranus) caused illumination (Uranus).

While we cannot be sure what happened exactly in real life at the pump in 1887, in reel life, in the film we see Annie spelling into Helen's right hand [which is more associated with the left brain] doing what that side of the brain does—language, Logos/scio--knowing]. On the other hand, literally, Helen is holding the pitcher under the pump, while the water is flowing over it, onto her left hand, which is more associated with the right brain and [doing what it does, intuitively apprehending things in their wholeness [Eros/con—withness] and there we have it—a synaesthia occurs. The literal tension of opposite hands, opposite sides of the brain and opposite ways of perceiving, along with the shock of the cold water, gave us the ability to see the transcendent function in action, as it did what it was named to do, transcend opposites!

Emotion also plays a part, the brain pays attention when emotions are heightened, and perhaps the intensity of the frustration helped Helen's brain to pay more attention or different attention, because her limbic system had the proper amount of arousal. This instance was not just fun and games, as it usually was when Helen and Annie were playing their finger games; the intense emotions helped Helen's brain pay extra attention and perhaps this was the extra ingredient that was necessary.

The nature of water itself may perhaps have played a part. We come from water, it is one of the initial conditions that made life possible. Our bodies are more than 75% water when we are young, and as we age, we literally dry out (USGS, 2013). Future study might shed light on whether the structure of water itself played a part on that miraculous occasion. There is increasing research that water holds memory and can be affected by emotion, and that is research for another day, but what I am alluding to is different.

Neuroscience has shown that it is useful to have many ways into the neural net when you want to access information (Rock, 2006). That is why it is useful to make hand written notes, and embed things in different ways, being able to associate knowledge to as many things as possible, so that these neural nets get stickier.

In this regard, water would have been relatively unique, in comparison with other words that Helen was learning. Helen would have come to have it spelled to her in a variety of contexts—the stream, in a mug or cup, in the wash basin, and the pump. So perhaps Helen was able to access this information for all of the above reasons. We will never know exactly what happened, but only that it did happen, and we will turn and give the last word on this subject to Rilke, to express poetically what transpired in Tuscumbia.

> Just as the winged energy of delight
> carried you over many chasms early on,
> now raise the daringly imagined arch
> holding up the astounding bridges.
> Miracle doesn't lie only in the amazing
> living through and defeat of danger;
> miracles become miracles in the clear
> achievement that is earned.

To work with things is not hubris
 when building the association between words:
denser and denser the pattern becomes—
being carried along is not enough. Take your well-disciplined strengths
and stretch them between two
opposing poles. Because inside human beings
is where God learns. (Rilke, 1924, p. 236)

Let us now continue on, and follow Helen in her first few moments of her eureka experience. Like Archimedes, she is euphoric, and running around ecstatically.

Scene 2: Reunited And It Feels So Good

Helen runs headlong to the pump, a tree, the step, with Annie following her and spelling the words to her. Then Helen begins to ring the bell and is off running again. Annie shouts "Mrs. Keller, Mrs. Keller." Helen is down on the lawn again. Her parents rush out to join her there, with Aunt Ev and Jimmy on the porch. Annie spells *m-o-t-h-e-r* and *f-a-t-h-e-r* into Helen's hand.

Annie shouts to them as they embrace her "She knows, she knows." Helen has had her breakthrough. The miracle moment has occurred, she has transformed into a linguistic being, she is reunited with her family in a new way—Grof's BPM IV, the Death Rebirth experience, where new vistas open up [See Appendix E]. Helen's parents hug and kiss her, a wave of emotion overcomes them, like the ending sequence in the film *Twister* (de Bont, 1996), they have weathered the storm, and the problematic relationship is remade anew. No longer "a phantom, living in a no world," she is *Helen* (Keller, 1955). The former torrents of rage and frustration will now be channeled into new tributaries of learning.

Helen now leaves her parents' embrace and searches out Annie and points to her, wanting to know her name. Annie spells *t-e-a-c-h-e-r* into Helen's hand. *Teacher*, this is how she will be known to Helen for the rest of her life. Helen spells it back to her, and Annie softly nods yes. Tears of gratitude stream down Helen's face, as she turns back to her parents. Annie goes to sit at the pump. Her parents embrace Helen again, and she searches for the keys from her mother. She spells *t-e-a-c-h-e-r* into her mother's hand. Kate translates and then reluctantly lets Helen go. Kate, overcome with emotion, collapses onto the ground, supported by her husband.

Helen heads back to Annie with the keys and gives them to her. Helen feels the emotions on Annie's face, and then her father comes and scoops Helen up and carries her into the house. The family is together again. James lingers outside on the porch, silently nodding and acknowledging Annie.

Helen and Annie have battled many times since their first meeting, struggling through the wilderness, in search of meaning. They have emerged from the underworld of the unconscious transformed in the process. Through these battles, consciousness was created. This angel has blessed them both. Conforti (2013) said that the only way out of a possession is grace. Annie's name means just that [See Appendix D].

The key reappears in this scene again, and this time, an additional meaning is apparent, for *key* is also "used to symbolize freedom of access to a particular place and presented ceremonially as a formal honour or mark of respect by a representative of a city, organization, etc." (OED, 2013, *key*).

Helen through her unconscious communication has given Annie the freedom of access to her psyche, formally acknowledging Annie, as a mark of respect. Helen, intuitively knows the momentousness of this occasion. Annie, in identifying herself to Helen as *T-e-a-c-h-e-r,* has shown us what a teacher truly is: A teacher is a confluence of relatedness and eros, who holds the space for others to transform, who has the ability to go into the underworld when that is needed. One who fiercely protects the sanctity of the relationship and the space in which it occurs. One who can see patterns and reflect back what she sees.

A teacher is open to transformation herself and trusts her intuition. She helps her students to make sense of the chaos of their world, through giving them appropriate access to knowledge, presenting many possibilities in a variety of ways, re-kindling the innate desire to learn if it has been extinguished or lays dormant, and keeping the thirst for knowledge alive while negotiating often difficult passages.

A teacher is a portal for grace. Thus the teacher shares attributes with various gods—from the trickster and psychopomp qualities of Hermes, to the wisdom, protection, reflection and civilizing qualities of Athena, to the Wounded Healer aspects of Chiron, the one who has been there before, whose name interestingly enough means *hand* (Theoi, 2013, Chiron). Delving deeper into these archetypes and their interplay will have to wait, just as will an examination of the astrological significance of Annie's arrival and initial meeting and this miraculous moment, too.

Helen now has the ability to understand and to communicate with others. She now has words, objects to think with. She is able to name her experience and include others in her world. This will allow Helen's consciousness, and along with it, her knowledge to grow. Helen is thus able to relate to others and to her world in a new way. Her horizons have expanded.

In *The Creation of Consciousness: Jung's Myth for Modern Man,* Edward Edinger (1984) explained that meaning was what was most important for man. Jung felt that our desire for meaning and to make meaning was the new myth.

Aniela Jaffe (1975), in *The Myth of Meaning,* said that consciousness "plays a creative part in the evolution and differentiation of archetypal God-images. We might say that he [man] accomplished the miracle of a second theogony" (p. 139). Then quoting Jung from *Memories, Dreams, Reflections* Jaffe said, "Jung even speaks of the 'miracle of reflecting consciousness' in which the whole evolutionary trend of nature culminates." Jaffe, then went on to quote Meister Eckhart:

> The importance of consciousness is so great that one cannot help suspecting the element of meaning to be concealed somewhere within all the monstrous, apparently senseless biological turmoil, and that the road to its manifestation was ultimately found on the level of warm-blooded vertebrates possessed of a differentiated brain—found as if by chance, unintended and unforeseen, and yet somehow sensed, felt and groped for out of some dark urge. (pp. 139-140)

Reminding us that Jung used *consciousness* and *reflecting consciousness* as equivalent concepts, Jaffe, then, summarized Jung's thoughts, which gave rise to Van Eenwyk's (1997) möbius strip analogy of the chaotic nature of examining consciousness from within consciousness:

> Jung's myth of meaning is the myth of consciousness. . . . . It is consciousness that gives the world a meaning. "Without the reflecting consciousness of a man the world is a gigantic meaningless machine, for as we know man is the only creature that can discover meaning." . . . The answer to the question of meaning is not a scientific answer. Every

answer is a human interpretation or conjecture, a confession or a belief. It is created by consciousness, and its formulation is a myth. (pp. 140-141)

Back to Edinger (1984), who, like Percy (1975) looked at the word *consciousness*, and its etymological meaning "knowing with." This word combines *knowing*, from the Latin *scio*, which is logos-based and with *con*, from the Latin *cum* meaning *with* or *withness*, which is eros-based. The combination of these two together gives us the nature of consciousness.

By teaching Helen to communicate using words, Helen was able to join the human community in a new way. She was able to become conscious. Language and the relationship with her teacher gave her this. Although Annie had some guidance from Dr. Howe's work with Laura Bridgman, it only took her so far. Annie used her own personal experience to inform her.

Annie was able to read the patterns that she saw in the behavior of people around her; she was fierce in her stand for Helen's possibilities. She was firm in her resolve and set and defended appropriate boundaries, and had amazing perseverance.

Annie followed Helen's lead and taught Helen through the natural world around her, making learning something fun, using play to awaken Helen's mind to new possibilities. Annie knew what was at stake if she failed, not only for herself but for Helen. She was keenly aware of the possible outcomes and trajectories.

No matter what, Annie could not let either Helen or herself end up where she had been as a child. Learning had been the key to Annie's own freedom and she was unshakable in her belief that it would be Helen's, too. Annie was able, like Hermes, to lead Helen through the underworld and back out again, from chaos to a new order, a new attractor site.

"*I-L-O-V-E-H-E-L-E-N!*"

The final scene is at hand now. It is night, we see Annie out on the porch, sitting in a chair covered by her shawl. The last time we saw the shawl was when Annie had the nightmare on their first night in the garden house. Helen approaches Annie, who is curious. Helen now touches Annie's face, and then kisses her and climbing into Annie's arms. "Hush Little Baby" begins to play in the background as it had that first night. Holding her close, Annie spells *i-l-o-v-e-h-e-l-e-n* into Helen's hand. It is April 5, 1887; Annie has been there for 32 days.

This is Annie's lysis. Annie has transformed, too. She once again has someone to love. The resurrection that Annie spoke of with Michael Anagnos when we first saw her has occurred; yet the scope of Annie's resurrection was not as broad as Helen's rebirth into language. And in the end, I believe this goes back to initial conditions. Because of Annie's past, both physical and psychological, and the way it differed from Helen's, she was not able to leap as far.

Physically, the injury to Annie's eyes from her untreated childhood illness was too great and too advanced to allow her to break free from it. Although Annie had over a dozen operations, she eventually lost her battle for her sight and succumbed to blindness.

Whenever Annie talked of her past, she skipped over her traumatic time at Tewksbury, and the truly agonizing nature of her childhood. What Annie did for Helen, she could not do for herself. She sponsored Helen, brought a mature, loving human presence to help midwife the pain, anger, and confusion inside, while she was teaching Helen. She used the important energies of fierceness, tenderness, and playfulness to help transform Helen's life (Gilligan, 1997).

In the film and in her letters, Annie shared that she needed a teacher, too. Just as she felt that she needed someone to help lift the dark veil of ignorance from Helen, she also needed someone to sponsor her, to help her metabolize her experience to bring it into light and transform the *prima materia* of trauma—and resulting the heavy veil of depression that often clouded Annie's own vision throughout her life. Instead, Annie kept her traumatic past hidden from view and no one was able to help her with her intense burden.

At the beginning, Annie carries her own baggage, not allowing others to help her with it. We see this happen twice. In life, Annie did this as well, she carried her own psychological baggage, keeping things private that she might have shared with others at an appropriate time. This led in later life to depression. There was no one to sponsor her terrible gifts, and so they remained locked away, unable to transform.

Annie did not share the details of her life with others until she was well into her 60s. She did not tell Helen, who was the closest person to her in the world, about it until Helen was 50 years old, and had only shortly before shared her dark secrets with her biographer Nella Braddy (1933). Annie would not give anyone the chance to sponsor her, which they would have willingly and gladly done, especially Helen.

Like Moses, Annie was not able to really reach the Promised Land that she led Helen to, she would struggle with depression and illness and become blind before she died. Through Annie, Helen was able to find her way back to the human community and become an influential and inspiring member. Helen developed a powerful faith through her study of the work of Emanuel Swedenborg. Helen's (1927/1994) religion became the "light in her darkness," and provided her with the strength and optimism to endure her outwardly sightless and soundless existence. Helen could have sponsored her beloved teacher, Annie, if she had only been allowed in.

The major biographies that have been written about Annie (Nielsen, 2009; Braddy, 1933, Lash, 1980 and Hickok, 1961) have begun to bring to light the extraordinary nature of Annie's accomplishments. It is my hope that I have added a small part of depth psychological insight to that light, so that Annie might come out of the shadows, and that we might be able to more fully appreciate what she did, and possibly be able to apply it in our own lives and world.

PART III
FINAL CAMPFIRE

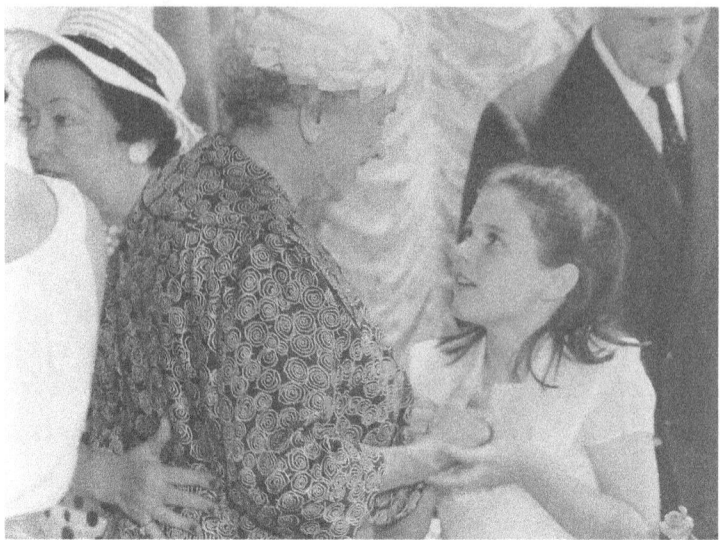

Figure 22: Helen Keller and Patty Duke on Helen's 80th

Like Helen Keller and Annie Sullivan, Anna Patty Duke is an amazing woman. Anna played both Helen and Annie in the film, *The Miracle Worker* and Helen in the Broadway play that inspired the film. She won many awards for these iconic performances, and has also directed the play.

Anna, diagnosed with bi-polar disorder in the 1980s, knew from her own experience the kind of suffering that Annie experienced, enduring archetypally similar life circumstances, and she has written poignantly about them. Yet despite her own difficulties, Duke, is a highly accomplished actor and activist. Duke was the president of the Screen Actor's Guild, and continues to be a tireless advocate for mental health education.

Because Duke was able to bring Helen so powerfully to life, others have been able to be touched by this profound story of the power of the human soul, of care, relatedness, strength, courage, commitment in many ways.

Duke is the person and the performance I remembered when I was inspired to use the film as an example of the transformation process. I have been touched and transformed in ways that I am forever grateful for and which I could never have anticipated.

Duke's performances, both as Helen and Annie have helped me to bring the story of these amazing women to life, and to show the transformative power of film to create consciousness and help us see with archetypal eyes.

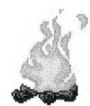

FINAL CAMPFIRE

Our journey has drawn to a close. In this chapter, I will summarize where we have been, reflecting on the lessons that have been learned, and will briefly mention or reiterate dreams for the future. Before doing that, I would like to put Annie into context and presence her true brilliance.

Annie and the Collective Unconscious

In a letter dated August 28, 1887, Annie was describing to her friend Sophia Hopkins what she was teaching Helen Keller, who had just turned 7, two months previously:

> I made her understand that all life comes from an egg. The mother bird lays her eggs in a nest and keeps them warm until the birdlings are hatched. . . . I told her that she could call the egg the cradle of life. Then I told her that other animals like the dog and cow, and human beings, do not lay their eggs, but nourish their young in their own bodies.

While there is nothing remarkable about a child learning about the "facts of life," it is useful to put this moment in context. The miracle at the pump, where Helen first understood that *w-a-t-e-r* spelled into her hand meant the substance that she felt with her other hand coming out of the pump, had happened only 4 months prior—114 days to be exact. Annie herself had just turned 21 that April and had only learned to read 7 years previously, due to being nearly blind for most of her life. While this in itself is notable, what follows a few sentences later, is rather more extraordinary:

> The subject was difficult, and my knowledge inadequate; but I am glad I didn't shirk my responsibility; for, stumbling, hesitating, and incomplete as my explanation was, it touched deep responsive chords in the soul of my little pupil, and **the readiness with which she comprehended the great facts of physical life confirmed me in the opinion that the child has dormant within him, when he comes into the world, all the experiences of the race. These experiences are like photographic negatives, until language develops them and brings out the memory-images.** [emphasis added] (Keller, 1903/2003, pp. 166-167)

The collective unconscious was not yet a gleam in Carl Jung's eye, for on this day, he was 12 years and 2 days old. He had entered his secondary studies in the spring of 1886, when Annie was graduating from Perkins as valedictorian of her class. At this time, Jung was quite possibly on his 6 month hiatus from school, while Sigmund Freud had just met Wilhelm Fliess, and had only recently gone to study with Charcot for a few months between October 1885-February 1886. This was long before Freud met Breuer, or had his dream of Irma's injection in 1895 (Ellenberger, 1970).

Yet, in America, April 1887 turned out not to be the cruelest month. As the South was reconstructing itself from the Civil War, another civil war had been fought, the victory was decisive and consciousness was the winner! A young girl gained the world and we are better for it. This is why I believe that not only can Annie Sullivan can be thought of as one of the patron saints of Archetypal Pattern Analysis, but of depth psychology, too.

The Miracle Worker's Enduring Legacy

The Miracle Worker (Penn, 1962; Gibson 1956/2008) portrays the beginning of Helen and Annie's work together, but that beginning was just a start of a much grander work. This book has sought to shed some light on that beginning—the consciousness that was created from the tension of opposites, the struggles and fierce battles that must be fought, the dark and terrifying wilderness that is encountered during the liminal times in the underworld. Yet as we have seen, the underworld nourishes seeds of consciousness, which can bear tremendous fruits. My own internal process mirrored their story. It has been a struggle, almost maddening at times, but I have changed, deepened and been led to new understandings and insights. It is my sincere hope that others will come to new understandings and appreciations of the transformation process that has played out in the preceding pages.

I have sought to do justice to the brilliance of both Annie, Helen, and William Gibson, as well as the unforgettable performances of the brilliant actors and actresses that have brought this story to light and etched it in our imaginations: especially Anne Bancroft and Anna Patty Duke.

Annie Sullivan was indeed a miracle, an orphan who was able to go beyond her traumatic initial conditions and use the eternally iterating plutonic memories of her childhood to free another child, who was tragically trapped in a typhonic "no world" of soundless darkness. Through the gift of language and symbols, Annie brought light into Helen's darkness and helped light the way for countless others. The light of their lives and the promise and possibility they portrayed, as well as the strength and courage required, were writ large on the screen. *The Miracle Worker* (Penn, 1962) has been a miracle for me in my own life. My only regret is that I could not thank some of the now departed amazing artists who brought this legendary story to light.

Following on from the archetype of beginnings explicated in *Threshold Experiences* (Conforti, 2007), I examined the archetype of the field of transformation, AKA the eternal return, using Dr. Stanislav Grof's cartography of the psyche and the perinatal dimension that he explicated as a map, along with Dr. Richard Tarnas's corresponding and complementary planetary archetypal complexes. In my own experience, these two men and their work have been wonderful teachers. These maps, one psychological, one astrological, have been and continue to be a light in my own darkness, helping me to know where I am, and to make meaning out of my own life, especially during liminal times.

A teacher can guide us through this unending cycle of death and rebirth. Teachers and teachings throughout the ages are available to us in the form of words. This is the world that Annie gave Helen. Here are Gibson's (1961) beautiful words, shown in the original text of the screenplay and the traditional courier type:

```
              I wanted to teach you.
    Oh... Everything the earth is full of, Helen.
       Everything on it that's ours for a wink.
          And what we are on it. The light
       we bring to it and leave behind in words.
             You can see 5000 years back
                in the light of words.
             Everything we feel, think,
               know, and share in words.
           So not a soul is in darkness,
           or done with even in the grave.
                    But I know.
                I know one word and
       I can put the world in your hand.
    And whatever it is to me, I won't take less.
```

We all need teachers, but they don't have to be what we normally think of as a teacher: they can be a word or image, a film or television show, a myth, a movie star, a website, someone you admire, a cause you are passionate about—anything that engages the imagination can be a teacher.

Through exploring this work, and the story of this teacher, I have been and continue to be transformed. Song lyrics speak to me and help me along, like Annie Sullivan patiently spelling over and over into Helen's hand, or Sam I am presenting the green eggs and ham to the unwilling I in Dr. Seuss's (Geisel, 1960) classic work.

Whatever or whoever either gives us meaning, or points us toward meaning, or helps us get back to meaning—they are a teacher. It is a relatedness that holds the space, creating the proper conditions, too. A teacher can be like a coach, someone to help us to envision and to a achieve a goal, a north star to follow and navigate by. In the eternal return of transformation, in the chaotic liminal times, one can easily get lost. Goals, teachers and coaches help us to find our way to new places, emotional spaces, and identities.

Putting oneself in play, and holding the tension of the opposites is necessary as well. In alchemy, the alchemists put many things in the retort. They mixed it around and then turned up the heat; and the pressure that was created did strange and weird things to these opposites.

The alchemists talked about it as the suffering of the sulfur. Our present moment mirrors this process. We need to be able to understand the transformation process so that we don't get caught and unconsciously project our inner turmoil out into the world. Consciousness is often a battle between opposites, where we struggle with becoming conscious ourselves. In speaking of the individuation of mankind, Jaffe (1975) noted:

> In addition, the boundless force of inertia opposes the desire for transformation and greater consciousness. It is the same in individual life: everyone who struggles to individuate and become more conscious is thwarted by this inhibiting and decelerating tendency in the unconscious. "The unconscious wants to flow into consciousness in order to reach the light, but at the same time, it continually thwarts itself, because it would rather remain unconscious. That is to say God wants to become man, but not quite." (p. 117)

Consciousness and the ability to reflect and record our reflections and share them is what life is truly about. We are able to find our way in the dark through the light of consciousness.

Dr. David Ulansey, in a course on the mystery traditions felt that the internet was an alchemical vessel. He spoke of it as being made of glass—the silicon connections—and like the alembic, retort, or crucible where the alchemist worked his magic on the *prima material*. He noted that were throwing everything into it, hoping to create the philosopher's stone. Perhaps we can create that alchemical transformation and change our world. Through the internet, we can perhaps find light, teachings and teachers of all kinds that will help us to create more consciousness, and add our light to the sum of light.

Each night we participate in the eternal return—in our dreams we are taken back to the primordial ouroboric state of unconsciousness—we iterate, feeding back the current day's activity into what went before. As we do, our brains participate in, as Goethe wrote—"formation, transformation, eternal mind's eternal recreation." This is the eternal play we are engaged in—it is the archetypal field of transformation.

We, too, are the dissipative structures chaos theory speaks of. Before and after we sleep, we cross over the thresholds, and these are powerful times, something to explore in the future. As we sleep, our brains are forming and reforming themselves, neural connections are rearranged and reformed, sometimes giving us dreams that we remember, symbols to help us transform.

Words themselves are symbols, so this might speak to the power of images—because they store so many words within them. And as Jung (and Hillman "riffing off" of him) affirmed "psyche is image" (Jung, 1946/1954/1981; Hillman, 1983a, 1992). Hillman exhorted us to stick with the image. Kaufmann (2009), and Conforti following him have sought to do this. Our entire endeavor of archetypal pattern analysis is centered on this thesis. In the future perhaps we can use these images to help ourselves transform as a species.

Perhaps we can work with the eternal return instead of constantly being thrashed by it, for after all, life is the eternal return. If we can only wake up and participate in it consciously, it might free us from compulsively repeating nongenerative patterns and unhelpfully projecting them out onto others. Eliade had it right [for those of you who have not made your way to the Initiation Excursion in Appendix E, you're missing out! And its not too late. . .]. Eliade (1952/1991) essentially thought that these iterations of the eternal return were an invitation of sorts to transcend the past patterns, to bifurcate and take the road less traveled, to finally try some green eggs and ham! As Romanyshyn (2007) noted, the hermeneutic circle is really an alchemical spiral, for we are always in the hermeneutic process, its own eternal return and once again—here we go again! By using the eternal return to free ourselves from it, we can then be on a higher iteration of the spiral. Speaking of spirals, Joseph Campbell, and the Hero's Journey was my initial inspiration to go to Pacifica, so it is fitting that he should make his way into this book, too. In *The Power of Myth*, Campbell (1988) said:

> Schopenhauer, in his splendid essay called "On An Apparent Intention in the Fate of the Individual," points out that when you reach an advanced age and look back over your lifetime, it can seem to have had a consistent order and plan, as though composed by some novelist. Events that when they occurred had seemed accidental and of little moment turn out to have been indispensable actors in the composition of a consistent plot. . . . the whole thing gears together like one big symphony, with everything unconsciously structuring everything else. And Schopenhauer concludes that it is as though our lives were the features of one great dream of a single dreamer in which all the dream characters dream, too; so that everything links to everything else, moved by the one will to live which is the universal will in nature.
>
> It's a magnificent idea—an idea that appears in India in the mythic image of the Net of Indra, which is a net of gems, where at every crossing of one thread over another there is a gem reflecting all the other reflective gems. Everything arises in mutual relation to everything else, so you can't blame anybody for anything. It is even as though there were a single intention behind it all, which always makes some kind of sense, though none of us knows what the sense might be, or has lived the life that he quite intended. . . . So each incarnation, you might say, has a potentiality, and the mission of life is to live that potentiality. How do you do it? My answer is, "Follow your bliss." There's something inside you that knows when you're in the center, that knows when you're on the beam or off the beam. (p. 229)

If we take the combined wisdom of Schopenhauer and Campbell, I believe that if we can understand the attractor sites that we are in, their landscapes and customs, and work with them, and we won't have to wait so long to look back. We can make sense of the endlessly returning patterns and then work with them, we can transform.

If we can't do it alone—which is most often the case—a teacher can be infinitely helpful; and as previously mentioned, a teacher, as one who educates, or draws out, can be almost anything; it doesn't have to be literalized into a human being! This is how I found my way to Pacifica and ultimately here.

As Annie Sullivan so powerfully realized, it is in the power of words, and as Walker Percy (1975) explicated further, words as symbols, that we are able to create consciousness, "to know with," as Edinger (1984) reminded us— together.

Dreaming My Possession Onwards. . .

There is so much more to be written, I will only mention a few of my longings here. Object relations and the work of Bion, Klein, and Winnicott could enrich our understanding, especially if we looked from a more clinical perspective at the relationship between Annie and Helen in terms of attachment dynamics and the intersubjective field. A deeper understanding of language acquisition and how Annie's approach to education might inform our own present day problems, are also fruitful areas to be pursued, not just with the deafblind as Pevsner did (2010), but in education overall.

Although I intended to focus on the "Aha" moment, I believe that neuroscience would have much to teach us in that regard, and will pursue that avenue in the future. This film provided so many richly symbolic moments that could be worked and reworked, deepened and seen through different depth lenses. Different archetypal energies were present that were mentioned only in passing, if at all.

Similarly, while I have looked at the teacher's role in the transformation process, I have only alluded to the specific archetypal roles of the teacher. I would seek in future work do an extended archetypal study of the gods that played through Annie: Chiron, Hermes, and Athena. Although Mayes (2010a, 2010b) hinted at some of these archetypes, and clearly presenced the need for a therapeutic classroom, as well as the need for educators to be conscious of the archetypal nature of their profession, a truly Hillman-esque study remains in the future. Also, as mentioned before, an astrological analysis awaits, which will certainly bring interesting insights.

There are many many parallels, but we have stayed too long already and that study must wait until another time. For now, as my teachers and mentors Veronica Goodchild and Robert Romanyshyn have recommended: "This is my best effort for now," and "For the moment, that's enough."

I choose to close this final campfire with an image. I have used image a couple of times before, as the front cover of two different papers: the first discussing the liminality of play—which was where I first encountered chaos theory; and the second on the autonomous psyche and the individuation process, playing with the film *Chocolat* (Hallstrom, 2000) as my canvas. The image is entitled "Prelude to the Kiss," It fittingly, shows the chocolate kiss's initial conditions, as it were. Its triangular shape, alludes to the transcendent function, its relational nature, and our campfires along the way, and the Greek Δ, as well as Walker Percy's (1975) conception of the triadic and tetradic nature of consciousness—"knowing with." In this image, we are back to my beginnings again, for my brother Ben created it. The autonomous psyche continues to work its magic, showing itself as it shines through powerful cinematic creations.

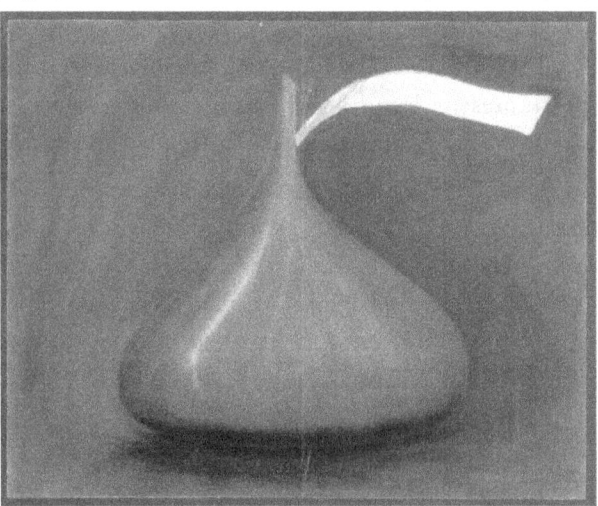

Figure 23: Prelude to the Kiss

There is so much more to *The Miracle Worker* (1962), it has so many more possibilities yet to explore. Because of this, I will end by quoting a favorite line from *Chocolat*: "But still the clever North Wind was not satisfied. The Wind spoke to Vianne of towns yet to be visited, friends in need yet to be discovered, battles yet to be fought by someone else, next time" [as she lets the ashes of her mother go] (Hallstrom, 2000). The journey has been bittersweet, my ego defeated many times, but consciousness has in the end won out, yet again.

I, too, must now let go, for now, although the autonomous psyche still is not satisfied. It speaks to me of things "not yet" written, things yet to be said, things yet to be discovered about *The Miracle Worker* (Penn, 1962), [as I press the save, and later attach and send buttons] by myself or someone else, next time!

T-E-A-C-H-E-R

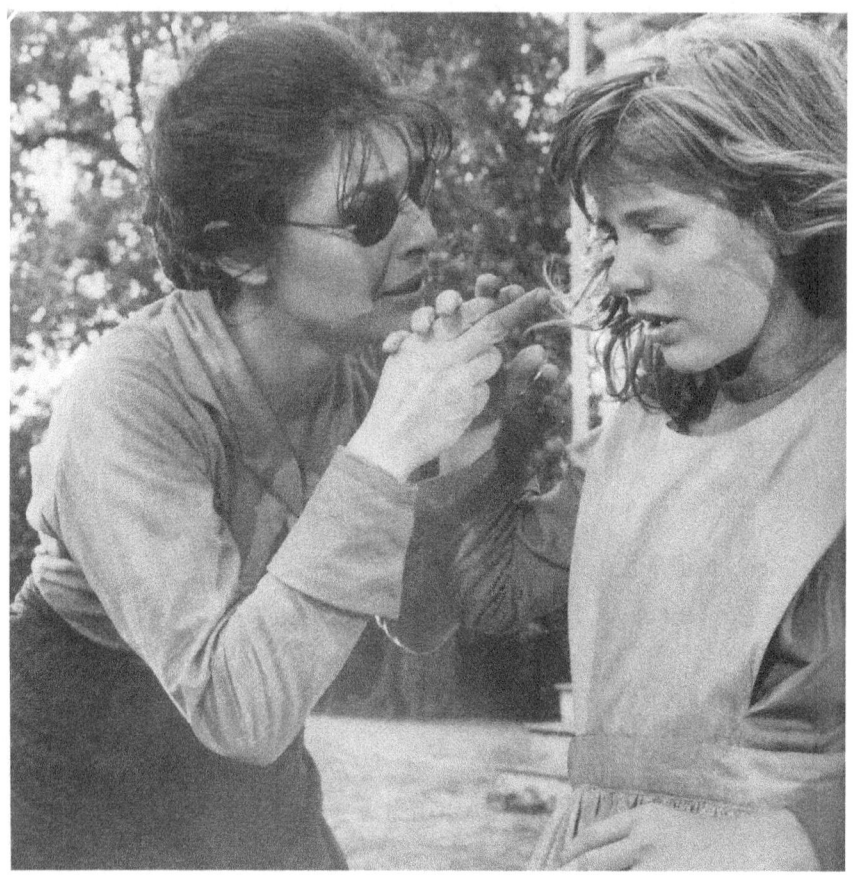

Figure 24: Bancroft and Duke

The moment when Annie names herself to Helen; the center of the collage cover.

APPENDICES

To the loving memory of Anne Bancroft, who began the decade of the 1960s portraying a young nearly blind teacher awakening consciousness in a child, to the end of the decade where in another iconic performance she awakened a different sort of consciousness in the youth of America— Here's to you Mrs. Robinson!

Figure 25: Anne Bancroft as Annie

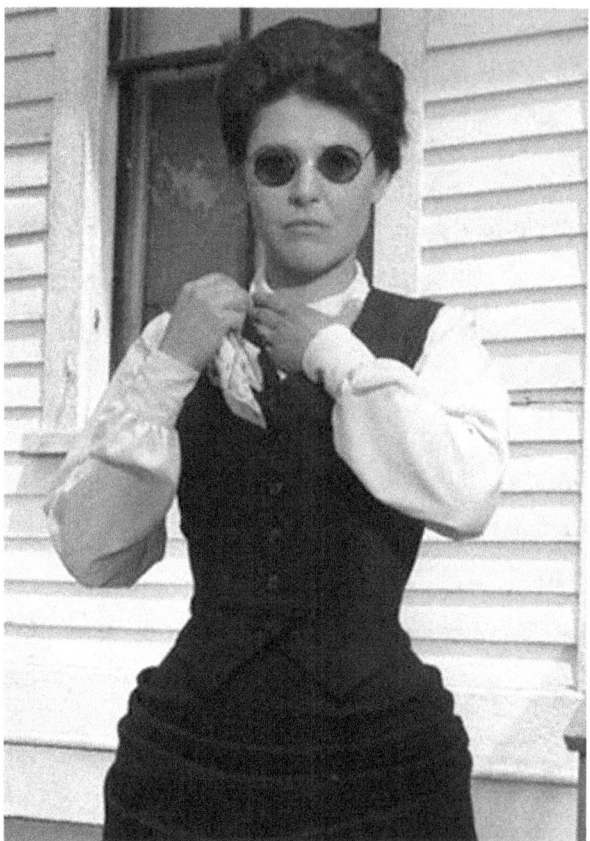

"I am beginning to suspect all elaborate and special systems of education. They seem to me to be built up on the supposition that every child is a kind of idiot who must be taught to think."

—Annie Sullivan, in *Story of My Life*, Letters

APPENDIX A: LEARNING FROM LEGENDARY LIVES

Such Stuff As Dreams Are Made Of

James Hillman (1983b), in *Healing Fictions*, showed that all of our depth psychological writing is at base poetic, and from Freud's *Dora* on, "case histories are a way of writing fiction" (p. 5). Long before Hillman was born, both Helen Keller and Annie Sullivan realized the storied nature of life. Each eloquently expressed, in similar words, that narratives of people's life are similar to dreams. Following this insight, which happened while psychoanalysis was still in its early infancy, I will examine the story that has become known to us through William Gibson's play and later film *The Miracle Worker*. Although I have chose to use the 1962 version, two other cinematic versions have been made, in 1979 and 2000, as well as another film *Black* (2004). I have chosen to let Helen and Annie express in their own words the reason for my choice. In *The Story of My Life*, Helen Keller (1903/2003) wrote:

> When I try to classify my earliest impressions, I find that fact and fancy look alike across the years that link the past with the present. The woman paints the child's experiences in her own fantasy. A few impressions stand out vividly from the first years of my life; but "the shadows of the prison-house are on the rest." Besides, many of the joys and sorrows of childhood have lost their poignancy; and many incidents of vital importance in my early education have been forgotten in the excitement of great discoveries. (p. 12)

Annie Sullivan, did not share her entire story with Helen until 1930, when she was 64 years old and Helen was 50. A reluctant biographical subject, Annie told her future biographer Nella Braddy (1933):

> The most conscientious biographer cannot tell the whole truth about his subject, because the subject himself has forgotten so much that was once impressive. He sees things differently; from day to day the aspect of life changes, what was important yesterday seems trivial today. A little while, and significant events and experiences take on a vagueness of a dream, thrilling episodes fade into silence, the precious hour of love is followed by pitiful speech, the tremulously whispered promise by sighs and tears. The flames leaping high with exultation turn to red ashes and

smoulder [sic] out because less and less frequently tended; the years pass; memories become dull aches. . . . Our early recollections of childhood are very similar to dreams—they are pictures. When we try to put them into words we must make connections and fill gaps. Time and place are lost, but an image remains. The truth of the matter is not what I tell you about it, but what you divine in regard to it. (p. xiii)

Rodas (2003) described the lives of Sullivan and Keller as a *palimpsest*. A palimpsest is defined as "1. A manuscript, typically of papyrus or parchment, that has been written on more than once, with the earlier writing incompletely erased and often legible." And "2. An object, place, or area that reflects its history." (AHD, 2009). The film will also reflect this, as we will see. Rodas explained:

In fact, Keller's sense of her own life, especially the early years described in *The Story of My Life*, which was the primary basis of Gibson's drama, is based largely not on her own personal memories, but rather on stories related to her by Sullivan and others. The "miracle" breakthrough moment described first in one of Sullivan's letters, then in Keller's text, and depicted finally as the dramatic climax of *The Miracle Worker*, is not actually a moment that Keller personally recollected, but was included in her early autobiography since it had become a part of her repertoire, one of the many stories from her teacher that lent meaning and context, that offered a pattern to the course of her life.

For these reasons, we ought to remember, when we consider any representation of Keller's life, that the boundary between the "real" and the fictional is often difficult to determine. Gibson's version of Keller's story is certainly based in fact, but it should not be thought of as an historical document. The same holds true, too, for other versions; descriptions of Keller's life, whether from Sullivan's writings, from biographies of Keller, or even from Keller's autobiographies ought each to be regarded as a kind of palimpsest, a document written, erased, and re-written so that there must always remain some question as to the nature of the original. (p. 10)

While Rodas is specifically commenting on the lives of these two extraordinary women, the same holds true in our own lives, where we essentially re-write our stories, combining and recombining versions, using memory fragments mixed with the memories of others.

"More Wonderful Than Any Fiction"

Klages (1989), in her dissertation *More Wonderful than Any Fiction: The Representation of Helen Keller*, examined the writings about Helen's life from a literary perspective, situating it in the wider cultural debate between the "feminine" idealist and "masculine" materialist modes. Biography, Klages argued can be "read like fiction," and quoting Tompkins, Klages noted that fictional texts "offer powerful examples of the way a culture thinks about itself, articulating and proposing solutions for the problems that shape a particular historical moment" (p. 9).

Klages proposed "the rhetoric used in a biographical work reflects and reshapes a certain system of values, what a particular life is shown to represent," and Klages further said that representations of Helen Keller

> can be read as Tompkins reads fiction, as portrayals of a certain version of reality. . . . [which] present the "facts" of her life and education in terms which reaffirm aspects of cultural values specific to a certain section of the American population. (p. 10)

By the 1950s, representations of Keller as the "embodiment of feminine sentimental and idealist traditions" had become problematic. Klages (1989) in her epilogue, without using the words *transcendent function* discussed how the play and later film resolved the contradiction

> between the celebration of Keller as an American saint who affirmed the importance of idealism, and the cultural emphasis on science which affirmed the centrality of objectivity. . . . by presenting a new and surprisingly different representation of Keller; The Miracle *Worker's* portrayal of the pre-linguistic deaf-blind child has shaped the meanings which the generations of Americans born after 1957 assign to the cultural sign "Helen Keller." (p. 12)

In the above quote, Klages is essentially describing what the *transcendent function* does. Jeffrey Miller (1991), partially quoting Jung, succinctly summed it up this way: "the 'union of conscious and unconscious contents' to produce a wholly new perspective, a 'living third thing'" (p. ii). Miller's dissertation is about Jung's original 1912 essay on transcendent function and its later revision in 1957/1981. Interestingly, Jung's revision occurs very close in time to Gibson's original teleplay (1955), Eliade's (1952/1991; 1954/1991; 1958/1995) work on initiation and the eternal return and Walker Percy's essay (1954) and Keller's (1955), own biography of Annie.

The Miracle Worker (Penn, 1962) does this not only in the literary and representational sense that Klages discussed, but it is also an example, par excellence of the transcendent function, of the creation of consciousness itself.

Ken Wilber (1999), referring mainly to Joseph Campbell's work, noted that myths can function either as signs or symbols. As signs, myths function as an upholder of tradition, initiating, confirming and strengthening the individual into mundane or normal levels of society and the same levels of self and reality. Alternatively, myths can act as symbols and help the experiencer transform and open up to transcendence. (pp. 452-454)

Indeed, *The Miracle Worker* (Penn, 1962) can produce wholly new perspectives. By exploring and amplifying this marvelous story, through the lenses of depth psychology, the new sciences, and other disciplines, this book has sought to dream onwards this particular myth, uncovering many implications and possible applications. Joseph Campbell, in *The Portable Jung*, summed it up this way: "The collective unconscious consists of mythological motifs or primordial (pre-dating mankind) images, for which reason the myths of all nations are its exponents. The whole of mythology could be taken as a sort of projection of the collective unconscious" (Jung, 1976, p. 39).

By engaging with myths consciously, we can perhaps, experience the transcendent function for ourselves. Nella Braddy (1933) in her biography of Anne Sullivan Macy wrote: "And now the legend begins. No one that far-off summer day [August 1886] knew that a miracle was about to be performed, but later, after the miracle was accomplished, many claimed that they had know all the time" (p. 105).

The mythic lives of Annie and Helen, as portrayed in this iconic film, are an example of Jung's myth, the creation of consciousness (Edinger, 1984). Put simply, the after many challenges and battles, the legendary student overcame the curse that had befallen her and was freed from a prison by an equally extraordinary young teacher one spring day at a water pump, when the key to language was given to her.

Since their lives were indeed legendary, it is only fitting that we transform their story, and the healing fiction created from it in *The Miracle Worker*, into a fairytale. [See Following Appendix B]

APPENDIX B: THE FAIRYTALE LIVES OF TEACHER AND STUDENT

Once upon a time, in a town called Tuscumbia, [which was originally called Ococoposa or Cold Water], a baby is born to a new mother Kate and her husband Arthur. Kate is in her early 20s, and Arthur, also known as Captain Keller or Capt'n, is 20 years her senior, for he had fought in a terrible war. At first all goes well until their young daughter Helen, is stricken by an illness at 19 months old and is cursed with blindness and deafness.

For years she lives as a "phantom" in a netherworld, helplessly groping and hopelessly unable to find her way. Her parents have tried to find help many times, but it has been unsuccessful, and in the meantime, out of love and pity cannot tolerate disciplining her, so she grows up as an unruly little animal, becoming more frustrated as she grows.

She lashes out with tantrums and rages, trying to communicate, but her attempts are frustrated. She is growing and her uncontrolled behavior is becoming dangerous. Her parents have been unable to find anyone to help her. Her mother then reads of a far away school where someone may be able to help. They travel far away to another doctor who sends them to yet another doctor, who invented a magical device for talking to people far away. He tells the parents to write to the school, and following his advice, her father goes home and writes the letter.

But back to our story. A young woman who has been nearly blind herself, is chosen and accepts the challenge. Her name is Annie, and she prepares herself for this task for half a year, studying the report of one who had accomplished such a nearly impossible task half a century before, with a more docile child, who was similarly afflicted. The wise older man who has chosen her for the task sees her off on her journey, giving her a gift—a garnet ring.

This young woman, Annie, will become the miracle worker. Her own harsh origins and struggles have given her the strength and courage she will need to work this miracle. She arrives at the family home after a long and arduous journey, quickly learning that this child is anything but docile. Annie will have to find her own way to break the spell, her own path through the woods, where it is darkest.

The child Helen, and indeed the whole family are under a spell, they are locked in a ouroboric dance of mutual unconsciousness, Helen can't see or hear others, and they in turn are essentially blind and deaf to her. Their love and pity has stripped them of any power to change the situation, which escalates as it endlessly repeats. They oscillate between the chaos created by the child and the peace bought at a cost of capitulating to this small tyrannical beast. Not only is the child almost unreachable due to her curse, but this second spell on the family is so strong that it is almost unbreakable.

This is the landscape into which our heroine, Annie enters. The young teacher's task is to rescue the child from eternal darkness and isolation. After a dragon battle with the young child, where Annie emerges triumphant, Annie realizes that she break the family curse, and must first rescue the child from the influence of her misguided family and teach her discipline. Annie then wrests the child from her parents, which she accomplishes through confronting them with the harsh reality of a probable future.

The secret weapon she uses is her own past experience; she has been there, she knows what will surely happen if they do not allow her to properly initiate the child into the world of understanding. Helen's embattled parents reluctantly allow the young teacher to take their daughter to a secluded cottage, where Annie will at first tame and then teach her young charge.

This is no easy task, because at first the young girl flees from Annie as if she were a wicked witch. The rebellious Helen however has met her match. Many battles of wills ensue, but Annie has been here before herself, and her passion and prior trauma give her the power to break Helen's spell. After a time, the first big change has occurred: Helen yields to and accepts discipline. This in itself is a miracle.

Annie works with Helen's own internal hunger to learn, to know, to understand. After two weeks of endlessly spelling words into the young child's curious fingers, Annie has still not succeeded in penetrating the cloak of darkness and ignorance that is holding Helen captive in this unreachable place of chaos and confusion. Helen, the "Phantom" is stuck in a liminal limbo, a no-world, she is not yet fully human, although she is no longer a beast.

Before the initiation can be completed, Helen's parents interrupt the process. Missing their daughter, and happy with her mere obedience, they insist she return home, against Annie's objections. Annie has lost this round; the tenuous discipline and learning that has been put in place is fragile and in danger of coming undone, and the family spell, like a powerful sun quickly pulls Helen back into its orbit. Helen again reverts back to a more unruly state. Annie battles back, and this time, has to teach Helen while she is still inside of and under this powerful spell.

Annie and Helen are both in a state of intense frustration, on the day that the miracle occurs. Helen does not understand, and Annie tries yet another way of trying to reach her struggling student. Helen still doesn't know that the finger game she is playing with Annie are words and that the words are the names for the things that Annie lets her feel as she spells the words into Helen's hand.

Annie is unbending as she leads Helen to the water pump; Annie spells a word which she has spelled many times before into the young girl's hand. Annie spells into her right hand W-A-T-E-R while placing Helen's left hand under the pump and operating the pump, as cold water splashes onto her small hand.

Finally, the miracle moment is at hand. Helen stands transfixed, she finally understands that the letters W-A-T-E-R are the word, which is the name of this thing that is flowing into her other hand. Helen spells it back into her own hand at first and then into Annie's.

At last, Helen knows. The spell of darkness and ignorance is broken. The miracle of language has been revealed to her. The rest is history. And another important word is learned a few moments later: Helen approaches Annie and points to her. Annie, as she has done thousands of times before gives Helen the name: into Helen's hand, Annie spells T-E-A-C-H-E-R.

Annie has also been released from a spell that day. Many years before, Annie lost her brother, who was Helen's age, and this love and her grief at its loss helped to free Helen. Now, Annie had someone to love again, her young pupil. She will devote the rest of her life to Helen, and Helen likewise is devoted to Annie, her teacher. Annie is known from then on to Helen and to many others as Teacher.

The story continues, but we will leave it here for now. Suffice it to say that together they will overcome great obstacles, accomplish great things and help many people worldwide, and serving as an inspiration, the student and the teacher, live on, their mythic lives celebrated in many books and movies. They have become immortal.

APPENDIX C: ANNIE SULLIVAN VALEDICTORY ADDRESS (DELIVERED JUNE 1, 1886)

Today we are standing face to face with the great problem of life. We have spent years in the endeavor to acquire the moral and intellectual discipline, by which we are enabled to distinguish truth from falsehood, receive higher and broader views of duty, and apply general principles to the diversified details of life. And now we are going out into the busy world, to take our share in life's burdens, and do our little to make that world better, wiser and happier.

We shall be most likely to succeed in this, if we obey the great law of our being. God has placed us here to grow, to expand, to progress. To a certain extent our growth is unconscious. We receive impressions and arrive at conclusions without any effort on our part; but we also have the power of controlling the course of our lives. We can educate ourselves; we can, by thought and perseverance, develop all the powers and capacities entrusted to us, and build for ourselves true and noble characters. Because we can, we must. It is a duty we owe to ourselves, to our country and to God.

All the wondrous physical, intellectual and moral endowments, with which man is blessed, will, by inevitable law, become useless, unless he uses and improves them. The muscles must be used, or they become unserviceable. The memory, understanding and judgment must be used, or they become feeble and inactive. If a love for truth and beauty and goodness is not cultivated, the mind loses the strength which comes from truth, the refinement which comes from beauty, and the happiness which comes from goodness.

Self-culture is a benefit, not only to the individual, but also to mankind. Every man who improves himself is aiding the progress of society, and every one who stands still, holds it back. The advancement of society always has its commencement in the individual soul. It is by battling with the circumstances, temptations and failures of the world, that the individual reaches his highest possibilities.

The search for knowledge, begun in school, must be continued through life in order to give symmetrical self-culture. For the abundant opportunities which have been afforded to us for broad self-improvement we are deeply grateful.

We thank His Excellency, the Governor, and the legislature of Massachusetts, and the governors and legislatures of the several New England states, for the most generous and efficient aid they have given our school. We thank our trustees for the zeal and invariable interest which they have shown in all that concerns our well-being. Directors, teachers and matrons: we enter life's battle-field determined to prove our gratitude to you, by lives devoted to duty, true in thought and deed to the noble principles you have taught us.

Schoolmates: though the dear happy years we have spent together are over, yet the ties of friendship, and an enduring love and reverence for our school, and the sacred memory of her whom God has called from her labor of love to be an unseen but constant inspiration to us through life, are bonds of union that time and a and absence will only strengthen.

Fellow-graduates: duty bids us go forth into active life. Let us go cheerfully, hopefully, and earnestly, and set ourselves to find our especial part. When we have found it, willingly and faithfully perform it; for every obstacle we overcome, every success we achieve tends to bring man closer to God and make life more as he would have it.

APPENDIX D: EXCURSION INTO ORIGINS

ORIGIN early 16th cent.: from French *origine*,

from Latin *origo*, origin-, from *oriri* 'to rise.'

"Note: The *origin* of something is the point from which it starts or sets out, or the person or thing from which it is ultimately derived (*the origin of a word*). It often applies to causes that were in operation before the thing itself was brought into being."

–Isaac and Sophie Koren
(July 14, 2013 synchronistic email invitation to a Salon)

Origins can refer to many things; it is often useful to orient oneself in time, place, and space. In this appendix, we will consider different origins, after first looking at the origin of *origins*. First the geographic origins of both Helen and Annie will be considered, and then the etymology of their names. Next, the inspiration and origins of this project will be described, to put things in context. In the future, I will add sections such as a timeline, using *metabletics*, or van den Bergian phenomenology (Pohn, 2006) to show how the world was gathered during this time, which will serve to situate us in the cultural and historical moment, and astrological charts will provide a more cosmic perspective for future consideration, too.

Taking my cue from the synchronicity of working on the initial conditions piece of this paper, with the arrival of the above quoted email. I thought it would be important to discuss origins. This is doubly true because one of the foundational texts in this program, *The Way of the Image*, discusses Yoram Kaufmann's (2009) orientational approach.

Beginnings are important. In chaos theory this is expressed as Sensitive Dependence on Initial Conditions (Van Eenywk, 1997). In the Assisi Institute Archetypal Pattern Analyst training program (AIAPA), they are one of the core concepts. We are interested in the orient of the image, the beginning of a dream, of a therapeutic encounter, a life, etc. (Conforti, Thresholds; AIAPA Initial Conditions). The AIAPA program grew out of Conforti's (2007) research on the importance of beginnings—the initial interviews in therapy for his Jungian analysis dissertation. Beginnings can give us clues to where we are and where we may be headed. So let us first orient ourselves to these origins.

The words *origin* and *orient* share a common root: *oriri*, meaning "to rise." *Orient* (n.) and orient (v.) refer to the east, from the 11th century Old French *orient*, and the Latin word *orientem*: "the rising sun, the east, part of the sky where the sun rises, comes from can be traced back to about 1400. *Origin* means "'ancestry, race,' from Old French *origine* 'origin, race,' and directly from Latin *originem* (nominative *origo*) 'a rise, commencement, beginning, source; descent, lineage, birth," from stem of *oriri* 'to rise, become visible, appear.'" The verb *orient* originally meant "to arrange facing east and comes from the French *s'orientier*, meaning "to take one's bearings," and later extended to "determine bearings." (Etymology online, 2013, *origin* and *orient*).

We now proceed to the physical place of the origins we are concerned with. Edward Casey (1993, 1997) followed the philosophical evolution of space and place, and presenced the importance of place in peoples lives. Chalquist (2007) in his dissertation turned book, looked to "the soul of place" using *terrapsychology*, a term he coined, as a method to attend to the relationship and recurring resonances between soul and place.

Geographic Origins

Tuscumbia, Alabama. Tuscumbia, the city of Helen's birth, was incorporated December 20, 1820 as Cold Water or Ococoposa. The name was changed six months later to Big Spring, and on December 31, 1822, it was changed a third time to Tuscumbia. McDonald (2007) related:

> There is a legend that the citizens were asked to select either the name "Annie," in honor of the infant daughter of Michael Dickson, who was the first white child born at that place, or the name "Tuscumbia" in honor of the old chief who was still living in the community. The name Tuscumbia won by a majority of one vote, and the Chickasaw chieftain was so pleased that he presented little Annie with a tiny pair of moccasins.

McDonald noted that *Tashka Ambi* possibly meaning "the warrior who kills," although a "source in Mississippi referred to him as one of the priesthood, being labeled as "Chief Rainmaker of the Chickasaw Tribe, and In the late 1780's that Chief Chief Tashka Ambi meaning "the warrior who kills." married Im Mi, whose full name was Im Mi Ah Key. The history of the name, is very interesting and symbolically prescient of the future events that would transpire almost 60 years hence: The original name, meaning, "cold water" was also the nature of the place, the underground spring coming up from the ground. This cold water coming up from under the ground was an important element in Helen's awakening, that fine Spring day in 1887. It is also interesting that Annie was an alternate name being considered for the town.

Agawam, Massachusetts. Agawam was the Anglicization of the native name of a large territory *Wonnesquamsauke*, from *wonne*, "pleasant," *asquam*, "water" and *auke*, "place." (Agawam [tribe], 2013) that belonged to a Native American tribe. The English named the tribe Agawam after the place name. "The Indian village originally sited on the west bank of the Connecticut River was known as Agawam, or Agawanus, Aggawom, Agawom, Onkowam, Igwam, and Auguam." Agawam is on the west side of the Connecticut River opposite of Springfield, Massachusetts, and incorporated as a town May 17, 1855. The Anne Sullivan Memorial— marker and statue dedicated to Helen Keller's Teacher, is on the corner of Springfield and South Westfield Streets (Agawam [MA], 2013).

The Riverside Hotel is located about 50 miles upriver from Agawam. I have traveled past Agawam 7 times in the past two years, presenting this paper will mark my graduation from the program and my 8th time to pass by Agawam. Each time I have come to the conferences, I have stayed at the Riverside Hotel and my final presentation was held there on the banks of the Connecticut River.

Tewksbury Almshouse and Perkins Institution. Tewksbury Almshouse, established in 1852 and opened in 1854, is located in Tewksbury, Massachusetts, which is bordered by the Merrimac River on the north and the Shawsheen River on the south. *Sawsheen* is said to mean "Great Spring" and also of interest is the fact that in 1857 a devastating tornado hit Tewksbury originating in a water-spout in Round Pond less than a mile away from the almshouse (CelebrateBoston.com, 2013).

Perkins Institution, now called Perkins School for the Blind, is located in Watertown, Massachusetts and was established in 1829 and began taking students in 1832. Laura Bridgman was born in Hanover, New Hampshire, but lived at Perkins most of her life, from October, 1837 until her death in 1889. Annie also lived there for about 7 years and she and Helen stayed there several times as well.

Karey Pohn

The common thread running through all of these locations is a relationship with water. These places are identified with water, except in the case of Tewksbury, but its proximity to water, and the tornado incident is reflective of the role that Tewksbury plays in the overall drama.

Etymological Roots

Helen. The etymology of Helen is problematic. The Greek for Helen is Ἑλένη Some thought it related to the moon (Selene Σελήνη), others attributed it as deriving from the noun ἑλένη meaning torch, and still others thought it might be connected to the root of *Venus*. Linda Lee Clader's (1979) investigations revealed connections to Indo-European etymology putting forth candidates such as a form of the

> root *wel, "to turn, roll" [3](or from that root's sense "to cover, enclose" — compare Varuna, Veles), or of *sel- "to flow, run". . . . would allow comparison to the Vedic Sanskrit Saraṇyū, a character who is abducted in Rigveda 10.17.2. Saraṇyū means "swift" and is derived from the adjective saraṇa ("running", "swift"), the feminine of which is saraṇā; this is in every sound cognate with Ἑλένα, ... The possible connection of Helen's name to ἑλένη ("torch"), as noted above, may also support the relationship of her name to Vedic svaranā ("the shining one"). [Wikipedia, 2013, Helen of Troy]

The Low German and Middle Dutch *helen* means to heal, as in *hale* or *whole*. The Oxford English Dictionary (2013, online) defines it as a transitive verb: "To make whole or sound in bodily condition; to free from disease or ailment, restore to health or soundness; to cure (of a disease or wound)." *Helen* was used as early as 1275 (OED, 2013, *Helen*). A popular website that provides histories behind names, cites various versions in different languages and reported that Helen is probably the feminine of *helenos* "the bright one" (Behind the Name, 2013, *Helen*).

Annie. Annie Sullivan was born and baptized as Johanna, but always called Anne or Annie. The feminine form of John, which is the "English form of *Iohannes*, the Latin form of the Greek name *Ιωαννης (Ioannes)*, itself derived from the Hebrew name יוֹחָנָן *(Yochanan)* meaning 'YAHWEH is gracious.'" Anne comes from the French form of ANNA. Imported to England in the 13th-century, it was also commonly spelled *Ann*, which derives from the Greek and Latin *Anna* which comes from the Hebrew Hannah, meaning "grace or graciously"[Etymology Online, Anne, Hannah]

APPENDIX E: GROF AND TARNAS BIRTH PROCESS AND PLANETARY ARCHETYPES

THE BIRTH PROCESS	PLANETARY ARCHETYPES
BPM I: PRIMAL UNION WITH MOTHER— AMNIOTIC UNIVERSE AND COSMIC UNITY	**NEPTUNE**
Intrauterine environment: tropical paradise / good womb, oceanic Apollonian ecstasy / cosmic unity / heaven and paradise / nature at its best / *unio mystica* / experiences of being a sea creature, whale, dolphin, fish, etcetera. *Also bad womb experiences (attempted abortions, toxic reactions, fetal crises, mother's emotional upheaval) universal threat, paranoid ideation, being poisoned, encounter with demonic forces and evil.	Transcendent ideal reality, imagination and spiritual, ocean of consciousness, dissolves boundaries / escapist fantasy, illusion, deception, *maya*, divine play, mystical bliss, madness and mysticism / thirst for transcendence, experience flow of love and compassion. Governs myth, dreams, symbols, watery things / narcissus, absorbed in own reflection, drug addict / selflessness and unworldliness / increased intuition, sensitive to everything, but projects onto others, too, weakening ego.
BPM II: COSMIC ENGULFMENT AND NO EXIT OR HELL— EXPULSION FROM PARADISE, FIRST STAGE OF BIRTH	**SATURN**
Womb before cervix opens: cosmic engulfment, immense physical and psychological suffering / helpless victim, hopelessness, no end situation / images of hell / feeling of entrapment, agonizing guilt and inferiority, apocalyptic view of world / concentration camps / meaninglessness, oppression, difficulty breathing / devouring or entangling archetypal monsters / giant spiders or boa constrictors / dark night of soul begins, abysmal despair, starvation, jail, whirlpool.	Limit, structure, necessity, material world, time, tradition, aging, death, ending of things / contracts and inhibits, oppresses and opposes, limits but strengthens, grounds, forges, gives gravitas to soul / defines, principle of judgment, planet of karma / cuts off from primal union, consuming power of time, stands alone and knows solitude, superego, inner judge / guardians of threshold / skeleton / disciplines and orders existence.
BPM III: DEATH-REBIRTH STRUGGLE— PROPULSION THROUGH THE BIRTH CANAL	**PLUTO**
Birth canal / death-rebirth struggle / tremendous pressure / volcanic forces / titanic life and death struggle / aggressive and sadomasochistic aspects, scatology, pornography, especially bondage / torture, war and bloody revolutions / intense sexual orgiastic feelings: agony and ecstasy fusion / demonic aspects, Walpurgis Night, satanic / vital threat, extreme danger, observer or identification with aggressor or victim / feelings of suffocation, anoxia, crushing and choking / Dionysian ecstasy, carnivals and harems / dying and being reborn / adrenaline rush, amusement park rides / mythological hero encounters, ego death / element of fire, phoenix rising, / death-rebirth deities.	Primordial energy, universal life force, impels evolution and transformation, elemental force, Dionysian energy, power itself / compels, empowers, overwhelms, transforms, destroys resurrects, death and rebirth / upheaval, breakdown & decay, purifying fire of catharsis, underworld, dark mysterious terrifying reality beneath surface / volcanic eruption / primal libido and aggression / id, boiling cauldron of instincts.
BPM IV: DEATH-REBIRTH EXPERIENCE— TERMINATION OF THE BIRTH PROCESS	**URANUS**
Crowning, final expulsion from birth canal / death-rebirth experience / ego death, total annihilation/union with the goddess / identification or encounter with Christ, Shiva, other deities / epiphanic ecstasy / expansion of space, illuminative ecstasy/radiant light, beautiful colors, or white & golden light / feelings of rebirth & redemption / escape from dangerous circumstance / humanitarian tendencies / divine epiphany / enormous decompression, expansion of space / visions of gigantic halls / peacock feathers / appreciation of simple way of life / sensory enhancement / brotherly feelings / manic activity, grandiose feelings, transition to elements of BPM I.	Change, freedom, rebellion, revolution / unexpected phenomenon, sudden surprises, insights, awakenings, breakthroughs, sudden breakup of established structure / invention & technology / individualism & originality / exciting, electric / Prometheus stole fire from heavens, rebellion against gods for greater freedom / changeability, restlessness, new experience / mediates creativity & innovation, eccentricity, genius, personal & cultural breakthrough / radical expansion of horizons.

APPENDIX F: HELENE SHULMAN'S (1997) COMPLEX SYSTEMS MODEL

Overview of the Text Diagrams

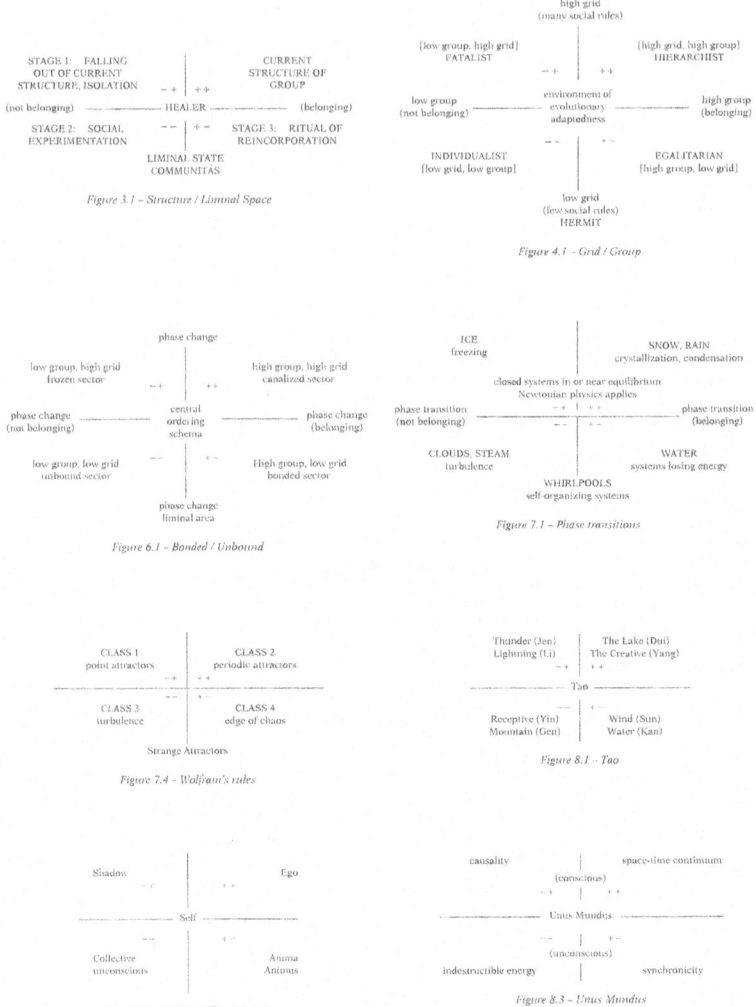

© Shulman, H. (1997) *Living at the edge of chaos: Complex systems in culture and psyche.* Zurich, Switzerland: Daimon Verlag.

APPENDIX G: GERONTOMORPHY/PEDAMORPHY TABLE

Gerontomorphy		Pedamorphy
Planetary Archetype: SATURN		**Planetary Archetypes: Pluto, occasionally Neptune & Uranus, too**
Look old when they are young	E	Retain youthful characteristics into adulthood
Adults	D	Children
Rigid in body and behavior	G	Soft bodied and variable behavior
Specialized	E	Generalized
Better adapted to the past		Better adapted to the future
Heavily armored	Of	Vulnerable to attack
Rough, cold, dry		Smooth, warm, moist
Asymmetrical	C	Symmetrical
Formed at birth	H	Metamorphic
Mortal, nonregenerative	A	Immortal, regenerative
Isolative	O	Congregative
Localized	S	Ubiquitious
Resistant to behavioural change		Ductile
Resistant to structural change	E	Speciative
Huxley: individuation

Westcott: differentiation diversification — separate life from its beginnings | D | Huxley: aggregation,

Wescott: coordination, reunification — return life to that which in its beginnings was most fruitful |
Left brain	G	Right brain
Specialized creodes organizing channels of function	E	Integrative networks, limbic system, closer to edge of chaos, emotion, attachment, love, territoriality, image formation, mythological thinking, sleep and dreaming all without conscious control. Busy ancient creative (Shulman, p. 128)
Thinking—cuts, categorizes, separates, "simpler" than feeling		Feeling—joins, connects, links, more complex
Cold brain	Of	Hot brain
Attention focusing capacity		Relaxation of attention and lowering of mental energy "abaissment du niveu mental"

Gerontomorphy		Pedamorphy
Planetary Archetype: SATURN		**Planetary Archetypes: Pluto, occasionally Neptune & Uranus, too**
Ergotropic—vigilant—fight/flight	C	Tropotropic—rest, calm, relaxation
Ego—fixed categories of space/time, is skeletal, structural and inhibition in its function, armored and defensive of its categories, independent, isolated and localizes everything into space/time	H	Unconscious—not sharp either/or categories, blurs things together, more hermaphoroditic, ubiquitous and creates a union of opposites, carried by emotions.
Ego control	A	Spontaneous impulse
Ego consciousness separating from integrating function. Separation/detatchment and agonizing confrontation through opposition that produces consciousness and insight	O	Merging, emotional relatedness and possibility of dreams and fantasies, integrative
Assimilation (Piaget in Montagu)	S	Accommodation (Piaget in Montagu)
Causality		Synchronicity
Rational	E	Irrational
Order/structure	D	Chaos/liminality
Yang/logos/masculine	G	Yin/eros/feminine
Wise old man/woman archetype	E	Child archetype
Convergent thinking (Montagu)		Divergent thinking (Montagu)
Rote learning—banking education (Montagu—Freire)	Of	Experiential learning—informal education (Montagu—Freire)
Conscious mind = adult		Unconscious organizing structure=Self = divine child=counterpole of the world
Normal waking consciousness	C	Holotropic Nonordinary states of consciousness (Grof) — Healing rituals which induce merger, trance states, access hidden healing energies
Out of balance	H	Contains secret source of balance, associated with divine child Divine child mediator, bringer of healing, (makes one whole), unites opposites—Healer accommodates both rational and irrational
Devouring gods who sacrifice their young	A	Asclepius' with extended family
One-sided	O	Between banks (Anzaldua)
Out of play	S	In play

© Pohn, 2006-2013, based on Shulman (1997) & Montague (1983)

APPENDIX H: EXTENDED EXCURSION INTO INITIATIONS— ETERNALLY DIPPING INTO THE CHAOTIC REALM

In this excursion, we dive more deeply into the waters of chaos, to more deeply partake in these eternally recurring dynamics that are at the heart of transformation. After exploring how rites of passage work in relation to the eternal return, we will take time to explore the liminal nature of thresholds, and finally explore how chaos theory fits into this picture—and how this process is actually related to archetypal dynamics themselves.

How Rites Of Passage Work— Their Relation To The Eternal Return

To reiterate what was said before, rites of passage are essentially engines of the transformation process. Through ritual they bring us back to a chaotic place, so that we can shed the old outworn order, renew ourselves and come to a new place—a new order, a new identity. Rites of passage are a ritualized form of the transformation process and bring us back to origins, and hence partake in the eternal return.

"The eternal return is a cyclical recurrence of what has been before, the periodic reversion to a timeless beginning. . . . It is repetition, and *anakuklosis*, eternal return" (Eliade, 1954/1991, p. 89). The moon appearing, waxing and waning, its disappearance and reappearance every month is a prime example of the eternal return, and this motif is also found in many myths—Christ, Demeter-Persephone, Osiris. This lunar structure is also seen in rites of renewal and initiation, as well as the death and rebirth mysteries. Van Eenwyk (1997) noted that this death rebirth theme is especially evident in rites of passage, "which seek to recapitulate the events that occurred at the beginning of time, when the chaotic deathlike state that existed before creation yielded to the emerging complexity of creation" (p. 159). This eternally returning pattern has a shadow side, it is like a never-ending merry go round that you where you cannot get off (Chapelle, 1993).

The only way to free oneself from this endless round is through an act of spiritual freedom, which Eliade (1952/1991) suggested we can use "this vision of infinite time, of the endless cycles of creations and destructions, this myth of the eternal return, as an 'instrument of knowledge' and as a means to liberation" (p. 68).

We can leap out of time and arrest its flow through paradox. Eliade (1952/1991) explained "the human condition is defined by the existence of opposites, and liberation from the human condition is equivalent to a non-conditioned state in which the opposites coincide" (p. 84). The paradoxical instant of enlightenment is compared in the Indian texts to lightning. The goal is then to transcend the opposites and polar tensions, and to unify the Real or to reintegrate the primordial One.

Jung (1988), when discussing a passage from *Thus Spoke Zarathustra*, about a river flowing back into itself, explained that the river "returns to the place where it started and so forms something like a circle—even if interrupted by many meanderings" (p. 1340) and then went on to explain:

> the idea that life, or the life of the psyche more probably, is an eternal return, a river which seeks its own source and not the goal, the end. It returns to the source, thereby producing a circular movement which brings back whatever has been. Here we can use another nice Greek term the apokatastasis, which means the return of everything that has been lost, a complete restoration of whatever has been. (p. 1341)

Chapelle (1993) in discussing the eternal return in *Nietzsche and Psychoanalysis* wrote that *Zarathustra* was Nietzsche's myth of the eternal return and that "to think eternal return thus comes to mean to think transformation" (p. 38). Chapelle also talked at length about the repetition compulsion, transference, the uncanny, Rank's double, and synchronicity as instances of the eternal return. Depth psychology itself, with its focus on origins—whether personal, in Freud's case, or archetypal, as in the cases of Jung and Hillman are all examples of this. Rank's work on the birth of the hero, and Grof's (1975, 2000) work with the perinatal and transpersonal dimensions of the psyche, combined with Tarnas's (2006) work surrounding outer planetary transits are similarly focused on this eternally recurring pattern. Jung's myth of the creation of consciousness, the individuation process, and the Job archetype are also, all variations of the eternal return theme.

Chapelle (1993) explained that for Freud, the compulsion to repeat, the "compulsion of destiny," was connected with psychological fate and the Greek Goddess of Necessity—Ananke:

> Etymology provides images of the ways in which the experience of necessity has been described: narrow, throat, surround, embrace,

strangle, ring, constrict, to wind around the neck as the neckband of a slave, chain, suffocation, chain-formed necklace, fetters lid around the neck of prisoners, necklace, cord binding yoked oxen. Repetition compulsions, then by virtue of their relation to psychological necessity, are the ways in which man is bound, enslaved, yoked, chained, fettered and fixated to personal destiny. In light of what we said earlier about the metaphoric nature of the compulsion to repeat, we can now say that the repetition compulsion fixates man into a personalized metaphor that must be enacted again and again. (Chapelle, 1993, pp. 116- 117)

This description exactly matches BPM II in Grof's cartography of the psyche, the first stage of birth, where the contractions have begun but the cervix has not yet open. Repetition compulsions are a vicious circle version of the eternal return, where there is no way out. This is what has been happening in Helen's life so far before Annie's arrival. This is the pattern that she and her family are caught in and that Annie is seeking to break. Stephen Gilligan (1997) in *The Courage to Love* explicated principals and practices of sponsorship, a mature loving human presence, without which the pattern continues to iterate:

The problem is that an unintegrated response repeats itself until integrated. On this point, nature seems eternally patient and forever cruel. It may take years, even generations, but a negative experience returns until human presence is brought to touch it with love and acceptance and integrate it. (p. 12)

Chapelle found that we fulfill our destiny by the paradoxical process of becoming who we are through the process of *convalescence*. We repress or forget what is intolerable to us and the work of therapy or any transformative work is then to convalesce, to remember or recollect ourselves:

Thus convalescence is related to nostalgia, the longing to return home, to where one belongs. Taken broadly, to convalesce refers to the return to one's origin, to the heart and core of one's identity. It means, in the end, to return to who one was and is and will be. Convalescence has to do with the fulfillment of personal destiny. (1993, pp. 163-164)

So it seems that the eternal return, like Sam I am, from *Green Eggs and Ham* (Seuss, 1960), keeps on repeating until you accept your destiny and become who you are, by returning home to yourself.

To reiterate what was mentioned earlier—no one seemed to consciously realize that the garden house, was actually the house of Helen's own beginnings: the same house that Helen lived in as a baby and young child, both before and after her illness. Indeed, it bears repeating that William Gibson, author of the play and screenplay did not realize that the location of Helen's initiatory incubation was the self same house, until he visited Tuscumbia in 2008 (Gibson, 2008, interview)! It is not known whether Annie knew this or not, in Helen's biography (1903/2003), or other writings, Helen also never identifies it as such, and other biographers did not either.

To reiterate, Annie, in separating Helen from her parents and taking Helen to a new environment, is essentially reenacting a ritual rite of passage, although unconsciously. This age old vehicleof transformation—of separation, liminality, and return—is one of the major keys allow Annie to work her alchemical magic. Annie now has a proper container in which to teach Helen. With the *uncanny synchronicity* of Helen's rite of passage occurring in the actual physical place of her origins, we will now leave the eternal return and step over the threshold into the liminality phase while we can.

Liminality And Thresholds Again

Again, *liminality*, the transition phase of rites of passage come from the Latin *limen*, meaning in between, which van Gennep (1909/1960) noted and it bears repeating, means threshold, a doorway, or entranceway.

In my dissertation I wrote extensively about the origins of *threshold*, as liminality has been an ongoing theme in my work:

Thresholds are also a piece of hardwood or stone at the bottom of a doorway. Separating grains or seeds from their stalks, husks, etc. it is called *threshing*, which is usually done by slapping the stalks against something. The Indo-European root for threshold is *ter II*: with some derivatives referring to twisting, boring, or drilling and piercing, and other referring to the rubbing of cereal grain to remove the husks, and thence to the process of threshing either by the trampling of oxen or by flailing with flails, to rub, turn. *Thresh* and *threshold* come from the Germanic *threskan* to thresh or to tread (AHD, 2000, p. 2051), while other derivatives of *ter II* are from the Greek *tornos*, meaning a tool for drawing a circle, lathe, and the Latin *tornare*, to turn as in a lathe. From *tornos* and *tornare* come words like *tornado, return, turn, detour* and *attorney* (Shipley, 1988, pp. 407-408). By looking at the etymology of threshold, we can anticipate that the stage of liminality, is not always pleasant. But grains do get set free of their old structures when they are threshed and then new things can be made from them or they can be planted and the cycle will continue. (Pohn, 2006)

Again, it bears repeating that Helen's old way of being, the old order [which is anything but orderly], needs to die, but it is not going down without a fight. Helen's thrashing around like a typhonic tornado clearly shows the chaotic nature of this stage.

The interval of liminality, constitutes a moment of "pure potentiality" where the past is momentarily negated, suspended, or abrogated and the future has not yet begun" and in this instant, "everything, as it were, trembles in the balance." (Turner, 1982, p. 44)

Turner (1982) explained that as liminality is an ambiguous state, it "may be for many the acme of insecurity, the breakthrough of chaos into cosmos of disorder into order, [rather] than the milieu of creative interhuman or transhuman satisfactions and achievements." Although the structures of society inhibit us in certain ways, they also "provide security," while "liminality may be the scene of disease, despair, death, suicide, the breakdown without compensatory replacement of the normative, well-defined social ties and bonds." The bottom line is that "liminality is both more creative and more destructive than the structural norm" (pp. 46-47).

During liminality, anti-structure, a breaking down of structure occurs, which is Plutonic in nature. During rites of passage, this breaking down of structure occurs within the group of initiands, whose condition Turner described:

Initiands are often considered to be dark invisible, like the sun or moon in eclipse, or the moon between phases, at the "dark of the moon"; . . . Some of the practices . . . are instruction in a secret language, various non-verbal symbolic genres such as dancing, painting. . . with symbolic patterns and structures which amount to teaching about the structure of the cosmos and their culture as a part and product of it . . . liminality may involve a complex sequence of episodes in sacred space-time, and it may also include subversive and ludic (or playful) events. "The 'antistructure' represents the latent system of potential alternatives from which novelty will arise when contingencies in the normative system require it. . . . It is the precursor of innovative normative forms. It is the source of new culture [pp. 18-19]" (1982, p. 28)

During the time that she in in the garden house with Annie, Helen learns a secret language, and nonverbal symbolic gestures, as well as learning through playful events. But that cannot happen until after Annie reestablishes contact with Helen.

Being trapped alone with Annie, in an unfamiliar place, with no way out, pushes Helen far from equilibrium. This perturbation, the is attempt to introduce order, leads the situation into more chaos, deterministic chaos, which sends the system far from equilibrium and in the end, a transformation will occur bringing the system to a new order.

As previously mentioned, rituals take place takes place in a sacred space that has been specifically marked out and is away from the normal everyday life. Like the retort in alchemy and the cocoon or chrysalis which moths and butterflies construct, this separate space or structure or place is necessary because the process of transformation is often messy. Jung (1934/1954) himself described what a difficult and costly thing the journey towards becoming more conscious is, and also said:

> We also are part and parcel of this amazing nature, and, like it, carry within us the seeds of the unpredictable.

> Our personality develops in the course of life from germs that are hard or impossible to discern, and it is only our deeds that reveal who we are. . . . Just as the child must develop in order to be educated, so the personality must begin to sprout before it can be trained. And this is where the danger begins. For we are handling something unpredictable, we do not know how and in what direction the budding personality will develop, and we have learned enough of nature and the world to be somewhat chary of both.

> . . . The development of personality from the germ-state to full consciousness is at once a charisma and a curse, because its first fruit is the conscious and unavoidable segregation of the single individual from the undifferentiated and unconscious herd. This means isolation, and there is no more comforting word for it. Neither family nor society nor position can save him from this fate, . . . The development of personality is a favour that must be paid for dearly. (pp. 172-173, paras.

289-294)

In the natural world, the process takes place instinctually. In humans it is much more helpful to have someone to guide or sponsor you. Because something has to die, an old identity, or way of being, this necessitates a descent into the underworld and so having a guide or teacher to assist is of utmost importance. Jung (1946/1954) emphasized the importance of this when he said:

> So long as you feel human contact, the atmosphere of mutual contact, there is no danger; and even if you have to face the terrors of insanity, or the shadowy menace of suicide, there is still that area of human faith, that certainty of understanding and of being understood, no matter how black the night. (p. 97, para. 181)

Van Eenwyk (1997) noted that the oscillations back and forth between opposites, are often felt as suffering. Stephen Gilligan (1997), who used Annie Sullivan as a model for sponsorship concurred, and provides a clue to how to navigate this dark place. He noted that Self Relations assumes :

> that suffering is a major way in which life awakens within a person. Something is trying to wake up, but it needs human presence and sponsorship to be realized. . . . Self-Relations emphasizes that perhaps the greatest gift of human consciousness is the capacity to transform experience. Thus we look to develop ways to accept and attend to symptoms as gifts, albeit "terrible gifts" that we would not wish on our worst enemies. We practice accepting such gifts as a means to realize a deeper understanding and connection to self and world. (p. 54)

The guide, psychopomp, shaman, or teacher has been there, and they know the territory—and will keep the process on track and keep the initiate from getting lost in the liminal landscape, which is often intense and frightening.

Annie, as we have seen, is very familiar with this territory, having essentially grown up here. Annie spent the majority of her formative years until she was fourteen years old in the liminal landscape of illness, death, more death, abandonment and more death and the to top it all off, the traumas of Tewksbury; and she was almost literally blind and in physical pain most of the time.

How Chaos Theory Figures Into The Equation.

In *Archetypes and Strange Attractors*, Van Eenwyk (1997) noted that there are parallels between the in-between, liminal, threshold nature in the transition stages of these rites, and the fractal nature and dimensions of chaos.

> The oscillatory dynamics (tension of opposites) that generate myths and rituals enliven them as well, by bringing up new possibilities. Thus creation occurs over and over again. So the eternal return is an iterative dynamic: it allows the present to be fed back it the original equation. (pp. 113-114)

Jung felt that there were two kinds of dynamics operating in the psyche: cyclical and developmental. The cyclical processes, which Van Eenwyk (1997) called the *synchronic* aspects of individuation "constantly repeat themselves through the establishment of the tension of opposites, their resolution and the subsequent appearance of new tensions between the resolution and new possibilities." The developmental processes that Van Eenwyk termed *diachronic* "build upon the synchronic dynamics and move through time . . . they begin somewhere and end up somewhere else" (p. 16).

Van Eenwyk (1997) explicated "while all archetypal processes generate feedback dynamics, *the eternal return is the epitome of all such aspects of archetypal processes. It is the archetype of archetypal dynamics, so to speak*" (p. 114 emphasis added)! Van Eenwyk also revealed that not only does the myth of the eternal return symbolize "creation and rejuvenation," but "creation and rejuvenation are themselves symbolic of a basic characteristic of dynamic systems. In the new mythology of chaos theory, this is imagined as recurring cycles of chaos and order" (p. 114).

Van Eenwyk (1997) also explored the dynamics of symbols in depth. Symbols are very complex and have their feet in both worlds, consciousness and the unconscious, and mediate between them by participating in both (p. 111). Symbols are liminal, occurring between individual and environment. They are "interfaces not only "between synchronic and diachronic dynamics, but between psychic structure and personal experience, between past and present, order and chaos" (pp. 88-89). Since symbols are produced by the psyche, their dynamics will reflect the dynamics of the psyche; because we cannot observe archetypes directly, we observe symbols.

The same is true of strange attractors, as Stewart (2002) noted: we cannot observe them directly, only their observables (p. 130). Symbols are transformers, they "transform the process of perception" (Van Eenwyk, 1997, p. 102), helping the psyche to "form itself by drawing it to perspectives and experiences that promote growth" (p. 85). As they transcend categories, symbols take us to places that are difficult to define. They are "stargates that point beyond themselves" (pp. 70-71) and have a compelling influence on us as "they mobilize our psychic energy" (p. 90), and thus they lead us through life. Symbols, as Jung believed, give us access to and expose us to what is absent in our lives, which is not easy, because it "involves a descent into the unconscious, a 'dark night of the soul' on the course of the 'hero's journey.' In short it is an encounter with the shadow" (p. 85).

Van Eenwyk elaborated: "When the ego gains access to the unconscious through symbols, the unconscious gains access to the ego. Thus begins the process of fragmentation, dismemberment, and chaos" (p. 115). He described the process of archetypal dynamics as a dance or play of opposites as it were, between consciousness and the unconscious going back and forth, first one way and then back around the next. This oscillation is an iterative process, and these synchronic dynamics are what fuel the psyche and lead to psychological growth.

Just as in chaos theory, where we get new patterns emerging from chaos, so too, with symbols, at some point something new springs from something old, which as Jung noted was the result of the underlying archetype. Van Eenwyk convincingly demonstrated the usefulness of chaos theory in understanding Jung's ideas.

While discussing the oscillating nature of the tension of opposites, Van Eenwyk (1997) observed that the oscillations can create a cascade of bifurcations that lead to chaos. He further discussed Jung's familiarity with this phenomenon, noting that Jung

> considered it to be an integral part of the individuation process. He cited precedents in alchemy, shamanism, and mystical experience, all of which contain references to fragmentation, dismemberment, even "the return to chaos." Furthermore we know that when a cascade continues to intensify, patterns that were once part of the original tension of opposites may again appear amid the chaos. Jung described this aspect of psychodynamics as a descent into the chaos of the unconscious that

could lead to increased psychological functioning. (p. 112)

The eternal return is the prototypical example of the descent to chaos to create more order. Van Eenwyk (1997) noted that symbols, as the mechanism through which psychological growth takes place:

> move us from the security of the known to the limitless potential for being. They offer us the opportunity, ever again to participate in the eternal return. The ease with which we are able to entertain the chaotic experience of symbols determines the ease with which new order can enter our lives" (p. 171).

Jung (1988) in discussing Nietzsche's *Zarathustra* said "the eternal return belongs with the symbol of the ring, the ring of rings, the ring of eternal Recurrence . . . now this ring is the idea of totality and it is the idea of individuation naturally, an individuation symbol" (p. 1044). Van Eenwyk (1997) noted that individuation is a repetitive process that "constantly destabilizes us so that we can take advantages of potentials for growth that we might not otherwise see. No wonder it feels so chaotic" (p. 36). Van Eenwyk also explained that underlying all rebirth symbolism is the transcendent function, and quoting Jung, remarked that the transcendent function refers to transitions from one attitude to another, and is not used in the metaphysical sense (p. 38).

REFERENCE LIST

*Note: References to OED refer to the Oxford English Dictionary. (2013). Retrieved from www.oed.com. The word that is looked up will be specified in the citation. The same convention applies to Wikipedia references.

Aaron, P. (Director). (2009). *The miracle worker* [1979 Television Movie/DVD]. Hollywood, CA: NBC/Shout Factory.

Amar, S. (2007). *Bedside dream dictionary.* New York, NY: Skyhorse.

American Federation for the Blind. (2010). Ask Keller February 2005. Retrieved from Braille Bug http://www.braillebug.org/askkeller.asp?issueid=20052

AHD. (2000). Appendix I: Indo-European roots. In *The American heritage dictionary of the English language* (4th ed.). http://www.bartleby.com/61/roots/IE117.html

Behind the Name. (2013). Behind the name: The etymology and history of first names. Retrieved from http://www.behindthename.com/name/helen

Bettelheim, B. (1991). Master teacher and prodigious pupil. In *Freud's Vienna and other essays* (pp. 156-165). New York, NY: Vintage Books.

Bhansali, S. L. (Director). (2005a). *Black* [Feature film]. Applause Bhansali / Yash Raj Films.

Bhansali, S. L. (2005b). *Black* [Movie Trailer]. Retrieved from http://black.indiatimes.com/main.htm

Bion, W. R. (1962). *Learning from experience.* PEP Archive.

Bond, D. S. (2003). The archetype of renewal: Psychological reflections on the aging, death and rebirth of the king. Toronto, Ontario: Inner City Books.

Braddy, N. (1933). *Annie Sullivan Macy: The story behind Helen Keller.* Garden City, NY: Doubleday, Doran.

Briggs, J., & Peat, F. D. (1989). Turbulent mirror: An illustrated guide to chaos theory and the science of wholeness. New York, NY: Harper & Row.

Campbell, J. (1988). *The power of myth.* New York, NY: Doubleday.

Casey, E. S. (1993). *Getting back into place: Toward a renewed understanding of the place-world.* Bloominton: University of Indiana Press.

Casey, E. S. (1997). *The fate of place: A philosophical history.* Los Angeles: University of California Press.

CelebrateBoston.com (2013). *Tewksbury tornado of 1857.* Retrieved from http://www.celebrateboston.com/disasters/tewksbury-tornado-1857.htm

Chalquist, C. (2007). *Terrapsychology: Reengaging the soul of place.* New Orleans, LA: Spring Journal Books.

Chapelle, D. (1993). *Nietzsche and psychoanalysis.* Albany: State University of New York Press.

Chevalier, J. and Gheerbrandt, A. (1996). *The Penguin dictionary of symbols* (J. Buchanan-Brown, Trans.). New York, NY: Penguin Books.

Chiron. (2013). Theoi.com website. Retrieved from http://www.theoi.com/Georgikos/KentaurosKheiron.html

Clemens, S. L. (1937). Helen Keller and Napoleon: Two most interesting people of the Nineteenth Century. In *A.A.S.A. Official Report of the American Association of School Administrators* (p. 65).

Clemons, S. L. (1903). Letter to Helen Keller- March 17, 1903. *Letters of Note.* Retrieved from http://www.lettersofnote.com/2012/05/bulk-of-all-human-utterances-is.html

Columbia University. (2012). *Orphic Mysteries. The Columbia electronic encyclopedia,* 6th ed.). Retrieved from http://www.infoplease.com/encyclopedia/society/orphic-mysteries.html

Conforti, M. (1999). *Field, form and fate: Patterns in mind, nature and psyche.* Woodstock, CT: Spring.

Conforti, M. (2007). *Thresholds experiences: The archetype of beginnings.* Assisi Institute Press.

Conforti, M. (2010). The four parts of a dream. Retrieved from http://www.experiencefestival.com/wp/article/the-four-parts-of-a-dream

Davachi, L. Kiefer, T., Rock, D., & Rock, L. (2011). Learning that lasts through AGES. *Neuroleadership Journal 3.* Retrieved from *www.davidrock.net/resources/*

Davidson, G. (1971). *Dictionary of angels.* New York, NY: Free Press.

De Bont, J. (Director). (1996). *Twister* [Feature Film]. United States: Warner Brothers.

De Bont, J. (Director). (2003). *Lara Croft and the cradle of life* [Feature Film]. United States: Paramount.

Dickens, C. (1842). *American notes.* Retrieved from http://www.gutenberg.org/files/675/675-h/675-h.htm

Dickenson, E. (2013). *There is a pain so utter.* Retrieved from http://en.wikipedia.org/wiki/There_is_a_pain_%E2%80%94_so_utter_%E2%80%94

Doors, The. (1967). *Break on through* (to the other side) [Song/Album]. United States: Elecktra Records.

Dreamtation. (2013). Spoon. Retrieved from http://www.dreamtation.com/docs/4659.htm

Edinger, E. (1984). *The creation of consciousness: Jung's myth for modern man.* Toronto, Canada: Inner City Books.

Eliade, M. (1991). *Images and symbols: Studies in religious symbolism* (P. Mairet, Trans.). Princeton, NJ: Princeton University Press. (Original work published 1952)

Eliade, M. (1991). *The myth of the eternal return or, cosmos and history* (W. Trask, Trans.). Princeton, NJ: Princeton University Press. (Original work published 1954)

Eliade, M. (1995). *Rites and symbols of initiation: The mysteries of birth and rebirth* (W. Trask, Trans.). Woodstock, CT: Spring. (Original work published 1958)

Ellenberger, H. F. (1970). *The discovery of the unconscious: The history and evolution of dynamic psychiatry.* New York, NY: Basic Books.

Eros, (2013). Theoi.com website. Retrieved from http://www.theoi.com/Protogenos/Eros.html

Etymology online. (2013). Anne to Anna. Retrieved from http://www.etymonline.com/index.php?term=Anna&allowed_in_frame=0

Etymology online. (2013). Orient. Retrieved from http://www.etymonline.com/index.php?allowed_in_frame=0&search=orient&searchmode=term

Etymology online. (2013). Origin. Retrieved from
http://www.etymonline.com/index.php?allowed_in_frame=0&search=origin&searchmode=term

Fleming, V. (director). (1939). *The wizard of Oz* [DVD]. United States: MGM/UA Home Video.

Freud, S. (1997). *Dora: An analysis of a case of hysteria*. New York, NY: Touchstone. (Original work published 1905)

Frost, R. (1916). The road not taken. In *Mountain interval*. Retrieved December 1, 2005 from
http://www.americanpoems.com/poets/robertfrost/theroadnot.shtml

Geisel, T. (1960). *Green eggs and ham*. New York, NY: Beginner Books/Random House.

Gibson, W. (1959). Prefatory: A hit and a flop. In *Two plays and a preface: The miracle worker and Dinny and the witches* (pp. 3-22). New York, NY: Athenaeum.

Gibson, W. (1961). *The miracle worker* [Screenplay, Revision 5/8/61]. Unpublished.

Gibson, W. (2008). Interview at Helen Keller Birthplace. Retrieved from
http://www.youtube.com/watch?v=zqeMxBL28gM

Gibson, W. (2008). *The miracle worker: A play*. New York, NY: Scribner. (0riginal work published 1956).

Gilligan, S. G. (1997), *The courage to love: Principles and practices of self-relations psychotherapy*. New York, NY: W. W. Norton.

Grof, S. (1975). *Realms of the human unconscious: Observations from LSD research*. New York, NY: Viking Press.

Grof, S. (1998). *The cosmic game: Explorations on the frontiers of human consciousness*. Albany: State University of New York Press.

Grof, S. (2000). *Psychology of the future: Lessons from modern consciousness research*. Albany: State University of New York Press.

Grof, S. (2006). Psyche and cosmos: Holotropic states of consciousness, archetypal psychology, and transit astrology. Retrieved from
http://www.cosmicplay.net/artpdfs/Grof%20-%20Psyche%20and%20Cosmos.pdf

Grof, S. & Grof, C. (1990). *The stormy search for the self: A guide to personal growth through transformational crisis*. New York, NY: G.B. Putnam & Sons.

Grof, S., & Tarnas, R. (2002, March 17-22). *Psyche and cosmos* [Seminar]. Big Sur, CA: Esalen Institute.

Hallstrom, L. (Director). (2000). *Chocolat.* [DVD] United States: Buena Vista Home Entertainment.

Hamilton, N. (Director). (2005). *Unconquered: Helen Keller in her story and VISIONS in silent darkness* [Documentary/DVD]. United States: Nobility Films.

Hansen, G. P. (2001). *The trickster and the paranormal.* Philadelphia, PA: Xlibris.

Hermann, D. (1999). *Helen Keller: A life.* Chicago, IL: University of Chicago Press.

Hickok, L. A. (1961). *The touch of magic: The story of Helen Keller's great teacher Anne Sullivan Macy.* New York, NY: Dodd, Mead.

Hiller, A. (Director). (1979). *The Inlaws* [Feature Film]. United States: Warner Brothers.

Hillman, J. (1983a). *Archetypal psychology: A brief account.* Woodstock, CT: Spring.

Hillman, J. (1983b). *Healing fictions.* Woodstock, CT: Spring.

Hillman, J. (1992). *Revisioning psychology.* New York, NY: Harper Perennial. (Original work published 1975)

Hinshelwood, R. D. (1991). *A Dictionary of Kleinian thought* (2nd ed.). Northvale, NJ: Jason Aronson.

Iliades, C. (2013). How stress affects digestion. Retrieved from http://www.everydayhealth.com/health-report/better-digestion/how-stress-affects-digestion.aspx

Jaffe, A. (1975). *The myth of meaning: Jung and the expansion of consciousness* (R.C.F. Hull, Trans.). New York, NY: Penguin.

Jewels For Me. (2013). Garnet. Retrieved from http://www.jewelsforme.com/garnet-history.asp

Jones, T., & Schmidt, H. (1990). *The fantasticks* (30th anniversary ed.). New York, NY: Applause Books. (Original work published in 1960)

Jung, C. G. (1972). On the psychology of the unconscious (2nd ed.) (R. F. C. Hull, Trans.). In H. Read et al. (Series Eds.), *The collected works of C. G. Jung* (Vol. 7, pp. 3-119). Princeton, NJ: Princeton University Press. (Original work published 1917 / revised 1943)

Jung, C. G. (1976). Symbols of transformation (2nd ed.) (R. F. C. Hull, Trans.). In H. Read et al. (Series Eds.), *The collected works of C. G. Jung* (Vol. 5). Princeton, NJ: Princeton University Press. (Original work published 1912 / revised 1952)

Jung, C. G. (1976). *The portable Jung* (R.C. F. Hull, Trans., J. Campbell, Ed.). New York, NY: Penguin Books.

Jung, C. G. (1981). The transcendent function (2nd ed.) (R. F. C. Hull, Trans.). In H. Read et al. (Series Eds.), *The collected works of C. G. Jung* (Vol. 8, pp. 67-92). Princeton, NJ: Princeton University Press. (Original paper written 1916 / revised 1957)

Jung, C. G. (1988). *Nietzsche's Zarathustra: Notes of the seminar given in 1934-1939* (J. Jarrett, Ed.). Princeton, NJ: Princeton University Press.

Jung, C. G. (1990). The psychology of the child archetype (2nd ed.) (R. F. C. Hull, Trans.). In H. Read et al. (Series Eds.), *The collected works of C. G. Jung* (Vol. 9, Part 1, pp. 151-181). Princeton, NJ: Princeton University Press. (Original work published 1951)

Karas, S. A. (1991). *The solstice evergreen.* Lower Lake, CA: Aslan.

Kaufmann, Y. (2009). The way of the image: The orientational approach to the psyche. New York, NY: Zahav Books.

Keller, H. (1903). *Optimism.* Retrieved from http://www.gutenberg.org/files/31622/31622-h/31622-h.htm

Keller, H. (1938). *Helen Keller's journal: 1936-1937.* New York, NY: Doubleday, Doran.

Keller, H. (1955). *Teacher: Anne Sullivan Macy.* Garden City, NY: Doubleday.

Keller, H. (1994). *Light in my darkness* (R. Silverman, Ed.). West Chester, PA: Chrysalis Books. (Original work published 1927).

Keller, H. (2003). *Story of my life: With supplementary accounts by Anne Sulivan her teacher and John Albert Macy* (Restored Classic, R. Shattuck, Ed., with D. Herman). New York, NY: W.W. Norton. (Original work published 1903)

Keller, H. (2011). *To live, to think, to hope: Inspirational quotes by Helen Keller* (M. B. Gordon, Ed.). Createspace.

Kerényi, K. (1988). *Athene: Virgin and mother in Greek religion* (M. Stein, Trans.). Woodstock, CT: Spring. (Original work published 1952)

Klages, M. (1989). *More wonderful than any fiction: The representation of Helen Keller* (Doctoral Dissertation). Retrieved from UMI Dissertations. AAT: 9011527.

Langs, R. (1983). *Unconscious Communication in Everyday Life.* New York: Jason Aronson.

Lash, J. P. (1980). *Helen and teacher: The story of Helen Keller and Anne Macy Sullivan.* Cambridge, MA: Perseus Press.

Lévi-Strauss, C. (1966). *The savage mind (La pensée sauvage).* Oxford, England: Oxford University Press. (Original work published in 1962)

Lininger, M. (Ed.). (2013. Spoons—Etiquette Scholar. Retrieved from http://www.etiquettescholar.com/dining_etiquette/table_setting/place_setting/flatware/spoons.html

Locomotive General. (2013). Civil war era steam locomotive the "General" specifications. Retrieved from http://www.locomotivegeneral.com/faq.html

Lucas, G. (Director). (1977). *Star wars* [Feature Film]. United States: Twentieth Century Fox.

Masters, E. L. (1938). *Mark Twain: A portrait.* New York, NY: Biblo & Tannen.

Mayes, C. (2010a). *Inside education: Depth psychology in teaching and learning.* Madison, WI: Atwood.

Mayes, C. (2010b). *The archetypal hero's journey in teaching and learning: A study in Jungian pedagogy.* Madison, WI: Atwood.

Mercer, 1954. Something's gotta give. Retrieved from http://www.sing365.com/music/lyric.nsf/Something%27s-Gotta-Give-lyrics-Frank-Sinatra/9DBAFCC787394D7B482569200004CE80

Mihajlovski, D. (2010). Defensive legends: The greatest defensive players in NBA history. Retrieved from http://bleacherreport.com/articles/519667-defensive-legendsthe-greatest-defensive-players-in-the-nba-history/

Miller, J. C. (2001). The transcendent function: The emergence of the third in depth psychology. *Dissertations Abstracts International, 62*(05), p. 2471B. (UMI No. 3015796).

Montague, A. (1983). *Growing young.* New York, NY: McGraw Hill.

Moore, T. (1992). *Care of the soul: A guide for cultivating depth and sacredness in everyday life.* New York, NY: HarperCollins.

Moustakas, C. L. (1990). *Heuristic research: design, methodology and applications.* Thousand Oaks, CA: Sage.

Neumann, E. (1990). *The child: The structure and dynamics of the nascent personality* (R. Manheim, Trans). Boston, MA: Shambala. (Original work published 1963)

Neumann, E. (1995). *The origins and history of consciousness* (R.C.F. Hull, Trans.). Princeton, NJ: Princeton University Press. (Original work published 1949).

Nielsen, K. (2009). *Beyond the miracle worker: The remarkable story of Anne Sullivan Macy and her extraordinary friendship with Helen Keller.* Boston, MA: Beacon Press.

Nietzsche, F. (1978). *Thus spoke Zarathustra: A book for none and all* (W. Kaufmann, Trans.). New York, NY: Penguin Books. (Original work published 1892)

O'Connell, M. & Airey, R. (2012). *Complete dictionary of signs and symbols.* London, UK: Anness.

Odajnyk, W. (1976). *Jung and politics: The political and social ideas of C. G. Jung.* New York, NY: Harper & Row.

Ogden, Thomas, H. (2004). On holding and containing, being and dreaming. *International Journal of Psycho-Analysis, 85* (6), 1349-1365.

Ormell, C. (1996). Eight metaphors of education. *Educational Research 38*(1), 67-75.

Penn, A. (Director). (1957*) The miracle worker* [Television Production]. Playhouse 90: Season 1, Episode 19. Los Angeles, CA: CBS/Screen Gems.

Penn, A. (Director). (1962). *The miracle worker* [Feature Film]. MGM.

Percy, W. (1975). *The message in the bottle: How queer man is, how queer language is, and what one has to do with the other.* New York, NY: Farrar, Straus and Giroux.

Perkins Institution. (1843). *Eleventh annual report the trustees Perkins institution and Massachusetts asylum for the blind.* Retrieved from http://www.disabilitymuseum.org/dhm/lib/detail.html?id=2294&page =all

Perkins Institution. (1845). *Thirteenth annual report the trustees Perkins institution and Massachusetts asylum for the blind.* Retrieved from http://www.disabilitymuseum.org/dhm/lib/detail.html?id=2304

Pevsner, D. (2010). Comparison of Annie Sullivan's teaching strategies for literacy and communication to the current outcome performance indicators in deaf-blindness: An exploratory mixed-methods study (Doctoral Dissertation). Retrieved from UMI Dissertations: AAT 3407818].

Pohn, K. (2002). The phenomenology of play. Unpublished paper. Carpinteria, CA: Pacifica Graduate Institute.

Pohn, K. (2003). But wait there's more: Musing on the mysteries at the dawning of the age of Aquarius. Unpublished paper. Carpinteria, CA: Pacifica Graduate Institute.

Pohn, K. (2006). *Playing the cosmic game: Exploring the archetypal aspects of play through the kaleidoscope of culture* (Doctoral Dissertation) Retrieved from UMI Dissertations AAT: 264654. [Complete Dissertation as website: www.cosmicplay.net]. Carpinteria, CA: Pacifica Graduate Institute.

Polanyi, M. (1966). *The tacit dimension.* New York, NY: Doubleday.

Price, P. (Director). (2005). *Shining soul: Helen Keller's spiritual life and legacy* [Documentary/DVD]. Swedenborg Foundation.

PRTHS. (2013). *The Pennsylvania railroad technical & historical society* http://prrthsdiscussionweb30239.yuku.com/topic/454/steam-locomotive-horsepower#.UfcU9lNNiGI

Pugh, A., & Crow, L. (2000). *The real Helen Keller* [Documentary Film/streaming]. Retrieved from http://www.cultureunplugged.com/play/2920/The-Real-Helen-Keller

Ramis, H. (1993). *Groundhog day* [Feature Film]. United States: Columbia Pictures.

Random History. (2013). From benches to barstools: A history of chairs, posture, and society. Retrieved from http://www.randomhistory.com/2008/11/11_chair.html

Rank, O. (1970). *The myth of the birth of the hero; A psychological interpretation of mythology* (F. Robbins & S. E. Jelliffe, Trans.). New York, NY: The Journal of Nervous and Mental Disease. (Original work published 1909)

Rank, O. (1993). *The trauma of birth.* New York, NY: Dover. (Original work published 1924)

Rilke, R. M. (1992). Just as the winged energy of delight (R. Bly, Trans.). In R. Bly, J. Hillman, & M. Meade (Eds.), *Rag & bone shop of the heart* (p. 236). New York, NY: Harper Perennial. (Original work published 1924)

Rilke, R. M. (1993). *Letters to a young poet* (Revised ed.) (M.D. Herter, Trans.). New York, NY: W. W. Norton. (Original work published 1934)

Rock, D. (2006). *Quiet leadership: Six steps to transforming performance at work.* New York, NY: Harpercollins.

Rock, D. (2008). SCARF: A brain based model for collaborating with and influencing others. *Neuroleadership Journal 1.* Retrieved from www.davidrock.net/resources/

Rock, D. (February, 2011). Neuroscience provides fresh insights into the 'aha' moment. *T+D. Neuroleadership Journal 1. www.davidrock.net/resources/*

Rock, D., & Cox, C. (2012). SCARF in 2012: Updating the social neuroscience of collaborating with others. . *Neuroleadership Journal 4.* Retrieved from *www.davidrock.net/resources/*

Rodas, J. M. (2003). *Generation BAM study guide for the miracle worker.* New York, NY: Brooklyn Academy of Music.

Sharp, D. (1991). *C. G. Jung lexicon: A primer of terms and concepts.* Toronto, Ontario: Inner City Books.

Shipley, J. T. (1984). *The origins of English words: A discursive dictionary of Indo-European roots.* Baltimore, MD: The Johns Hopkins University Press.

Shulman, H. (1997). *Living at the edges of chaos: Complex systems in culture and psyche.* Einsiedeln, Switzerland: Daimon Verlag.

Spielberg, S. (Director). (1993). *Jurassic park* [Motion Picture]. United States: Universal Pictures.

Stein, M. (1983). *In midlife: A Jungian perspective.* Woodstock, CT: Spring.

Stevenson, R. (Director). (1964). *Mary Poppins* [Feature Film]. Burbank, CA: Disney.

Stewart, I. (2002). *Does god play dice? The new mathematics of chaos.* Malden, MA: Blackwell.

Sullivan, M. (2011). *Lillibet's dream.* Santa Cruz, CA: Hanford Mead.

Tarnas, R. (1995). *Prometheus the awakener: An essay on the archetypal meaning of the planet Uranus.* Woodstock, CT: Spring.

Tarnas, R. (2006). *Cosmos and psyche: Intimations of a new world view.* New York: Viking.

Tass, N. (Director). (2000). *The miracle worker* [Television Movie]. Burbank, CA: Disney.

Turner, V. (1969). *The ritual process: Structure and anti-structure*. Ithaca, NY: Cornell University Press.

Turner, V. (1982b). *From ritual to theater: The human seriousness of play*. New York, NY: Performing Arts Journal.

Turner, V. (1987/88). Body Brain and Culture. In *Anthropology of Performance*. (pp. 156-177). New York: PAJ.

USDI. (2013). Ivy Green. On National Registraion of Historic Places." [*USDI/NPS NRHP Registration Form Ivy Green] http://pdfhost.focus.nps.gov/docs/NHLS/Text/70000101.pdf

USGS. (2013). The water in you. Retrieved from http://ga.water.usgs.gov/edu/propertyyou.html

Van Eenwyk, J. R. (1997). *Archetypes and strange attractors*. Toronto, Canada: Inner City Books.

van Gennep, A. (1960). *The rites of passage*. (M. B. Vizedom & G. L. Caffee, Trans.). Chicago, IL: The University of Chicago Press. (Original work published 1908)

Von Drachenfels, S. (2013). Napkins a brief history. Retrieved from http://www.foodreference.com/html/art-history-napkins-729.html by Suzanne

von Franz, M.-L. (1977). *Individuation in fairytales*. New York, NY: Spring.

von Franz, M.-L. (1994). *Archetypal dimensions of the psyche*. Boston, MA: Shambala.

Waite, H. E. (1959). *Valiant companions. Helen Keller and Anne Sullivan Macy*. Philadelphia, PA: Macrae Smith.

Wikipedia, (2013). *Tewksbury, Massachusetts*. Retrieved from http://en.wikipedia.org/wiki/Tewksbury,_Massachusetts

Wikipedia. (2013). Robert Langs. Retrieved from http://en.wikipedia.org/wiki/Robert_Langs

Wikipedia. (2013a). *Agawam, Massachusettes*. Retrieved from http://en.wikipedia.org/wiki/Agawam_%28tribe%29

Wikipedia. (2013b). *Agawam tribe*. Retrieved from http://en.wikipedia.org/wiki/Agawam,_Massachusetts

Wikipedia. (2013). Horsepower. Retrieved from http://en.wikipedia.org/wiki/Horsepower

Wikipedia. (2013). Steam locomotive. Retrieved from
http://en.wikipedia.org/wiki/Steam_locomotive#United_States

Wilber, K. (1996). *Up from eden: A transpersonal view of human evolution*. Boston,
MA: Shambala.

Winnicott, D. W. (1999). *Playing and reality*. New York, NY: Routledge.
(Original work published 1971)

Yahoo.com (2013). Horsepower calculations. Retrieved from
http://uk.answers.yahoo.com/question/index?qid=20090824060203AA
itayE

BIBLIOGRAPHY

Bolen, J. S. (1999). *Ring of power: Symbols and themes love vs. power in Wagner's Ring circle and in us—A Jungian-feminist perspective.* York Beach, ME: Nicholas-Hays.

Briggs, J. (1992). *Fractals: The patterns of chaos: A new aesthetic of art, science, and nature.* New York, NY: Simon & Schuster.

Briggs, J., & Peat, F. D. (1984). *Looking glass universe: The emerging science of wholeness.* New York, NY: Simon & Schuster.

Briggs, J., & Peat, F. D. (2000). *Seven life lessons of chaos: Spiritual wisdom from the science of change.* New York, NY: Harper Perennial.

Brown, N. O. (1990). *Hermes the thief: The evolution of a myth.* Great Barrington, MA: Lindisfarne Press.

Chaudhuri, H. (1977). *The evolution of integral consciousness.* Wheaton, IL: Quest Books.

Combs, A., & Holland, M. (2001). *Synchronicity: Through the eyes of science, myth, and the trickster* (3rd ed.). New York, NY: Marlowe.

Doty, W. G. (1980). Hermes heteronymous appellations. In J. Hillman (Ed.), *Facing the gods* (pp. 115-133). Dallas, TX: Spring.

Doty, W. G. (1993). A lifetime of trouble-making: Hermes as trickster. In W. J. Hynes & W. G. Doty (Eds.), *Mythical trickster figures: Contours, contexts, and criticisms* (pp. 46-65). Tuscaloosa: University of Alabama Press.

Doty, W. G., & Hynes, W. J. (1993). Historical overview of theoretical issues: The problem of the trickster. In W. J. Hynes & W. G. Doty (Eds.), *Mythical trickster figures: Contours, contexts, and criticisms* (pp. 13-32). Tuscaloosa: University of Alabama Press.

Edelman, S. (1998). *Turning the gorgon: A meditation on shame.* Woodstock, CT: Spring.

Edinger, E. (1992a). *Ego and archetype.* Boston, MA: Shambala.

Edinger, E. (1992b). *Transformation of the god-image: An elucidation of Jung's answer to Job.* Toronto, Ontario: Inner City Books

Eliade, M. (1963). *Myth and reality* (W. Trask, Trans.). New York, NY: Harper & Row.

Freeman, W. (1995). The kiss of chaos and the sleeping beauty of psychology. In F.D. Abraham & A. R. Gilgen (Eds.), *Chaos theory in psychology* (pp. 19-29). Westport, CT: Praeger.

hiHillman, J. (1996). *The soul's code: In search of character and calling.* New York, NY: Random House.

Hynes, W. J. (1993). Mapping the characteristics of mythical tricksters: A heuristic guide. In W. J. Hynes & W. G. Doty (Eds.), *Mythical trickster figures: Contours, contexts, and criticisms* (pp. 13-32). Tuscaloosa: University of Alabama Press.

Hynes W. J., & Doty, W. G. (1993a). Inconclusive conclusions: Tricksters—metaplayers and revealers. In W. J. Hynes & W. G. Doty (Eds.), *Mythical trickster figures: Contours, contexts, and criticisms* (pp. 202-218). Tuscaloosa: University of Alabama Press.

Hynes W. J., & Doty, W. G. (1993b). Introducing the fascinating and perplexing trickster figure. In W. J. Hynes & W. G. Doty (Eds.), *Mythical trickster figures: Contours, contexts, and criticisms* (pp. 1-12). Tuscaloosa: University of Alabama Press.

Hynes, W. J., & Doty, W. G. (1993c). *Mythical trickster figures: Contours, contexts, and criticisms.* Tuscaloosa: University of Alabama Press.

Jantsch, E. (1980). *The self-organizing universe: Scientific and human implications of the emerging paradigm of evolution.* New York, NY: Permagon Press.

Jung, C. G. (1978). Mind and earth (2nd ed.) (R. F. C. Hull, Trans.). In H. Read et al. (Series Eds.), *The collected works of C. G. Jung* (Vol. 10, pp. 29-49). Princeton, NJ: Princeton University Press. (Original work published 1931)

Jung, C. G. (1981). On the nature of the psyche (R. F. C. Hull, Trans.). In H. Read et al. (Series Eds.), *The collected works of C. G. Jung* (Vol. 8, pp. 159-234). Princeton, NJ: Princeton University Press. (Original work published 1946 / revised 1954)

Jung, C. G. (1981). Synchronicity: An acausal connecting principle (2nd ed.) (R. F. C. Hull, Trans.). In H. Read et al. (Series Eds.), *The collected works of C. G. Jung* (Vol. 8, pp. 417-519). Princeton, NJ: Princeton University Press. (Original work published 1952)

Jung, C. G. (1989). *Memories, dreams, reflections.* (A. Jaffe, Ed.; R. Winston & C. Winston, Trans.). New York, NY: Random House. (Original work published 1961)

Jung, C. G. (1989). The answer to Job (2nd ed.) (R. F. C. Hull, Trans.). In H. Read et al. (Series Eds.), *The collected works of C. G. Jung* (Vol. 11, pp. 355-

470). Princeton, NJ: Princeton University Press. (Original work published 1952)

Jung, C. G. (1990). Concerning rebirth (2nd ed.) (R. F. C. Hull, Trans.). In H. Read et al. (Series Eds.), *The collected works of C. G. Jung* (Vol. 9, Part I, pp. 113-150.). Princeton, NJ: Princeton University Press. (Original work published 1950)

Jung, C. G. (1990). On the psychology of the trickster figure (2nd ed.) (R. F. C. Hull, Trans.). In H. Read et al. (Series Eds.), *The collected works of C. G. Jung* (Vol. 9, Part I, pp. 255-274.). Princeton, NJ: Princeton University Press. (Original work published as lecture 1940/1954)

Jurich, M. (1998). *Scheherazade's sisters: Trickster heroines and their stories in world literature.* Westport, CT: Greenwood Press.

Kerényi, K. (1993). Kore. In C. G. Jung & K. Kerényi *Essays on a science of mythology: The myths of the divine child and the divine maiden* (R. F. C. Hull, Trans.) (pp. 101-151). Princeton, NJ: Princeton University Press. (Original published in 1963)

Kerényi, K. (1996). *Dionysus: Archetypal image of indestructible life.* Princeton, NJ: Princeton University Press. (Original Work published 1976)

Kerényi, K. (2003). *Hermes guide of souls* (Revised ed.) (M. Stein, Trans.). Putnam, CT: Spring. (Original work published 1976)

Koch, C. (2006). Change management - Understanding the science of change. CIO. Com Retrieved from http://web.archive.org/web/20070503034856/http://www.cio.com/article/print/24975

Koestler, A. (1976). Association and dissociation. In J. S. Bruner, A. Jolly, & K. Sylva (Eds.), *Play—Its role in development and evolution* (pp. 643-649). New York, NY: Basic Books.

Laszlo, E. (2003). *The connectivity hypothesis: Foundations of an integral science of quantum, cosmos, life, and consciousness.* Albany: State University of New York Press.

Laszlo, E. (2004). *Science and the akashic field: An integral theory of everything.* Rochester, VT: Inner Traditions.

Lopez-Pedraza, R. (1977). *Hermes and his children.* Irving, TX: Spring.

McNeely, D.A. (1996). *Mercury rising: Women, evil, and the trickster gods.* Woodstock, CT: Spring.

Miller, D. L. (1996). The bricoleur in the tennis court: Pedagogy in postmodern context. *1996 Conference on values in higher education.* Retrieved

Karey Pohn

November 11, 2003 from
http://web.utk.edu/~unistudy/ethics96/dlm1.html

Paulsen, A. (1966). The spirit Mercury in relation to the individuation process. *Spring 1966*, 107-120. New York, NY: Analytical Psychology Club.

Peat, F. D. (1987). *Synchronicity: The bridge between matter and mind*. New York, NY: Bantam Books.

Prigogine, I., & Stengers, I. (1984). *Order out of chaos: Man's new dialogue with nature*. New York, NY: Bantam Books.

Rowland, S. (2008). Introduction. In S. Rowland (Ed.) *Psyche and the arts: Jungian approaches to music, architecture, literature, painting and film* (pp. 1-11). New York, NY: Routledge.

Rowland, S. (2010). *C. G. Jung in the humanities: Taking the soul's path*. New Orleans, LA: Spring Journal. Books.

Shalit, E. (2002). *The complex: Path of transformation from archetype to ego*. Toronto, Ontario: Inner City Books.

Stein, M. (1973). The devouring father. In P. Berry (Ed.), *Fathers and mothers: Five papers on the archetypal background of family psychology* (pp. 64-74). Zurich, Switzerland: Spring.

Turner, V. (1982a). *Celebration, studies in festivity and ritual*. Washington, DC: Smithsonian Institution Press.

von Franz, M.-L. (1977). *The feminine in fairytales*. Dallas, TX: Spring.

von Franz, M.-L. (1980). *The psychological meaning of redemption motifs in fairytales*. Toronto, Ontario: Inner City Books.

von Franz, M.-L. (1997). *Archetypal patterns in fairytales*. Toronto, Ontario: Inner City Books.

von Franz, M.-L. (1999). *The cat: A tale of feminine redemption*. Toronto, Ontario: Inner City Books.

Wagner, D. (2012). *The "miracle worker" and the transcendentalist: Annie Sullivan, Franklin Sanborn, and the education of Helen Keller*. Boulder, CO: Paradigm.

Whitmont, E. C. (1993). *The alchemy of healing: Psyche and soma*. Berkeley, CA: North Atlantic Books.

Wickes, F. (1988). *The inner world of choice* (3rd ed.). Boston, MA: Sigo Press.

ABOUT THE AUTHOR

Karey Pohn, JD, PhD, RPCC is depth psychologist who specializes in looking more deeply into the archetypal nature of cultural creations. She is an adjunct faculty member at both Pacifica Graduate Institute and Antioch University, Los Angeles where she teaches courses and qualitative research methods and dissertation development.

Karey is passionate about play, entertainment, and transformation. She believes that play holds the key to our future, both personally and culturally. Karey's doctoral work was on the archetypal aspects of play, which focused on the death/rebirth process and was based on the work of Drs. Stanislav Grof and Richard Tarnas. Karey's dissertation is a website www.cosmicplay.net that explores the promise, pitfalls, and transformative power of play through the cultural creations of Disneyland, and the films *Chicago* and *Mary Poppins*. Karey is currently creating a game to dream this work onwards, and make it more accessible to others.

A personal & executive coach as well as a consultant for the past 20 years, Karey's latest passion has been diving deeper into neuroscience as a Results Professional Certified Coach to help people to be able to play more, think better, and realize their dreams. She earned her Certificate in the Foundations of Neuroleadership and is also pursuing an Executive Masters in Neuroleadership with the Neuroleadership Institute.

A lifelong learner, Karey's curiosity about the lives of Annie Sullivan and Helen Keller has turned into something of possession and her research is still ongoing.

Karey Pohn

www.ingramcontent.com/pod-product-compliance
Lightning Source LLC
Chambersburg PA
CBHW060835170526
45158CB00001B/174